T0316946

Human Resource Policy

Human Resource Policy

Connecting Strategy with
Real-World Practice

Mike Fazey

ANTHEM PRESS

Anthem Press
An imprint of Wimbledon Publishing Company
www.anthempress.com

This edition first published in UK and USA 2020
by ANTHEM PRESS
75–76 Blackfriars Road, London SE1 8HA, UK
or PO Box 9779, London SW19 7ZG, UK
and
244 Madison Ave #116, New York, NY 10016, USA

British Library Cataloguing-in-Publication Data
A catalogue record for this book is available from the British Library.

ISBN-13: 978-1-78527-235-6 (Hbk)
ISBN-10: 1-78527-235-7 (Hbk)
ISBN-13: 978-1-78527-236-3 (Pbk)
ISBN-10: 1-78527-236-5 (Pbk)

This title is also available as an e-book.

CONTENTS

FIGURES

TABLES

PREFACE

Purpose

I was prompted to write this book by the lack of any texts or reference books that focus specifically on HR policymaking and policy management. While there are many books about HRM, most of them pay little attention, if any, to the issues around developing, writing, implementing and managing policies. There are also very few journal articles or other policy-specific readings in the HRM literature.

Most organisations, irrespective of their size, have HR policy manuals. My experience as a practitioner is that these policy manuals often languish on shelves or in computer files somewhere, with most people in the organisation being unaware of what they contain. In other words, the policy manual is not a living document. But it should be. The fundamental theme of this book is that HR policies anchor all HR practices, whether operational or strategic. Practising HR without a decent set of policies is like building a house without foundations – it's likely to fall over at any time.

Structure

This book has three parts: Part I looks at HR policy from a conceptual perspective. What is it? Why do we need it? What influences the shape of HR policies? This part also examines how policy connects with HR strategy and HR practice, as well as broader management issues.

Part II focuses on processes – how policies are conceived, produced and introduced. The basic message is that policymaking needs to be systematic in order to make policies dynamic and relevant. This part also examines a number of policy management issues and problems and discusses how these can best be addressed.

Part III looks at the main types of HR policies that most organisations need and discusses the various policy options that might be included. The emphasis in this part of the book is on translating our theoretical understanding of business and people management principles into policies that can underpin workforce strategies as well as broader business strategies.

All three parts include learning activities such as discussion questions and case studies.

Overall, the intent is to move readers through the realm of HR policy-making, from concept to application – to bridge the gap between theory and practice.

Target audiences

This book has two main target audiences: first, HR practitioners, particularly early-career practitioners, or anyone who wants to broaden their understanding of the role and potential of HR policy and develop their policy-making and policy management skills.

The second intended audience is students of HRM, management or other business disciplines who have completed an introductory HRM course and have a broad conceptual understanding of its role and functions. This book will help students apply their theoretical learning and begin their professional careers with some practical skills and knowledge that can be used in the workplace.

While many of the examples discussed in the book are drawn from the Australian context, the basic principles and policy issues are applicable anywhere, and the literature that underpins them is global, drawn from authors in the United Kingdom, the United States, Canada, Europe, South America and New Zealand. The book is, therefore, a useful resource for students and practitioners no matter where they are.

Part I

POLICY CONCEPTS

Chapter 1

INTRODUCTION TO HR POLICY

Policymaking and policy management are fundamental to the role of contemporary HR practitioners, yet there is little formal education or training available in this area. Traditionally, HR practitioners have learned these skills informally – by trial and error, by learning as they go. As a result, the quality of HR policies in organisations tends to vary considerably. However, as HR becomes more complex and the demands placed on it increase, the policy challenges become correspondingly greater.

Various competency models describing the skills and attributes required by HR professionals have been developed over the years. Ulrich et al. (2015) have examined many of these and discerned six 'domains' that appear to be common: business; personal; HR tools, practices and processes; HR information systems and analytics; change; and organisation and culture. Policy skills could conceivably fall within the domain of 'HR tools, practices and processes', though as Vu (2017) has pointed out, HR competency models have evolved away from functional competencies (such as policy writing) towards higher level strategic competencies.

It seems evident that, within HR's new strategic identity, HR policymaking and policy management have been relegated to being lesser, non-strategic functions. Nonetheless, research by Kramar and Steane (2012) has found that HR practitioners continue to regard the policy function as a legitimate and necessary part of HR's role.

Although modern conceptions of HRM cast it as a strategic function, the reality is that it must be both strategic and operational (Lemmergaard 2009).

The major tenet of this book is that while HR policy is perhaps less sexy than HR strategy, policy is strategy's essential partner and is absolutely fundamental to effective HR. Policy's importance goes beyond its connection to strategy. This book recognises the complexity of policymaking and policy management and the high degree of connectedness between HR policy and broader organisational management issues. While it is certainly true that HR policies deal with operational matters, this is by no means the extent of their role, their relevance or their potential.

What is HR policy?

The word 'policy' is used in different ways in different contexts. The following dictionary definitions give a good flavour of what we mean by policy in a general context:

- a course of action pursued for a specific reason
- a plan for a course of action, especially one of an organisation or government; a course of action thought to be prudent or tactically advantageous
- a statement of principles for action; a position that guides the decision-making and activities of an organisation
- a course or principle of action adopted by a government, party, business or individual

More specifically, HR policy has been conceived in a variety of ways. Cooper (2012) sees HR policies as being 'statements of the acceptable ways of dealing with recurring situations'. Boxall and Purcell (2016) see them as part of the equation that determines individual performance and, ultimately, organisational outcomes. Boselie (2010) sees HRM as operating at both micro and strategic levels, with the policy function falling within the realm of micro-HRM. Cascio and Boudreau (2012) see HR policy as providing the vehicle through which organisations can differentiate themselves and their practices in the labour market. Vanderstraeten (2019) sees HR policies as vehicles for integrating different systems and practices, as well as making the intentions of the organisation clear.

As we have already observed, the relationship between HR policy and HR strategy is a close and important one. We explore the nature of that relationship further in Chapter 3. Suffice it to say at this point that policies are the instruments through which HR strategies are brought to life. HR policies can also be seen as embodying an organisation's philosophy of people management and its culture, a relationship we also explore later in the book. The terms policy and procedure are also linked and often referred to as a single concept. However, despite the fact that the dividing line between them can be somewhat fuzzy, the two are not synonymous. Procedures tend to include things like administrative processes, documentation requirements and details of decision-making and approval processes. Although policies and procedures are sometimes combined in a single document, it is not the intention of this book to explore procedures because they are essentially administrative in nature and will vary from organisation to organisation.

Reasons for HR policies

Stone (2017) has proposed the following reasons for having HR policies:

- to reassure employees that they will be treated fairly and objectively
- to help managers to make quick and consistent decisions
- to give managers the confidence to resolve problems and to defend their decisions

McConnell (2005) has identified six purposes for HR policies:

- to provide clear communication between the organisation and its employees regarding conditions of employment
- to form a basis for treating employees fairly and equally
- to act as a set of guidelines for supervisors and managers
- to create a basis for developing employee handbooks
- to form a context for supervisor training programmes and employee induction

These are all good reasons. A point worth noting is that HR policies are as much a resource for employees as they are for managers or HR practitioners. Knowing the 'rules of the game' and understanding the rationale for those rules help employees appreciate the nature of the psychological contract that they have with their employer. Unlike employment contracts that specify things like pay, hours of work and entitlements, psychological contracts are implicit – no formal contract is signed that outlines the nature of the relationship. HR policies, however, can give insight into that relationship and provide a means by which an organisation can be held accountable for the decisions it makes concerning its people.

There are also other reasons for HR policies that emphasise the connections between HRM and broader management and organisational issues (Figure 1.1).

Reason 1: HR policies enable business and HR strategies and help to align decision-making with organisational objectives.

Reason 2: HR policies help to protect the organisation from litigation and adverse legal findings as well as other financial, strategic and operational risks.

Reason 3: HR policies help to define and shape the culture of the organisation.

Reason 4: HR policies can help to foster innovation and creativity.

Reason 5: HR policies help to ensure that the organisation functions in an ethical way.

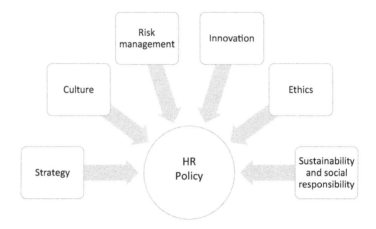

Figure 1.1 HR policy connections.

Reason 6: HR policies can help to define and underpin the organisation's approach to sustainability and social responsibility.

An important point to note is that some of these are potentialities rather than realities in many organisations. It remains common for HR to be perceived as being peripheral to mainstream business and to be mainly concerned with administrative or organisational housekeeping matters. HR policy's potential for connecting with a range of management issues outside the normal scope of HRM can, therefore, help to demonstrate its value from a business perspective and to raise its profile.

We explore these connections further in coming chapters.

Types of HR policies

Broadly speaking, HR policies can be classified into two types:

1. *Compliance policies* ensure that the organisation meets its legal obligations as an employer and adheres to whatever government or industry employment regulations apply. They also protect the legal rights of employees.
2. *Strategic policies* help to facilitate change and to shape the culture of the organisation, as well as reflecting its long-term needs in relation to the management of its workforce.

This is not to say that specific HR policies fall neatly into one or the other category. In fact, most policies have elements of both. Nonetheless, the existence of two distinct types of policy casts HR in dual policy roles. On the one hand, HR can be seen as the *policy police*, ensuring that the organisation complies with legal and regulatory requirements. At the same time, however, it is also striving to be a *strategic business partner*, contributing directly to business success. The two roles sit uncomfortably with one another at times. Compliance policies can be seen to be a hindrance to business success. Indeed, HR's historical focus on compliance has rather tarnished its image, as Hammonds (2005) has pointed out in no uncertain terms: 'The human resources trade long ago proved itself, at best, a necessary evil – and at worst, a dark, bureaucratic force that blindly enforces nonsensical rules, resists creativity and impedes constructive change.' This might seem a harsh view, but it should not be dismissed. The reality is that there are tensions between what HR needs to do as the policy police and what it strives to do as a strategic business partner. Learning to manage those tensions is fundamental to HR achieving the credibility and influence it seeks. We explore this issue further in Chapter 13.

Hammonds's views also imply a couple of important things about the way that compliance policies have traditionally been managed. The first implication is that the rationale for the policies themselves is not understood ('nonsensical rules'). The second implication is that HR appears to be either ignorant of, or uninterested in, the issues the policies might create for line managers and indeed employees themselves ('blindly enforces'). This brings to mind an HR profession with an ivory tower mentality, handing down edicts from on high, concerned only with following the rules and unaware or unconcerned about the stifling effects they might have on people, processes and business outcomes.

In Australia, a 2007 study undertaken by the Australian Human Resources Institute (AHRI) found that 45 per cent of HR practitioners and 73 per cent of managers and employees believed that HR was ineffective. The report also observed that 'there is a perception that the primary role of HR is to make the rules and hand out penalties' (AHRI 2007). Clearly this is an image of HR that needs to be shed. Good policy practice is one avenue through which HR practitioners can break down perceptions like these.

As Figure 1.2 shows, policies can be good or bad. Transparency, flexibility and a sensible approach to implementation and management are the hallmarks of good HR policies. It is also true that a fundamentally good policy that is badly managed is as potentially damaging as a policy that is inherently bad.

Most medium-sized and large organisations have HR policy manuals and/or employee handbooks that outline their people management policies. The scope of those policies can vary greatly depending on the size of the organisation, the

Table 1.1 Typical HR policy areas

Codes of conduct/ethics	Equity and diversity
Dress codes	Workplace flexibility
Discipline	Staffing
Grievance and dispute resolution	Learning and development
Attendance management	Succession management
Leave management	Work health, safety and well-being
Performance management	Privacy
Remuneration and rewards	Social media

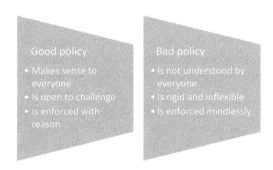

Figure 1.2 Good and bad policy.

nature of its HR function and a range of other factors. Typically, organisations need policies covering the areas listed in Table 1.1.

We explore each of these policy areas in Part III. As with most aspects of HR, there are strong connections between different policy areas. Individual policies need to be consistent with each other and collectively form a coherent blueprint for the management of people across the organisation. This underlines the need for policies to be developed and managed in a coordinated way rather than in a piecemeal fashion, which is unfortunately the case in some organisations where policies have been developed ad hoc, often as a response to problems. A systematic process for developing, implementing and reviewing policies is an essential part of the policy management process; this is the focus of Part II of this book.

Who needs HR policies, and how many policies should there be?

There are no hard and fast rules about how big an organisation should be before it needs a set of HR policies. Obviously a small business with a handful of employees would see little value in formalising its people management in this way. On the other hand, a large corporation with thousands of employees would be very foolish not to have a comprehensive set of HR policies. But where is the transition point? As a general rule of thumb, it could be argued that when an organisation becomes big enough to engage at least one HR specialist, then it is big enough to have HR policies. After all, there seems little value in having a set of policies without there being anyone to manage them, and it is unlikely that a CEO or a line manager would have the time or the inclination to do this. Decisions about the point at which it becomes necessary to engage an HR specialist are usually made by business owners or CEOs, and again, there are no hard and fast rules. In most cases, an organisation that has a hundred or more employees would probably need an HR specialist, but smaller organisations might also consider it worthwhile. Ultimately, it depends on the nature of the business, the nature of the workforce and the preferences of the owner or CEO.

The question of how many policies there should be is equally vexing. Generally speaking, the larger the organisation, the more comprehensive its policies need to be. Clearly a larger workforce is a more complex one with more potential for people management issues to arise. A larger organisation also has more HR systems and processes that need to be backed by policies (e.g. remuneration and performance management). By contrast, an organisation with only a hundred or so employees may only need a few well-chosen policies. Choosing which policies are required depends on the nature of the business. For instance, a business engaged in manufacturing, which employs people to operate machinery or do other physically demanding work, would need a safety policy, but a business where the employees are all white-collar workers engaged in administrative or knowledge-based work would probably consider a safety policy to be unnecessary. The nature and complexity of the policies might vary too. For instance, the staffing policy for a local building company might be very much simpler than that for a global corporation that engages and deploys staff internationally.

The basic message is that the number and nature of HR policies should always match the needs of the organisation. One size does not fit all. This underlines the importance of policy competence for HR practitioners regardless of the size or type of organisation they work in. The capacity to make sound judgements about policy needs and to develop policies appropriate to the organisation is paramount.

Policy priorities

A recent global survey of HR professionals identified a range of workforce issues that need to be addressed. These are summarised in Table 1.2. The second column indicates the percentage of respondents that identified the

Table 1.2 Global HR priorities

Issue	Percentage of respondents
Change management	46
Business efficiency	37
Culture development	58
Capability and competence management	35
Flexible employment	14
Management development	39
Diversity	20
Industrial relations	12
Performance management	52
Employee retention and motivation	48
Downsizing	12
HR systems and processes	42
Organisational growth	34
Talent management	57
Employee engagement	56
Succession management	38
Training and education	34
Performance metrics	21
Recruitment	50

Source: Harvey Nash HR Survey (2017).

issue as a priority. Most of these issues can be addressed, either directly or indirectly, through policy.

Wilson (2010) has observed that employee demand for flexibility, changing expectations in relation to ethics and social responsibility, government regulation and skills development will be among the top forces determining the shape of future workplaces in the period up to 2020. HR policy will be essential to addressing these issues.

Summary

- Policymaking and policy management are fundamental skills for the HR professional, but they appear to have been marginalised in modern HR competency frameworks.
- HR policies enable strategies and help to connect HR with other areas of management.
- Broadly speaking, there are two categories of HR policy: *Compliance* policies and *strategic* policies. This creates dual policy roles for HR which are sometimes difficult to reconcile.

- HR policies can cover a wide range of issues, and so it is important that the policies are developed with reference to one another and that they form a consistent, coherent blueprint for people management in the organisation.
- Smaller organisations probably don't need formal HR policies until the workforce is big enough to warrant the employment of an HR specialist. This often happens when the workforce reaches around a hundred employees, but it can vary either way.
- As a general rule of thumb, the larger the organisation, the more comprehensive a set of policies it needs.
- Regardless of the nature and size of the organisation, policies need to be purpose-built for the organisation and its specific circumstances and needs. One size never fits all.

Discussion questions

1. Discuss the view that organisations should have as few HR policies as possible. Is it better to allow decision-making flexibility in relation to people management rather than to try to regulate the relationship between employees and managers too much?
2. As an employee, would you rather work in an organisation that had a comprehensive set of HR policies, or one that had few or none at all? Why?
3. As a manager, would you rather work in an organisation that had a comprehensive set of HR policies, or one that had few or none at all? Why?

References

AHRI. 2007. *HRPulse Research Report No.1, Extreme Makeover: Does HR Need to Improve its Image?* Melbourne: Australian Human Resources Institute.

Boselie, P. 2010. *Strategic Human Resource Management: A Balanced Approach.* New York: McGraw Hill, pp. 4–6.

Boxall, P., and Purcell, J. 2016. *Strategy and Human Resource Management* (4th edn). Basingstoke: Palgrave MacMillan, pp. 250–52.

Cascio, W., and Boudreau, J. 2012. *A Short Introduction to Strategic Human Resource Management.* Cambridge: Cambridge University Press, pp. 83–106.

Cooper, K. 2012. 'The business of HRM'. In J. Bryson and R. Ryan (eds), *Human Resource Management in the Workplace.* Auckland: Pearson, pp. 278–79.

Hammonds, K. 2005. 'Why we hate HR'. *Fast Company Magazine,* Issue 97 (August): 40–47.

Harvey Nash HR Survey. 2017. https://www.harveynash.com/group/mediacentre/HR_survey2017.pdf (accessed 4 February 2019).

Kramar, R., and Steane, P. 2012. 'Emerging HRM skills in Australia'. *Asia Pacific Journal of Business Administration* 4(2): 139–57.

Lemmergaard, J. 2009. 'From administrative expert to strategic partner'. *Employee Relations* 31(2): 182–96.

McConnell, J. 2005. *How to Develop Essential HR Policies and Procedures*. New York: American Management Association, pp. 1–2.

Stone, R. 2017. *Human Resource Management* (9th edn). Milton, Queensland: Wiley, p. 37.

Ulrich, D., Brockbank, W., Ulrich, M. and Kryscynski, J. 2015. 'Toward a synthesis of HR competency models: The common HR "food groups"'. *People and Strategy* 38(4): 56–65.

Vanderstraeten, A. 2019. *Strategic HRM and Performance: A Conceptual Framework*. London: Red Globe Press.

Vu, G. 2017. 'A critical review of human resource competency model: Evolvement in required competencies for human resource professionals'. *Journal of Economics, Business and Management* 5(12): 357–65.

Wilson, P. 2010. *People@work 2020. The Future of Work and the Changing Workplace: Challenges for Australian HR Practitioners* (White Paper). Melbourne: Australian Human Resources Institute, pp. 39–45.

Chapter 2

CONTEXTUAL FACTORS INFLUENCING POLICY

No organisation exists in a vacuum. Every organisation is part of a society and the complex systems that underpin that society. Consequently, HR policy is influenced by a range of external forces that reflect local, national and global factors. Those factors can be broadly divided into four categories as outlined in Figure 2.1.

In effect, these contextual factors place constraints on HR policies. The context dictates the parameters of business policy and consequently, the parameters of HR policy. Obviously, HR policymakers need to be aware of these contextual constraints because the consequences of ignoring them can be serious, for example, prosecution, public censure and failure to compete in the marketplace.

Law

Perhaps the most fundamental contextual factor affecting HR policy is the legal framework that surrounds employment and business in general. Employment law is drawn from two main sources: common law and statute law.

Common law (or case law) is derived from decisions made in courts. These decisions establish precedents based on fundamental principles that are applicable generally. In an HR context, case law decisions provide the basis for understanding the legal principles that apply to employment scenarios and the obligations that the employment relationship imposes on both employers and employees. HR policies, therefore, need to reflect those obligations (Table 2.1).

Case law deals with a vast range of issues concerning employment relationship and is very complex. Courts and tribunals hand down hundreds of decisions each year. HR policies need to reflect these case law decisions, but it is impossible for most HR practitioners to be aware of each such decision. For this reason, it is prudent for businesses to develop and maintain a relationship with an employment law specialist who can advise on the legal validity of HR policies; however, this is really only a viable option for larger organisations.

Figure 2.1 Contextual factors influencing policy.

Table 2.1 Common law employment obligations

Employer obligations	Employee obligations
To pay wages and reasonable expenses	To obey lawful directions given by the employer
To give reasonable notice of termination	To conduct themselves appropriately at work
To take reasonable care for the safety and health of employees	To use the skills for which they were employed
To indemnify the employee against losses incurred while undertaking their duties	To indemnify the employer against losses incurred while undertaking their duties (except where specific legislation precludes this)
To co-operate with employees and not act in a way that would damage the employment relationship	To co-operate with the employer and not act in a way that would damage the employment relationship
To provide work for employees paid by commission or piece rates	To behave with fidelity and good faith (e.g. not accept bribes or disclose commercially confidential information)

Source: Adapted from Stone (2017, 153–54).

Smaller organisations can seek advice from industry and employer support bodies or from government agencies responsible for employment matters.

Indeed, the legal status of HR policies is a fundamental issue to consider. Case law supports the notion that HR policies form part of the employment contract and are legally binding. For this reason, HR policies should not attempt to cover issues like employment conditions which are usually enshrined in employment contracts and/or agreements. Rather, policies should deal with matters that fall within what is generally accepted as being management prerogative (Melbourne et al. 2008).

Table 2.2 Types of statute laws

Statute law	Description
Industrial relations	Covers setting of pay and conditions, minimum employee entitlements, grounds for dismissal, parameters for industrial action
Anti-discrimination	Outlaws discrimination in employment based on gender, race, age, disability and a range of other grounds
Work health and safety	Prescribes specific employer responsibilities for creating and maintaining a safe, healthy work environment and for managing safety and health issues
Privacy	Protects employee information

Statute law is legislation enacted by federal or state governments. Various types of statute laws affect employment and, therefore, HR policy. The main ones are outlined in Table 2.2.

In addition, public sector employment is usually regulated by another layer of legislation in many jurisdictions, particularly those that embrace the Westminster system of government. The main purpose of this additional legislation is to help prevent the politicisation of the public sector by making all employment processes rigorous and transparent.

Non-employment laws can also impact indirectly on HR policy. For instance, the criminal code and laws covering fair trade practices, financial integrity and corporate governance can be reflected in policies such as codes of conduct and codes of ethics, and taxation laws can affect remuneration and reward policies.

Industrial relations law is the most volatile of statute law areas affecting HR policy. One of the reasons for this is that industrial relations is an ideological battlefield for the two sides of politics, and so whenever there is a change of government, there is inevitably significant legislative reform to reshape the system. In Australia, for example, the implementation of the Fair Work Act has meant that there is now an industrial relations framework that emphasises collective bargaining and more central regulation. From the beginning of 2010, employers and employees covered by the federal system have been subject to new National Employment Standards (NES) and a revamped 'modern awards' system that together act as a safety net, guaranteeing certain employment conditions. The NES includes:

- a 38-hour standard working week
- a right for employees with family responsibilities to request flexible work arrangements

- a right to up to 12 months unpaid parental leave
- a minimum of 4 weeks' annual leave
- entitlements to personal/carers' leave, compassionate leave, long service leave and paid leave on public holidays
- entitlements to a minimum of 4 weeks' notice of termination and to up to 16 weeks' redundancy pay (Stewart 2018)

Modern awards cover the detail of employment arrangements, including wage rates, overtime and penalty rates, rosters, allowances and procedures for consultation and dispute resolution. They, however, do not cover higher income earners – in 2018/19, this means anyone earning more than $145,400 per year. The threshold is indexed annually. Employers have reported that the standards have affected the content of employment contracts and the development of policies in areas such as workplace flexibility (AHRI 2010).

Approaches to the regulation of the employment relationship vary considerably in different parts of the world, but the same policy challenges exist in all jurisdictions as the regulatory framework changes and adapts to political, social and economic changes.

Legislation in other areas tends to be less volatile. Some anti-discrimination laws, for example, have been in place since the 1970s and have changed little in that time. Nonetheless, amendments do occur from time to time, and HR policymakers need to keep track of changes that might require policies to be revised.

The scenario we have just discussed in relation to the Fair Work Act is a good example of how a high profile government policy leads to significant legislative change, and subsequently, to new compliance requirements for organisations. However, not all government policy is as high profile as industrial relations policy, nor is it always enshrined in legislation. Government policies in the areas outlined in Figure 2.2 reflect governments' interventionist roles in the economy and society.

Governments set the context for employment, and their interests are multifaceted. Generally speaking, all governments seek to intervene in the labour market to some extent in the pursuit of economic, social and political objectives. In fact, labour market issues can be seen as being at the intersection of economic and social policy. All governments want to achieve positive economic and social outcomes, and perhaps just as importantly, to be seen by the electorate to be striving for them. Among governments' primary interests are:

- labour market participation
- unemployment

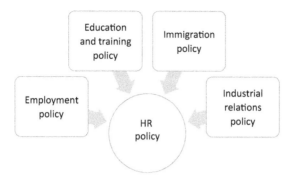

Figure 2.2 Government policy areas impacting on HR policy.

- access to the labour market for the disadvantaged
- labour supply and demand
- skills development
- skills shortages

Government agencies responsible for employment, education and training are usually charged with responsibility for pursuing these interests. Approaches vary according to political ideology and socio-economic factors. While some governments adopt a 'social market' approach which is more directly interventionist, others tend to favour a 'free market' approach which is more concerned with creating conditions favourable to employment than intervening directly in the labour market. The trend over the past 30 or so years has been away from social market interventions, though this approach has not disappeared entirely. There is a view that labour market programmes, such as those traditionally used as part of social market-oriented policies, actually have limited impact in modifying the labour market (Burtless 2002). But despite this, governments will probably continue to develop and implement these programmes because of the political aspect – they want to be seen to be doing something tangible about an issue that is high profile and that can potentially affect anyone.

In addition, government agencies responsible for immigration administer policies concerning skilled migration to help meet current and future skills needs for business and industry (Table 2.3). These policies can also impact directly or indirectly on workplaces. In recent years and despite the economic downturn of 2008/2009, an increasing number of employers in countries with developed economies have sought skilled workers from overseas. Indeed, the demand for skilled migrants is expected to increase over the next 20 years as economies continue to grow and large numbers of skilled people exit the

Table 2.3 HR policies potentially influenced by government policies

Government policy area	HR policy area
Employment	Staffing (recruitment, selection)
Education and training	Staffing (recruitment); training and development
Immigration and citizenship	Staffing (recruitment, international staffing); equity and diversity
Industrial relations	Staffing (employment, termination); remuneration and rewards; workplace flexibility; leave management; attendance management

workforce through retirement. Increased skilled migration (as well as other forms of migration) will inevitably lead to a more diverse community, which will in turn lead to more diverse and more culturally complex organisations. Both these developments present challenges for HR.

Economic conditions

Changes in business and labour market conditions can significantly affect HR policies, especially those that are primarily strategic in nature. During periods of strong economic growth, organisations tend to focus more on the future; therefore policies geared towards development gain ascendancy. Good economic times often coincide with a competitive labour market, and so organisations need to adjust their policies and practices in order to compete for scarce labour and skills.

By contrast, difficult economic times cause organisations to focus much more on the present and be driven by survival rather than growth. We saw this happen in 2008/2009, when the global financial crisis sent most developed economies into recession. As Balthazard (2009) has pointed out in commenting on the Canadian context, HR policy priorities changed almost overnight, emphasising the need to reduce labour costs, manage terminations and redundancies and deal with an anxious workforce. Similar policy priorities were pursued by companies in Europe, the United Kingdom and the United States. Interestingly, the Australian experience was somewhat different, with fewer redundancies and cost-cutting policies and more of a 'steady as she goes' mentality. This might be explained by the fact that the economic downturn was less pronounced in Australia than in most other developed countries. It might also be because Australian organisations that had struggled to recruit and retain employees in the preceding period didn't want to lose those assets, knowing that the demographics of the workforce would mean probable skill and labour shortages in the near future, regardless of economic conditions.

Previous experiences, however, have not been as positive. In fact, many HR practitioners have become somewhat fatalistic about the consequences of economic downturns – HR strategies are often the first to be cut, meaning that certain HR policies (the more strategic ones) are scaled back or even abolished.

As a general principle, economically difficult times lead to HR policies which are more austere and more short term in their focus. However, economically prosperous times lead to HR policies which are more expansive and geared towards facilitating future growth. The tendency to downgrade HR policies during economic downturns creates some interesting challenges for HR. While short-term cost cutting is, in some ways, an obvious response to reduced revenue, the medium to long-term implications of doing so can be quite negative. For example, policies that support attraction and retention strategies, if downgraded or discontinued, will obviously decrease an organisation's capacity to attract and retain.

While organisations might argue that policy downgrades are temporary measures, chopping and changing policies can create an uncertain employment environment that has a long-term effect on the organisation's reputation as an employer, and hence, on its capacity to compete in the labour market when economic conditions improve. This illustrates the need for policies to be sustainable rather than being knee-jerk reactions to economic and labour market fluctuations. Policies that are too generous may, in fact, be detrimental if they cannot be sustained. HR practitioners, therefore, need to be sensitive to the impact of economic conditions and to the fact that fluctuations are inevitable. Ideally, HR should strive to create and maintain stable, sustainable policies that can withstand these fluctuations without massive changes. This is not to suggest that HR policies should be unchanging. Indeed, they should be reviewed regularly. The challenge is to strike an appropriate balance that makes radical changes the exception rather than the rule.

Societal values

As well as the legal, political and economic contexts we have already discussed, organisations also exist within a social context. While this context influences many aspects of business, it could be argued that societal values and issues are particularly relevant to HR, because HR is fundamentally about people. It could also be argued that the values of business can affect the values of the society in which they exist. Pearson and Chatterjee (2001) found that in India, the values of the competitive market economy had undermined broader societal values that had previously been constant. India is, of course, a developing economy, and so it is perhaps understandable that the newly introduced values of the free market might have a pronounced effect on traditional societal values. If this is a universal phenomenon, it could be argued that in developed economies, societal values may already have been modified to some degree by the values of capitalism. Even so, tensions between business and societal values are common in developed economies, and this has implications for HR policy.

It is difficult to define a society's values in concrete terms. In Australia, for example, Holland et al. (2007) have found that workers' values embrace a unitarist philosophy – a belief that employer and employee interests are fundamentally compatible. Hence, the dominant Australian work values emphasise involvement, engagement and the pursuit of mutual interest. Many HR policy areas potentially encompass these values: staffing (including recruitment, selection, employment and termination), remuneration and rewards, equity and diversity, discipline, grievance and dispute resolution. The pressures of economic conditions and business imperatives can challenge these values at times, but where HR policies run counter to these societal and work values, tensions arise. In other countries, of course, there may be very different values at play. Indeed, this is one of the challenges of international HRM – adapting policies and practices to the prevailing cultural values rather than applying a 'one size fits all' approach, which may be entirely unsuitable in some places.

The impact of national cultures

Societal values stem, at least in part, from broader national cultures. Theorists have developed a range of frameworks for understanding the differences between national cultures. Perhaps the best known of these is Hofstede (2001) who has spent more than 30 years researching cultural differences. His framework comprises six dimensions, outlined below (Figure 2.3).

Cultural differences can influence both the way HR policies are developed and implemented and the content of those policies. For example, in high power distance countries such as Malaysia, Saudi Arabia and China, people accept that there are hierarchies of power, and leadership is rarely questioned. In cultures like these, HR policies will typically be developed unilaterally and implemented as *faits accompli*. In low power distance countries such as Denmark, Australia and the United Kingdom, HR policies are more likely to be developed consultatively and to be questioned or challenged. The policies themselves will generally include communication processes and provisions designed to make decision-making as transparent as possible, as well as provisions allowing decisions to be challenged and reviewed. Such provisions would not appear in policies within high power distance cultures.

Figure 2.3 Hofstede's cultural dimensions.

Remuneration and reward policies in individualistic cultures such as the United States will typically emphasise rewarding individual achievement, whereas those in collectivist cultures such as India are more likely to emphasise group rewards such as team bonuses. Similarly, performance management policies in individualistic cultures will typically focus on individual performance, whereas those in collectivist cultures are more likely to focus on team performance.

Organisations in cultures with low uncertainty avoidance such as Singapore and Jamaica (i.e. cultures in which people are comfortable with ambiguity) may have very few HR policies, and those policies are likely to be broad statements of principle rather than providing specific rules or procedures. The opposite would be true in cultures with high uncertainty avoidance (i.e. where people tend to want certainty and detail) such as France and Greece.

HR's monitoring role

As we have already discussed, difficult circumstances may require some policy revision, but this should not be at the expense of the fundamental values that underpin the policies. Indeed, it is HR's role to ensure that this does not happen. Thus, HR needs to adopt a 'societal value orientation' in which managerial decisions are tempered by consideration of the social consequences of those decisions (Kang and James 2007). Moral considerations notwithstanding, from a practical perspective, the consequences of HR policies conflicting with societal values can be damaging to an organisation's public image and reputation as well as to its ability to attract and retain employees.

While values tend to be relatively constant, other social issues arise from time to time that also impact on HR policies. Workforce demographics is perhaps the most significant social issue driving HR policy at present (Sheehan et al. 2006). Issues related to the ageing of the workforce, generational change and diversity have, therefore, tended to dominate HR strategy development in recent years. A growing social demand for better work–life/work–family balance is also influencing HR policies in many organisations, and is being increasingly seen as an effective attraction and retention tool as well as being something that is socially desirable (Hill et al. 2008; Richman et al. 2008). Hence, HR policies in areas like parental leave, equity and diversity, workplace flexibility, training and development, succession management and employee well-being are being influenced by social changes. The status of these policies is also increasing. Traditionally, these types of policies have been seen as being in the 'warm fuzzy' category, but their strategic importance is now more widely recognised as organisations come to grips with the impact of social changes.

One view to emerge in recent years is that HR should not only interpret social and public policy issues but also assume more of an anticipatory role – identifying emerging contextual issues and taking action to position the organisation to deal with them effectively (Beaumont 2005). This is a genuine strategic policy role that represents an opportunity for the development of policies that connect HR to the broader strategic management of the organisation.

Summary

- HR policy is influenced by a range of legal, political, economic and societal factors which are outside the organisation.
- The legal context includes statute law (formal legislation) and common or case law, both of which can be very complex.
- Four main types of legislation influence HR policy – industrial relations, anti-discrimination, occupational safety and health and privacy.
- Government policy in the areas of employment, education and training, immigration and citizenship and industrial relations can also influence the shape of HR policy.
- Positive economic conditions tend to breed HR policies geared towards enhancing attraction, retention, employee engagement, employee development and other future-oriented aspects of HR.
- By contrast, difficult economic conditions often lead to the scaling back or discontinuation of these kinds of strategic policies in favour of policies geared towards cost control and short-term survival. However, policies which are too severe may hinder the organisation's ability to respond quickly to improved market conditions when they come.
- The way an organisation manages its people is generally reflective of the values of the society in which it exists, though there is some evidence to suggest that societal values can actually be affected by the values of the market economy. Economic values can sometimes appear to be inconsistent with social values, creating tension within organisations.

- HR policies that are inconsistent with societal values can have negative consequences. For this reason, HR policymakers need to approach policy development and review with a 'societal value orientation'.
- Social issues connected with the ageing workforce and a growing demand for better work–life balance are also exerting strong influence on organisational HR policies.

Discussion questions

1. If organisations are constrained by the same legal, political, economic and societal factors, how can they differentiate themselves from one another in the marketplace? Is there enough scope remaining for organisations to develop distinct identities as employers?
2. Should economic factors always override other factors? Is it simply a fact of life that HR policies need to become less generous when times are tough?
3. What kinds of HR policies and practices might put an organisation in conflict with prevailing societal values in your country?

References

AHRI. 2010. *Impact of the Fair Work Act within Australian Workplaces*. Melbourne: Australian Human Resources Institute.

Balthazard, C. 2009. 'Future economic growth from a human resources perspective'. *Canadian Manager* (Summer): 7.

Beaumont, R. 2005. 'A challenge to HR: Building the company's external dimension'. In M. Losey, S. Meisinger and D. Ulrich (eds), *The Future of Human Resource Management*. Hoboken: John Wiley, pp. 333–40.

Burtless, G. 2002. 'Innovations in labour market policies: The Australian way – comments on an OECD report'. *Australian Economic Review* 35(1): 97–104.

Hill, E., Grzywacz, J., Allen, S., Blanchard, V., Matz-Costa, C., Shulkin, S. and Pitt-Catsouphes, M. 2008. 'Defining and conceptualizing workplace flexibility'. *Community, Work and Family* 11(2): 149–63.

Hofstede, G. 2001. *Culture's Consequences: Comparing Values, Behaviors, Institutions and Organisations Across Nations* (2nd edn). Thousand Oaks, CA: Sage.

Holland, P., Sheehan, C., Donohue, R. and Pyman, A. 2007. *Contemporary Issues and Challenges in HRM*. Prahran: Tilde University Press, pp. 222–40.

Kang, G., and James, J. 2007. 'Revisiting the concept of societal orientation: Conceptualization and delineation'. *Journal of Business Ethics* 73: 301–18.

Melbourne, S., Rubinstein, N. and Martin, G. 2008. 'Policies and procedures'. In CCH Australia, *Australian Master Human Resources Guide* (6th edn), pp. 675–86.

Pearson, C., & Chatterjee, S. 2001. 'Perceived societal values of Indian managers: Some empirical evidence of responses to economic reform'. *International Journal of Social Economics* 28(4): 368–79.

Richman, A., Civian, J., Shannon, L., Hill, E. and Brennan, R. 2008. 'The relationship of perceived flexibility, supportive work-life policies, and use of formal flexible

arrangements and occasional flexibility to employee engagement and expected retention'. *Community, Work and Family* 11(2): 183–97.

Sheehan, C., Holland, P. and De Cieri, H. 2006. 'Current developments in HRM in Australian
organisations'. *Asia Pacific Journal of Human Resources* 44(2): 132–52.

Stewart, A. 2018. *Stewart's Guide to Employment Law* (6th edn). Leichhardt: Federation
Press, chapter 7.

Stone, R. 2017. *Human Resource Management* (9th edn). Milton: John Wiley and Sons,
pp. 153–54.

Chapter 3

POLICY AND STRATEGY

In this chapter we explore the relationship between HR policy and organisational strategy. It is important to have a clear conceptual understanding of the two in order to know how they interact with one another. The words 'policy' and 'strategy' are sometimes used interchangeably; indeed, dictionary definitions of the terms are very similar. But in a business context, policy and strategy are not the same.

It is also useful to distinguish between business strategy and HR strategy, recognising that business strategy encompasses the full range of organisational functions (such as production, customer service, sales, technology, finance and marketing) as well as HR strategies. For our purposes, the following definitions are useful:

Business strategy: A blueprint for defining organisational goals and future directions.

HR strategy: Deliberate measures taken to address specific workforce issues that have strategic importance for the organisation.

HR policy: Actions, processes and decision-making guidelines that give life to HR strategies and demonstrate how the organisation will achieve its strategic HR objectives.

Business strategy and HR strategy

Business strategies reflect the challenges faced by an organisation to survive and thrive in its particular industry or context. While the specifics will vary across industries, sectors and organisations, there are some common themes. Kramar et al. (2014) have suggested four key competitive challenges for contemporary companies (see Figure 3.1).

Significantly, two of the four competitive challenges (HR innovation; attraction and retention) relate directly to the workforce, and so they have direct implications for HR policy. The other two also have workforce implications. Nankervis et al. (2017) have pointed out that there are different ways of

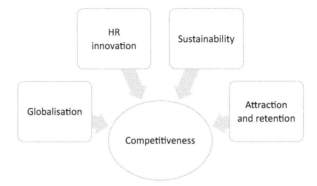

Figure 3.1 Competitive challenges for contemporary companies.

Figure 3.2 Business strategy drivers.

conceiving business strategy. The three-part model of business strategy drivers shown in Figure 3.2 is based on concepts originally developed by Porter (1985) and further refined by Storey and Sisson (1990).

These are all fairly abstract terms, of course. They are not meant to capture the specifics of organisational business plans, which are usually expressed as key performance indicators (KPIs) or in tangible terms of some other kind. We discuss these shortly.

Research by Mithen and Edwards (2003) among Australian CEOs has suggested that the top seven business success factors are:

- recruiting and retaining skilled employees
- increasing customer satisfaction
- employing and developing leaders
- sustaining a competitive advantage

- managing risk
- managing change and corporate culture
- becoming more innovative

In addition, the research also found that according to Australian HR managers, the major HR challenges facing Australian organisations are (in order of importance):

- labour supply
- productivity
- profitability and sustainability
- leadership and management
- globalisation
- recruitment, retention and talent management

These two sets of responses indicate a strong connection between the workforce and strategically significant business issues

Gratton and Truss (2003) have pointed out that not only do HR strategies and their attendant policies need to be consistent with business goals (vertical alignment) and with each other (horizontal alignment), but there also needs to be action (i.e. people need to actually carry them out). This might seem self-evident, but anyone who has worked in an organisation will know that simply having a strategy or a policy does not necessarily mean that the strategy or policy is enacted. This is a theme we explore further in Part II of this book as we discuss policy processes, including implementation.

Jorgensen (2005) has argued for a 'workforce policy architecture' that embraces six themes: quality and balance; procedures; compensation; people; work; and opportunity. These are designed to work together to create a high-performance environment in which productivity and commitment are enhanced. This kind of approach implies that, regardless of specific business strategies, there are certain fundamentally desirable cultural characteristics that can be activated through HR strategies and policies.

Although logic suggests a linear relationship between business strategy and HR strategy, there is a view that this is too simplistic, and that there is, in fact, a 'mutually informative' relationship between the two (Lemmergaard 2009). This shows that HR strategy is not simply a vehicle for achieving prescribed business outcomes. Indeed, Boxall and Purcell (2016) contend that HR has both economic and sociopolitical goals. The economic goals concern things like cost-effective labour, organisational flexibility and a workforce that delivers a competitive advantage. The sociopolitical goals revolve around social legitimacy (managing the workforce in a way that meets legal and social expectations) and managerial power (the tendency for management to act politically to increase its influence as a stakeholder over time). Inevitably, there is tension between these different goals.

The strategic role of HR

The reconception of HR as a strategic function is perhaps the most significant development in the profession's history. The term 'strategic business partner' has become common as a description of this new role and has even begun to be reflected in job titles. Interestingly, Ulrich's competency framework does not use the term. Rather, it describes a 'strategic positioner' who understands the business context and acts 'from the outside in' (Ulrich et al. 2012). The transition has not been an easy one. Indeed, Labedz and Lee (2011) have found that HR professionals 'lack a robust, integrated HR strategic perspective'. One of the responses to this redefinition of the role has been to devolve transactional people management functions to line managers, freeing up HR to focus on more strategic work. However, this move has had a mixed reception from line managers (Kulik and Bainbridge 2006).

As business partners, HR practitioners have needed to develop the ability to influence rather than simply impose administrative requirements (Wright 2008). HR practitioners who have assumed the mantle of strategic business partners do, however, have a distinct tendency to continue their involvement with issues concerning employee well-being. Indeed, this has been rationalised as being part of a legitimate strategic function because it enhances employee engagement and helps to maintain productivity and reduce staff turnover (Brown et al. 2009). This is consistent with Ulrich and Brockbank's (2009) view that focusing on the business side of the equation at the expense of the people side will negatively affect HR's ability to influence organisational performance.

From a policy perspective, acting as a strategic business partner should enhance HR's capacity to target strategically significant areas and to develop effective strategic policies. The biggest challenge is to get the business/people balance right. Brown et al.'s (2009) research indicates that at least some HR practitioners are attempting to do that by assuming the role of internal consultant. The need for a similar approach to policy could also be argued. HR policy portfolios that emphasise the business side of the equation at the expense of the people side (and vice versa) will be less effective than policies that balance the two appropriately.

Measurement

As we mentioned earlier, business strategies are usually defined by KPIs which are routinely measured to assess organisational performance. The adage that

Balanced scorecard	Triple bottom line
• Financial	• Economic/financial
• Processes	• Social
• Customers	• Environmental
• Learning and growing	

Figure 3.3 Multidimensional organisational measurement methods.

'what gets measured gets done' illustrates the effectiveness of KPIs in focusing attention and effort on those aspects of performance that are considered to be important. Traditionally, organisations have measured performance in financial terms (i.e. profit and loss, expenditure against budget allocations etc.), but organisational measurement today tends to be multidimensional. The recognition that organisational performance is more than just financial performance has led to the development of more holistic approaches to measurement such as the balanced scorecard and the triple bottom line. Both these methodologies seek to capture business data that indicate performance across a range of different categories as summarised in Figure 3.3.

Workforce measures are generally included as part of the 'learning and growth' category in the balanced scorecard methodology and within the 'social' category of the triple bottom line approach. Although methodologies like these have their critics, they have been adopted by a significant number of organisations. Others have developed their own KPIs based on a multidimensional philosophy but without necessarily adhering to a particular theoretical framework. Ultimately, organisations make their own judgments about what HR measures are strategically important. Table 3.1 outlines some of the potential workforce measures that might fall within this category.

HR might routinely measure all or most of these (especially if the organisation has a good HR information system), but it is unlikely that organisations would include them all in their overall KPIs. Whichever HR indicators are measured as part of the organisation's performance measurement matrix, they should have HR policies underpinning them.

Policies as strategy enablers

HR policy can be seen as the bridge between HR strategy and HR practice (Figure 3.4).

Without policies to back them, strategies are really little more than statements of good intention. Desirable strategic outcomes can only be achieved through action, and it is this action which policy describes and regulates. Perhaps more than anything else, HR policies help to ensure that the organisation's approach

Table 3.1 Possible strategic HR measures

HR area	Possible strategic measures
Staffing	Employee numbers and demographics
	Employee turnover
	Leave liability
	Employment patterns (i.e. F/T, P/T, casual etc.)
	Number of applicants per vacancy
	Vacancy filling times
Remuneration	Salary costs
	Average salary per employee, per occupational group, per division
	Salary differentials
	Overtime costs
Learning and development	Number of hours of training
	Types of learning/training activity
	Percentage of employees participating in learning/training
	Expenditure per person, per division
	Employee qualifications and study
Health, safety and well-being	Accident/incident rates
	Workers' compensation claims
	Workers' compensation costs
	Absence rates
	Grievances
Performance management	Percentage of appraisals completed
	Distribution of appraisal ratings
	360 degree feedback outcomes
	Performance bonuses awarded
Equity and diversity	Ratios of employees from different groups (women, ethnic and cultural groups, age groups)
	Number of grievances relating to equal employment opportunity (EEO)
	Turnover among members of EEO groups

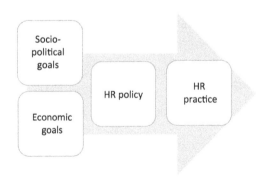

Figure 3.4 Relationship of policy to strategy.

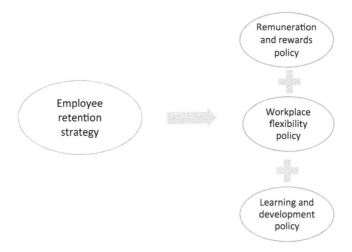

Figure 3.5 An example of how policies combine to facilitate strategy.

to its strategic objectives is coherent and consistent. They promote a shared understanding of HR strategies and a common approach to the way those strategies are translated into action.

The relationship between policy and strategy is somewhat more complex than 'one strategy = one policy'. In fact, there may be several policies that contribute to one strategic objective, as in the example in Figure 3.5.

In addition, individual policies may contribute to more than one strategic objective. In the example in Figure 3.5, for instance, the remuneration and rewards policy might also accommodate the requirements of a strategy to improve productivity, the workplace flexibility policy might address the organisation's diversity objectives and the training and development policy might also relate to a strategic objective to develop the next generation of leaders. So, strategic policies are interconnected, combining in different ways to support different strategic objectives. This high degree of interconnectedness adds further complexity to the policy function and places the onus on HR to ensure that coherence and consistency are maintained as the context changes and business objectives change.

It should also be remembered that HR policy is not solely about supporting business strategy (i.e. economic goals). There are also legal, regulatory, social and ethical considerations (i.e. sociopolitical goals). Policies need to take proper account of those factors as well as supporting strategic business objectives. After all, there is no value in developing a policy that addresses a business priority but is not legally or ethically defensible or that lacks what Boxall and Purcell (2016) call 'social legitimacy'. Indeed, it is part of HR's role to ensure that the organisation's people management practices do not leave it vulnerable to adverse consequences – an issue we explore further in Chapter 4.

Summary

- HR issues are among the most significant strategic issues identified by contemporary CEOs.
- Most organisational objectives are ultimately achieved through people, and so the management of people is an important strategic factor.
- HR policy is the link between HR strategy and HR practice. HR policies give life to HR strategies and ensure that there is a common understanding of their meaning and intent and a consistent approach to the way they are enacted.
- HR policies often combine to address a specific strategic objective.
- It is common for individual HR policies to underpin several different strategies simultaneously.
- Although there is a strong link between business strategy and HR policy, the role of policy also includes facilitating compliance with applicable laws and regulations as well as ethical and social standards. Policies, therefore, need to balance all of these considerations.

Learning activity – linking strategy and policy

Purpose and process

The purpose of this exercise is to help you think about the relationship between HR policy and HR strategy. Table 1 outlines the various types of HR policies that we'll be exploring in this book. Table 2 lists the strategic HR objectives for a large hypothetical organisation in the mining and resources sector. These objectives have been classified as part of the organisation's strategic planning and risk management processes; they identify a number of key workforce issues that need to be addressed to enable the organisation to achieve its business objectives. Your task is to consider each of the strategic objectives and identify the kinds of policies that would facilitate them. You do not have to design the strategies; just identify the policies that relate to them.

Remember:

Don't think 'one strategy = one policy'. Usually two or more policies combine to transform strategic objectives into actions.
- One HR policy might actually contribute to several strategies.

- Obviously you don't have access to the details of the policies themselves. That isn't necessary for the purposes of this exercise because we're thinking conceptually. Identify which policies would support which strategies. Outline the rationale for each choice you make.

Table B3.1 HR policies

Attendance management policy	Leave management policy
Code of conduct/ethics	Performance management policy
Discipline policy	Remuneration and rewards policy
Dress code	Staffing policy (recruitment, selection, employment, termination)
Work health, safety and well-being policy	Succession management policy
Equity and diversity policy	Workplace flexibility policy
Grievance and dispute resolution policy	Social media policy
Learning and development policy	

Table B3.2 Strategic objectives

1. Preparing the next generation of leaders
2. Reducing staff turnover
3. Reducing absenteeism
4. Increasing the representation of women in management and leadership roles
5. Reducing workers' compensation claims
6. Increasing labour market competitiveness for engineering and accounting roles
7. Encouraging older workers to stay with the company rather than take early retirement

References

Boxall, P., and Purcell, J. 2016. *Strategy and Human Resource Management* (4th edn). Basingstoke: Palgrave MacMillan, pp. 8–17.

Brown, M., Metz, I., Cregan, C. and Kulik, C. 2009. 'Irreconcilable differences? Strategic human resource management and employee wellbeing'. *Asia Pacific Journal of Human Resources* 47(3): 270–94.

Gratton, L., and Truss, C. 2003. 'The three dimensional people strategy: Putting human resources policies into action'. *Academy of Management Executive* 17(3): 74–86.

Jorgensen, B. 2005. 'Attract, retain and innovate: A workforce policy architecture adapted to modern conditions'. *Foresight* 7(5): 21–31.

Kramar, R., Bartram, T. and De Cieri, H. 2014. *Human Resource Management: Strategy, People Performance* (5th edn). North Ryde: McGraw Hill, pp. 25–28.

Kulik, C., and Bainbridge, H. 2006. 'HR and the line: The distribution of HR activities in Australian organisations'. *Asia Pacific Journal of Human Resources* 44(2): 240–56.

Labedz, C., and Lee, J. 2011. 'The mental models of HR professionals as strategic partners'. *Journal of Management and Organization* 17(1): 56–76.

Lemmergaard, J. 2009. 'From administrative expert to strategic partner'. *Employee Relations* 31(2): 182–96.

Mithen, J., and Edwards, D. 2003. *HR Creating Business Solutions: A Positioning Paper.* Melbourne: Australian Human Resources Institute.

Nankervis, A., Baird, M., Coffey, J. and Shields, J. 2017. *Human Resource Management: Strategy and Practice* (9th edn). South Melbourne: Cengage, pp. 18–22.

Porter, M. 1985. *Competitive Advantage: Creating and Sustaining Superior Performance.* New York: Free Press.

Storey, J., and Sisson, K. 1990. 'The limits to transformation: Human resource management in the British context'. *Industrial Relations Journal* 21(1): 60–65.

Ulrich, D., and Brockbank, W. 2009. 'The role of strategy architect in the strategic HR organization'. *People and Strategy* 32(1): 24–31.

Ulrich, D., Younger, J., Brockbank, W. and Ulrich, M. 2012. 'HR talent and the new HR competencies'. *Strategic HR Review* 11(4): 217–22.

Wright, C. 2008. 'Reinventing human resource management: Business partners, internal consultants and the limits to professionalization'. *Human Relations* 61(8): 1063–86.

Chapter 4

POLICY AND ORGANISATIONAL CULTURE

Theorists and researchers have devised numerous ways to classify organisational culture based on the structure, business strategies and management methods of organisations. One of the most important aspects of culture is the way in which the workforce is perceived and managed. Perhaps the most interesting characteristic of the relationship between HR policy and organisational culture is that it is two-way: the prevailing culture shapes HR policy, but equally, HR policy can influence and shape organisational culture. Indeed, HR policy can be a powerful catalyst for cultural change.

The introduction of new or revised policies can signal a shift in management thinking and help to bring about changes in the way the workforce is managed. In most cases, the messages that HR policies send about the organisation's culture are implicit. Organisations rarely attempt to define their cultures in an explicit way. Rather, the culture is implied by the decisions, actions and management policies of the organisation. Historically, the most explicit cultural statements about workforce management have tended to be empty platitudes like 'Our people are our most valuable resource'. Such statements have come to be viewed sceptically by employees, especially where the reality does not match the rhetoric. Indeed, as Gill (1999) has pointed out, it is common for organisations to espouse a culture that values employees as important sources of competitive advantage while managing those employees as mere commodities. If, as Begley and Boyd (2000) have asserted, actual corporate values regarding the workforce are articulated through HR policies, then employees will be more likely to draw their conclusions from those policies than from management rhetoric.

Approaches to HR culture

Policies that relate to the management of the workforce imply (broadly speaking) one of two particular philosophical positions. The two competing philosophies are perhaps best characterised by the Harvard Model (sometimes referred to as the Harvard Map of HRM) and the Michigan Model.

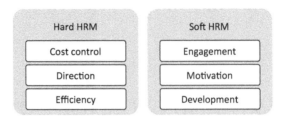

Figure 4.1 Soft and hard HR policy objectives.

The Harvard Model emerged from the so-called human relations school of management thought that was developed in the 1930s. The human relations school brought the social science of psychology to the business of managing people and emphasised issues such as motivation and job satisfaction as keys to employee performance. Taking that fundamental philosophy as its base, the Harvard Model sees employees as complex entities that cannot be managed like other resources. It proposes that people management policies and practices should have the ultimate objective of achieving commitment, competence and congruence, as well as cost effectiveness (Beer et al. 1984).

By contrast, the Michigan Model sees employees as resources to be managed in exactly the same way as any other resource. Drawing on strategic management theory, it emphasises cost control and efficiency, and advocates that people management policies and practices be directed exclusively to the achievement of business objectives (Tichy et al. 1982).

These philosophies have come to be seen as embodying *soft* and *hard* approaches to HRM (Figure 4.1). HR policies under these philosophies will inevitably vary in their objectives and focus.

In reality, however, it is not possible to characterise organisational HR culture as simply being one or the other. It is more accurate to see the two philosophies as being at opposite ends of a continuum. Organisational cultures tend not to occupy a fixed position on the continuum, but move backwards and forwards along it under the influence of contextual factors (such as those we discussed in Chapter 2) and internal factors (such as the values of the leadership group and the influence and status of HR). HR policies, therefore, will reflect the organisation's position on the continuum. Indeed, it is common for organisations to have some HR policies that clearly equate with a hard HRM philosophy and others that equate more with soft HRM. Clearly, there is potential for policies to conflict or send mixed messages, but this is not to say that hard and soft policies cannot coexist. One of HR's important policy management roles, therefore, is to maintain an appropriate balance between hard and soft policies and ensure that they do not clash with one another.

Human capital and intellectual capital

The concept of human capital (HC) has emerged from economic theory and has evolved to a point where it can be seen as an attempt to reconcile the different approaches to people management that we have just discussed. Traditionally, workforces have been seen as a cost of production. Contemporary HC theory sees the workforce as a capital asset, and so workforce costs are seen as investments which produce a tangible return for the organisation and contribute to its overall value. Indeed, numerous studies have shown a positive link between investment in HC development and organisational performance (Marimuthu et al. 2009; Agarwala 2003; Garavan et al. 2001).

An important difference between HC and other forms of capital is that, rather than being owned by the organisation, HC is engaged through the employment relationship. Part of that relationship is about recognising that an organisation's intellectual capital is not restricted to tangible assets like patents and intellectual property. Employees, too, possess stocks of intellectual capital (e.g. skills, knowledge and ideas) which they choose either to use or to withhold in the workplace. The nature of the employment relationship influences the extent to which this discretionary effort is applied. Burr and Girardi (2002), expanding on an earlier model developed by Ulrich (1998), have identified three aspects of intellectual capital which can all be affected by organisational culture and HR policy (see Figure 4.2).

The model suggests that, in order to optimise the intellectual capital that resides with people, organisations need to harness the capacity (competence) of employees, and their willingness to apply it (commitment), as well as giving them the opportunity to do so (control).

The implication of this model is that policies that enhance employee capacity and willingness, and which provide opportunity, will increase employee performance and, ultimately, organisational performance.

Psychological contracts

Unlike the formal employment contract, which is explicit, the psychological contract between employers and employees is implicit. The nature of psychological contracts has undergone significant change in recent times, moving from the *relational*, which is characterised by mutual commitment, to the *transactional*, which is based on an economic exchange (McShane and Travaglione 2003; Holland et al. 2015).

HR policies are indicators of the type of psychological contract that the organisation favours. Grant (1999) has pointed out that where there is a mismatch between the type of relationship explicitly espoused by the organisation

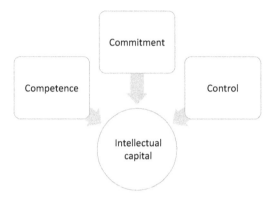

Figure 4.2 Dimensions of intellectual capital.

and employee perceptions of the reality of the relationship, there are inevitably negative consequences, such as cynicism, reduction in commitment and lower levels of employee engagement. This underlines the importance of alignment between policy and practice. This is a policy management issue that clearly falls within the purview of HR.

Notwithstanding these potential dangers, there is also a view that the trend towards transactional psychological contracts has negative long-term implications (Tsui and Wu 2005). This view places the onus on HR to develop policies and practices that emphasise reciprocity and are geared towards building long-term relationships between employers and employees. Importantly, Sonnenberg et al. (2011) have found that 'traditional' HR activities which are concerned with processes and systems are just as influential in shaping the psychological contract as HR practices that are specifically designed to enhance employee commitment. This indicates a significant role for HR policy, because it is through policy that these 'traditional' HR activities are regulated.

Workplace spirituality

One aspect of organisational culture which is gaining greater understanding and acceptance is spirituality. While for some, workplace spirituality is strongly connected with religious faith or other belief systems, for an increasing number of people, it is more about finding meaning and significance in their work and in the role of work in their lives. Organisations that embrace workplace spirituality essentially recognise that most people are driven by things deeper than financial reward and seek some sort of personal fulfilment in their lives and work.

Moore (2008) has asserted that the spiritual profiles of organisational leaders create the spiritual baseline for that organisation and that corporate cultures reflect the spiritual characteristics of the leadership group. These spiritual characteristics manifest themselves both in the way the organisation does business and in the way it perceives and manages its workforce.

According to Robbins et al. (2008), 'humanistic' policies and work practices that embrace workplace flexibility, collective rewards systems, equity, respect for individual differences and job security contribute significantly to the creation of a spiritual workplace. This implies a role for HR policy in developing and maintaining a culture where spirituality is embraced and nurtured.

Spirituality is very much on the soft side of the cultural continuum; thus it tends to be more congruent with 'softer' cultures than with 'harder' ones.

Cultural change

As we have mentioned earlier in this chapter, organisations' people management cultures tend to move backwards and forwards along the cultural continuum in response to internal and external influences. Sometimes a radical cultural shift is necessary – often as the result of a crisis. Changes like these are quite rightly led from the top, with changes to policies and management practices being modelled by the organisation's leaders (Waddell et al. 2011). Where cultural change is strategic in nature, HR policy clearly has an important role to play in defining and embedding cultural changes through the development and implementation of policies that are consistent with the strategy. This is consistent with the 'change champion' role outlined by Ulrich et al. (2012) as part of their strategic HRM competency framework. Under this framework, HR professionals are cast in the role of custodians of organisational culture. The role includes shaping a culture that is consistent with the organisation's strategic goals. Clearly, policy is an important tool in this process.

While it is difficult to argue against the logic of shaping culture to align it with strategic objectives, there is also a question of whether or not HR policy has a more fundamental culture-shaping role. After all, culture is not just about organisational strategy. It is also connected with the sorts of issues we have discussed in this chapter (the basic people management philosophy, the nature of the psychological contract and workplace spirituality). These are values-based concepts. Advocates of soft HRM philosophies or the 'people as assets, not resources' philosophy of HC theory or workplace spirituality would doubtless argue that HR should promote and uphold certain principles and values regardless of organisational strategy – and that such principles and values transcend business goals. This is not to suggest that HR should develop and enact policies that actively work against organisational objectives, but it does mean that, as stewards of culture, HR professionals need to balance values with business needs. This requires an ability to make meaningful connections between values-based cultural features and the achievement of business goals, and to successfully argue for them and gain support for them rather than attempting to implement them by stealth.

Summary

Although many organisations espouse a culture that values employees, it is common for policy and practice to be inconsistent with this, creating cynicism and negativity among employees.

- HR policy has a two-way relationship with culture – it reflects the prevailing culture but can also be used to change culture.
- People management cultures can be characterised as being 'hard' or 'soft', but rather than this being a simple dichotomy, it is more like a continuum. Most organisational cultures evolve in response to internal and external factors. They do not occupy a fixed position on the continuum.
- The workforce-related aspects of organisational cultures can be understood by looking at them through the lenses of theoretical frameworks that explore the relationship between employees and employers (e.g. human capital theory, intellectual capital theory, psychological contract theory and workplace spirituality theory).
- Modern conceptions of strategic HRM see HR professionals as custodians of organisational culture with the primary role of aligning culture with business objectives.
- A significant challenge for HR professionals operating as strategic business partners is to balance fundamental people management values with business needs.

Discussion questions

1. Is it true that people who are attracted to work in HR generally embrace soft HRM philosophies? If so, does this limit their potential to be genuine strategic business partners?
2. Is it possible to truly balance people-oriented values with hard business needs? Is 'balance' really just a compromise?
3. Is it necessary for all organisations to strive to engage, motivate and develop their employees? Is it possible to be successful from a business perspective without having a 'warm, fuzzy' relationship with the workforce?

4. Do all employees want a relational psychological contract with their employers? Aren't some people happy simply to do their jobs and collect their pay?

References

Agarwala, T. 2003. 'Innovative human resource practices and organizational commitment: An empirical investigation. *International Journal of Human Resource Management* 14(2): 175–97.

Beer, M., Spector, B., Lawrence, P., Mills, Q. and Walton, R. 1984. *Managing Human Assets*. Boston: Harvard Business Press.

Begley, T., and Boyd, D. 2000. 'Articulating corporate values through human resource policies'. *Business Horizons* (July/August): 8–12.

Burr, R., and Girardi, A. 2002. 'Intellectual capital: More than the interaction of competence x commitment'. *Australian Journal of Management* 27: 77–87.

Garavan, T. N., Morley, M., Gunnigle, P. and Collins, E. 2001. 'Human capital accumulation: The role of human resource development'. *Journal of European Industrial Training* 25(2/3/4): 48–68.

Gill, C. 1999. 'Use of hard and soft models of HRM to illustrate gaps between rhetoric and reality in workforce management'. WP99/13, Working Paper Series, RMIT University.

Grant, D. 1999. 'HRM rhetoric and the psychological contract: An employer perspective'. *International Journal of Human Resource Management* 10: 327–50.

Holland, P., Sheehan, C., Donohue, R., Pyman, A. and Allen, B. 2015. In *Contemporary Issues and Challenges in HRM* (3rd edn). Prahran: Tilde University Press, pp. 77–99.

Marimuthu, M., Arokiasamy, L. and Ismail, M. 2009. 'Human capital development and its impact on firm performance: Evidence from developmental economics'. *Journal of International Social Research* 2(8): 265–72.

McShane, S., and Travaglione, P. 2003. *Organisational Behaviour on the Pacific Rim*. Roseville: McGraw-Hill, pp. 596–99.

Moore, T. W. 2008. 'Individual differences and workplace spirituality: The homogenization of the corporate culture'. *Journal of Management and Marketing Research* 1: 79–93.

Robbins, S., Judge, T., Millett, B. and Waters-Marsh, T. 2008. *Organisational Behaviour*. New South Wales: Pearson Education Australia, French's Forest, pp. 596–98.

Sonnenberg, M., Koene, B. and Paauwe, J. 2011. 'Balancing HRM: The psychological contract of employees – a multi-level study'. *Personnel Review* 40(6): 664–83.

Tichy, N., Fombrun, C. and Devanna, M. 1982. 'Strategic human resource management'. *Sloan Management Review* 23(2): 47–61.

Tsui, A., and Wu, J. 2005. 'The new employment relationship versus the mutual investment approach: Implications for human resource management'. In M. Losey, S. Meisinger and D. Ulrich (eds), *The Future of Human Resource Management*. Hoboken: John Wiley and Sons, pp. 44–54.

Ulrich, D. 1998. 'Intellectual capital equals competence x commitment'. *Sloan Management Review* 39: 15–26.

Ulrich, D., Younger, J., Brockbank, W. and Ulrich, M. 2012. 'HR Talent and the new HR competencies'. *Strategic HR Review* 11(4): 217–22.

Waddell, D., Cummings, C. and Worley, C. 2011. *Organisational Change. Development and Transformation* (4th edn). South Melbourne: Cengage Learning Australia, pp. 325–27.

Chapter 5

POLICY AND RISK MANAGEMENT

Risk management is the process of systematically identifying and addressing business risks. Most organisations have some kind of formal risk management process, and some larger organisations employ risk management specialists to ensure that the organisation is equipped to manage risks effectively. Business risks can include factors such as natural disasters, systems failures, fraud, accidents or any event that has an adverse effect on the business. As we discussed in Chapter 3, CEOs place a high priority on risk management (Mithen and Edwards 2003; Nickson 2001); therefore it should be a concern for managers in all areas, including HR.

Risk management processes

Typically, the risk management process involves three stages (Figure 5.1). The usual outcome of the risk analysis stage is a matrix of risks and their risk ratings based on how likely they are to occur (shown on the vertical axis in Table 5.1) and the potential level of impact (shown on the horizontal axis).

Risks with high or extreme ratings will obviously be priorities at the risk treatment stage.

In recent times, workforce-related risks have become increasingly prominent in organisational risk assessments (CIPD 2006); therefore the role of HR in the risk management process has become all the more important.

Risk management and HR

In the past, risk management was seen as being primarily about risk mitigation (i.e. a mostly defensive function), but more recently it has begun to be conceived as a strategic function that is geared towards positioning the organisation for the future (KPMG 2010).

Within the sphere of HR, risk management has traditionally been associated with occupational safety and health, but today it is conceived much more broadly. Ernst and Young (2008) have identified four categories of risk related to the management of the workforce (Figure 5.2).

Table 5.1 Risk Assessment Matrix

	Insignificant	Minor	Moderate	Major	Catastrophic
Almost certain	M	H	H	E	E
Likely	M	M	H	H	E
Possible	L	M	M	H	E
Unlikely	L	M	M	M	H
Rare	L	L	M	M	M

Risk ratings: L = low; M = medium; H = high; E = extreme.

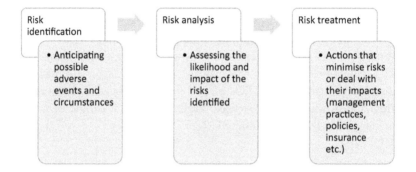

Figure 5.1 Typical risk management process.

Figure 5.2 Categories of HR risk.

Compliance risks are those risks posed by non-compliance with legislation, regulations or standards; financial risks are about workforce costs, budgets and value for money; operational risks are those which affect the productivity and efficiency of the organisation; and strategic risks are those that affect an organisation's sustainability and/or competitive position into the future. Ernst and Young's research has also revealed that the focus has shifted from managing compliance and financial risks to managing strategic risks, which is consistent with the evolution of HR as a strategic function.

Cascio and Boudreau (2012) have pointed out that risk management is an essential component of a genuinely strategic approach to human resource management. Despite this, however, a significant percentage of organisations do not review their HR risk profiles regularly – and some do not review them at all.

Stevens (2005) has also pointed out that HR needs to manage risks related to itself and its role within the organisation. Essentially, this more introspective aspect of risk management requires HR to be conscious of its impact on operations and of how it is perceived and to manage these factors actively. This implies that there are inherent risks for HR in being perceived negatively and not being seen to be making a tangible contribution to the organisation. As we discussed in Chapter 1, these risks are real and have the potential to undermine HR's status if not managed effectively. Balancing outward-looking and inward-looking approaches to risk management is very important. The danger of HR being too focused on itself is that it may actually exacerbate negative perceptions by being seen to be more concerned with organisational politics than with the effective management of the workforce. Therefore, HR's primary risk management efforts should be directed towards workforce risks.

Major HR risks

Research by the Chartered Institute of Personnel and Development (CIPD) and by Ernst and Young covering organisations in the United Kingdom, the United States and elsewhere in the developed world has revealed a fairly consistent set of HR risk issues. Using the framework we discussed in the previous section, Table 5.2 summarises the major HR risks commonly identified.

There are, of course, connections between the different risks. For example, compliance issues that lead to litigation or prosecution may damage the organisation's ability to recruit and retain, result in higher turnover or absence rates and lead to increased expenditure on recruitment and training.

In addition, Whicker and Andrews (2004) have identified 'knowledge risk' as a significant HR issue. Knowledge risk refers to loss of corporate knowledge either through underutilisation or as the result of people leaving. This is a particularly cogent issue because of the demographics of the workforce and the generational change that will be caused by the retirement en masse of workers from the baby boomer generation. This is primarily a strategic risk, but it could conceivably have impact across all four HR risk categories.

Table 5.2 Major HR risks

Risk category	Nature of risk
Compliance	Employee misconduct
	Employee litigation
	Prosecution
Financial	Unsustainable employment costs
	Increased workers' compensation costs
	Excessive expenditure on recruitment
	Insufficient return on investment in learning and development
Operational	High turnover
	Absenteeism
	Injury
	Industrial action
Strategic	Recruitment difficulties
	Retention problems
	Skills shortages
	Succession management difficulties

Earle (2009) has pointed out that there are also significant risks associated with remuneration, especially performance-linked remuneration such as bonuses. These risks include 'short-termism', in which inordinate emphasis is placed on rewarding short-term rather than long-term outcomes, as well as the risk of manipulation of outcomes by employees to give the appearance of meeting requirements for bonuses or other incentives. Flawed remuneration and reward systems carry significant risks as we have seen in the financial services industry in recent times. This is essentially a financial risk, but it too has possible impact across risk categories. Indeed, it could be argued that the effect on corporate reputation and customer confidence caused by the failure of remuneration and rewards systems is potentially more damaging than the financial aspect.

Vito (2008) has identified executive management ethics, health care costs, employee fraud and HR outsourcing as noteworthy risks that should be included in HR audits. Indeed, regular auditing is an effective way to identify emerging risks.

Policy responses to HR risks

In the main, HR risks are best addressed in a proactive way. That is, the emphasis should be on prevention rather than remediation. Policy is an effective vehicle for proactively addressing risks because it helps to prevent circumstances that give rise to risk by defining and underpinning management actions and behaviours

Table 5.3 HR policy/risk matrix (compliance risks)

	Employee misconduct	Employee litigation	Prosecution
Attendance management			
Code of conduct/ethics	X	X	X
Discipline	X	X	X
Dress code			
Employee privacy	X	X	X
Equity and diversity		X	X
Grievance	X	X	X
Leave management			
Health, safety and well-being			X
Performance management			
Remuneration/rewards			X
Social media	X	X	
Succession management			
Staffing (recruitment)			X
Staffing (selection)			
Staffing (employment)		X	X
Staffing (termination)	X	X	X
Learning and development			
Workplace flexibility			

that contribute to risk reduction. Every HR policy area has a risk management dimension. Tables 5.3–5.6 show how HR policies contribute to the management of different HR risks. We discuss their specific application in Part III.

In addition, Stevens (2005) points out that not having appropriate HR policies in place can lead to increased tension between employees and management and a consequent reduction in workplace harmony and productivity.

HR policies can also contribute to the management of other non-workforce-related business risks, particularly those connected with the protection of corporate reputation (e.g. code of ethics/code of conduct and dress code). Indeed, employment practices and people management issues in general have the potential to impact either positively or negatively on corporate reputation, and so HR policies that minimise the likelihood of controversy are useful from that perspective.

Issues and challenges for HR

Risk management is an area that has the potential to connect HR with other areas of management and to demonstrate HR's tangible contribution to the organisation. HR policies that address risk management issues can, therefore,

Table 5.4 HR policy/risk matrix (financial risks)

	Unsustainable employment costs	Increased workers' comp. costs	Excessive recruitment expenditure	Insufficient return on investment in learning and development
Attendance management	X			
Code of conduct/ethics				
Discipline				
Dress code				
Employee privacy				
Equity and diversity				
Grievance				
Leave management	X			
Health, safety and well-being		X		
Performance management				X
Remuneration/rewards	X			
Social media				
Succession management				X
Staffing (recruitment)			X	
Staffing (selection)			X	
Staffing (employment)	X			
Staffing (termination)				
Learning and development				X
Workplace flexibility	X			

enhance HR's relationship with management and improve its profile. One of the positive consequences of HR being actively involved in risk management is that it provides opportunities for greater understanding of why certain HR policies are desirable. This is particularly true for policies that have traditionally been seen as bureaucratic impositions (e.g. discipline, grievance, staffing, attendance management and performance management policies). Where these are understood to be protecting the organisation from adverse events such as litigation or prosecution, they are more likely to be accepted and less likely to create a negative view of HR.

However, there are also inherent risks in HR becoming too risk focused (CIPD 2006). An excessive emphasis on HR policies that reduce risk can have the effect of creating an inappropriately conservative and risk-averse culture that stifles innovation and actually reduces people's quality of work life. After all, HR policy is not solely a risk management function. It is also a vehicle for connecting HR to many other aspects of organisational management – such as the other topics covered in Part I of this book. Therefore, getting the right

Table 5.5 HR policy/risk matrix (operational risks)

	High turnover	Absenteeism	Injury	Industrial action
Attendance management		X		
Code of conduct/ethics				
Discipline				X
Dress code			X	
Employee privacy				X
Equity and diversity	X	X		
Grievance				
Leave management	X	X		
Health, safety and well-being			X	X
Performance management			X	
Remuneration/rewards	X			X
Social media				
Succession management				
Staffing (recruitment)				
Staffing (selection)				
Staffing (employment)				
Staffing (termination)				
Learning and development			X	
Workplace flexibility	X	X		X

Table 5.6 HR policy/risk matrix (strategic risks)

	Recruitment difficulties	Retention problems	Skills shortages	Succession and knowledge loss
Attendance management				
Code of conduct/ethics				
Discipline				
Dress code				
Employee privacy		X		
Equity and diversity	X	X		
Grievance		X		
Leave management				
Health, safety and well-being		X		
Performance management		X	X	X
Remuneration/rewards	X	X		
Social media				
Succession management		X	X	X
Staffing (recruitment)	X			
Staffing (selection)	X			
Staffing (employment)		X		
Staffing (termination)		X		
Learning and development	X	X	X	X
Workplace flexibility	X	X		X

balance is very important. Every organisation has a different risk profile which is shaped by the nature of its industry, its history and its strategic goals. HR policies, therefore, need to be consistent with the risk profile of the organisation.

We have argued in this chapter that risk-related HR policies should be proactive and geared towards prevention of adverse events. The reality is that not all adverse events are foreseeable, and so policy is sometimes reactive. When an unforeseen adverse event occurs, the immediate response is often to develop or amend policies 'so it won't happen again'. In circumstances like these, care needs to be taken that the policy response is not an overreaction. If the adverse event is unusual or has arisen because of unique circumstances, the likelihood of it recurring is probably very low. An inappropriately heavy-handed policy response may have the effect of imposing restrictions or processes that reduce efficiency and effectiveness in the name of addressing a risk that may never arise again. While it is always appropriate to review policies after critical incidents, the review process should include a proper assessment of future likelihood and potential impact, as in the normal risk management process, rather than being a knee-jerk reaction. Where workforce-related risks are concerned, it is clearly HR's role to ensure that policy responses to adverse events are appropriate.

Summary

- HR risk is no longer considered to be primarily about occupational safety and health – it is now recognised that HR risk is a much broader concept.
- HR risks can be divided into four categories: compliance risks, financial risks, operational risks and strategic risks.
- Strategic risks are of particular concern to CEOs at present because of the changing demographics of the workforce, the potentially devastating loss of corporate knowledge that this might precipitate and the emergence of skills and labour shortages in the near future.
- HR policies are effective risk treatments that focus on prevention rather than remediation.
- All HR policy areas have the potential to contribute in some way to risk management, though the risk management aspects of policy need to be balanced with other policy drivers.
- Although risk management can provide opportunities for HR policy to assume greater importance, it is important that HR not be overly focused on risk. Too great a risk focus can lead to the development of a risk-averse culture which is detrimental to innovation, change and employee morale.

Discussion questions

1. Consider the sorts of people-related things that can go wrong in organisations. What would be some of the most devastating ones? Can they be prevented through policy?
2. Are some HR risks inevitable? If so, discuss some examples. If a risk is inevitable, is it better to accept that and develop policies to deal with the aftermath rather than waste effort trying to prevent it?
3. Is it sufficient for HR to justify unpopular policies as being risk management policies and therefore necessary?
4. Are strategic risks more important than other categories of risk? If so, why? If not, why not?

References

Cascio, W., and Boudreau, J. 2012. *Short Introduction to Strategic Human Resource Management*. Cambridge: Cambridge University Press, pp. 21–23.
CIPD. 2006. *Risk and Performance: HR's Role in Managing Risk*. London: Chartered Institute of Personnel and Development.
Earle, J. 2009. 'The evolving role of risk management in the design and governance of compensation programs'. *Benefits Law Journal* 22(4): 44–56.
Ernst and Young. 2008. *2008 Global Human Resources Risk: From the Danger Zone to the Value Zone*. http://www.corporate-leaders.com/sitescene/custom/userfiles/file/2008_Global_Human_resource_risk.pdf.
KPMG. 2010. *Enterprise Risk Management: From Theory to Practice*. https://www.in.kpmg.com/SecureData/aci/Files/KPMG_ERM_Theory_Practices.pdf.
Mithen, J., and Edwards, D. 2003. *HR Creating Business Solutions: A Positioning Paper*. Melbourne: Australian Human Resources Institute.
Nickson, S. 2001. 'The human resources balancing act: Cooperation between risk management and human resources'. *Risk Management* 48(2): 25.
Stevens, J. 2005. *Managing Risk: The Human Resources Contribution*. London: LexisNexis.
Vito, K. 2008. 'The human resources audit'. *Internal Auditor* 65(2): 83–85.
Whicker, L., and Andrews, K. 2004. 'HRM in the knowledge economy: Realising the potential'. *Asia Pacific Journal of Human Resources* 42(2): 156–65.

Chapter 6

POLICY, CREATIVITY AND INNOVATION

We tend to associate creativity and innovation with companies at the cutting edge of dynamic industries such as biotechnology and information technology. However, creativity and innovation are important to almost all organisations, because regardless of whether the organisation is commercial, governmental or community-based, it needs to operate amid constantly changing conditions. This means it must continuously be developing new products, new services and new processes. Schaper and Volery (2007) see this as a three-stage process (outlined in Figure 6.1) where ideas are generated (creativity), assessed for their potential to be applied (innovation) and transformed into reality (entrepreneurship).

The capacity of organisations to undertake this process successfully is dependent on three interconnected factors – structure, culture and HR practices (Robbins et al. 2008). Innovative organisations tend to have flatter structures and more cross-functional teams. Their cultures encourage risk-taking and experimentation, and their HR practices promote original thinking and nurture creative, innovative behaviour.

Clearly, HR policy has an important role to play as it underpins HR practice. Indeed, HR interventions can be used effectively to move an organisation towards a more innovative culture (Hope Hailey 2001). Even so, as Searle and Ball (2003) have noted, organisations do not always make the connection between HR policy and creativity and innovation, which implies that there is a danger that some HR policies (which might be introduced for legitimate reasons) may have the unintended side effect of stifling creativity and innovation. This is obviously something that HR policymakers need to bear in mind (Figure 6.2).

Managing creative people

When we hear the term 'creative people', we tend to think of artists, musicians, writers and the like. Creativity is not limited to the arts, however. Indeed, most organisations would employ people with creative skills, especially those

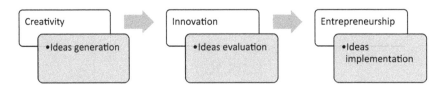

Figure 6.1 Evolution of new ideas in organisations.

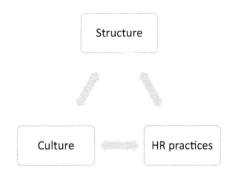

Figure 6.2 Factors affecting organisational creativity and innovation.

organisations that employ knowledge workers (i.e. people who work with their brains). The nature of knowledge workers and their work differs from those of workers whose jobs are more process oriented. It could be argued that knowledge workers, especially those with creative skills, are more challenging to manage because they require a good deal of operational autonomy and have high expectations (Newell et al. 2009). This view is supported by McLean (2005) and Hamel (2007), who also place strong emphasis on autonomy as a necessary precondition for creativity and innovation. Hamel also advocates purpose (the sense that one's work makes a difference) and community (a sense of belonging) as positive cultural features that contribute to a dynamic, engaging work environment that is conducive to innovation.

Westland (2008) has differentiated between different types of creative/ innovative roles in organisations. This role differentiation emphasises the fact that organisational creativity and innovation form a collective enterprise. Indeed, only very few individuals would have the skills or the energy to perform all of these roles. While it could be argued that only the 'ideas generators' are truly creative, the other roles are equally important because they facilitate the development and application of new ideas. After all, good ideas alone deliver no value whatsoever. They need to be converted from the conceptual to the concrete (Table 6.1).

Table 6.1 Creative/innovative roles

Role	Description
Idea generators	People who absorb data, imagine potentialities and see opportunities
Gatekeepers	People who communicate ideas across the organisation, or beyond it
Champions	People who see the potential of new ideas and actively promote them
Sponsors	People who deal with political obstacles and facilitate the development of ideas
Project managers	People who coordinate the practicalities and details of turning an idea into something tangible

The literature suggests that, in general, creative people (or those with creative potential) do not respond positively to highly regimented work environments or to 'command and control' management styles. Therefore, organisations wishing to develop a creative, innovative culture need to develop HR policies that support appropriate management practices. However, this is easier said than done. In reality, HR policies need to strike a balance that supports creativity and innovation without exposing the organisation to the kinds of risks we discussed in Chapter 5. The need for a balance between freedom and control is supported by the view that creativity and innovation do not happen in environments that are too structured or too disordered; rather they occur at some point between the two extremes (Clegg et al. 2005). Hence, HR policies designed to promote creativity and innovation can be seen as mechanisms for moderating both order and chaos.

Effects of HR practices

The fundamental role of HR policy in facilitating organisational creativity and innovation is to ensure that HR practices support creative, innovative behaviours by employees. But what kinds of HR practices will do this?

At a fundamental level, Cavagnoli (2011) has found that HR policies affect innovation by forming habits of behaviour and thought which are maintained and reinforced by reward systems.

Unsworth et al. (2005) have found that where employees understand that generating new ideas is a job requirement, it is more likely that creative behaviour will follow. This suggests that it is not sufficient simply to create conditions that lend themselves to creative, innovative behaviour. This has obvious implications for the way that jobs are defined and designed.

Beugelsdijk (2008) differentiates between incremental innovation and radical innovation and proposes that while there are commonalities, there are also some differences in the ways that HR practices affect them. Common positive effects result from job autonomy, workplace flexibility, and training and education (although training and education have a less pronounced effect on radical innovation in larger organisations). However, practices such as performance-based pay tend to have a positive effect only in relation to incremental innovation. In fact, research has found that it could actually have a negative effect on radical innovation. Job security was also found to be an important factor for both kinds of innovation, with short-term or 'standby' employment contracts having equally negative effects on both incremental and radical innovation. In a broader sense, this implies that employee retention (not just job tenure) is fundamental to innovation and that HR practices that enhance retention will also enhance innovation.

Learning and development has been identified by others as having a positive effect on organisational creativity and innovation. Gibb and Waight (2005) have contended that learning and development programmes need to develop the 'whole person' rather than be narrowly focused on operational matters, and that learning assessment that focuses only on adherence to regulations and standards can stifle creativity.

Performance management practices have also been found to affect creativity and innovation. According to Egan (2005), creativity is supported where performance evaluation is oriented towards employee development rather than simply focusing on outputs and outcomes. Hope Hailey (2001) has also noted that high-performing, innovative companies tend to favour frequent, informal performance appraisal, suggesting that, in innovative organisations, performance feedback is a cultural trait rather than an annual administrative process.

HR policies that support creativity and innovation

It should be noted at this point that HR policies and practices cannot by themselves create and sustain innovative organisations. As we have discussed earlier in this chapter, organisational creativity and innovation stem from the interactions of organisational structures, culture and HR practices. Clearly, there needs to be alignment between these three elements to achieve the desired outcome. Where HR policies and practices support creativity and innovation, but one or both of the other elements do not, the organisation will never be truly creative and innovative. This is one of the reasons that achieving a creative and innovative organisation is so difficult. Notwithstanding this, the following outlines the kinds of policies that underpin the HR practices that support creativity and innovation. Each of these policy areas is explored further in Part III.

Staffing policies

Staffing policies encompass recruitment, selection and employment practices and are perhaps the most fundamentally important policies in relation to creativity and innovation. As we have seen, autonomy is universally associated with creativity, and so key positions need to have job descriptions that reflect an operationally autonomous role. We have also seen that creativity is enhanced where there is an explicit job requirement to generate ideas. This also needs to be reflected in job descriptions. Similarly, selection criteria for key creative roles should reflect the kinds of personal characteristics and competencies that are consistent with creativity. Some organisations might wish to test for these characteristics and competencies, and if this is the case, it should be reflected in the selection policy.

Employment policies should emphasise long-term or ongoing job tenure. Short-term employment contracts actively diminish creativity and thus should be avoided.

Performance management policy

Performance criteria need to reflect the creative requirements of the position and be consistent with the job description in that regard. The process should be more forward-looking and have a strong emphasis on employees' future development rather than focusing exclusively on evaluating past performance. Given the research indicating that frequency of performance feedback is consistent with high-performing innovative organisations, performance management policies might aim to promote this by specifying more frequent performance reviews either by shortening the appraisal cycle or by inserting additional progress updates within the cycle.

Learning and development policy

Cross-functional training that enhances knowledge of systems and processes and how they interconnect is useful from an innovation perspective because it promotes a more holistic view of the business. This particularly aids the application of new ideas since it builds on the understanding of what is practicable. Job rotation and mobility programmes that allow people to actually apply their cross-functional learning will further enhance this understanding.

Access to personal and professional development opportunities that are oriented towards the future will also contribute to creative and innovative behaviours, and so policies need to support these types of activities. This may include supporting formal studies as well as attendance at conferences and networking events where people interact with peers in their profession or industry.

Workplace flexibility policy

A fundamental requirement for nurturing creativity and innovation is a workplace flexibility policy. In addition to the more common forms of flexibility such as flexible work hours and telecommuting, flexibility policies could also include provisions such as allowing people a certain amount of time each week to work on personal projects that could lead to innovation. As with most forms of workplace flexibility, practices like this require a good deal of trust to be shown between employer and employee. Management styles that tend towards micromanagement will negate the positive effects of flexibility, and so this is one area where congruence between policy, practice and culture is essential.

Remuneration and rewards policy

As we have discussed, the link between creativity, innovation and performance-based pay or incentives is quite tenuous. From a policy perspective, organisations need to make a judgement about whether or not to adopt a rewards approach as a means of stimulating creative, innovative behaviour. Of course, there may be other reasons to implement remuneration policies based on incentives, and these need to be considered alongside the requirement for creativity.

Perhaps one of the biggest negative issues for employees who create commercially viable innovations is that they don't share in the benefits that those innovations create for the organisation. This is more of a recognition issue than an incentive issue. It is natural for someone to feel aggrieved if their good work is not acknowledged and rewarded; therefore failing to recognise a creative contribution that results in positive commercial outcomes for the organisation is likely to have a negative effect on that employee's motivation and commitment. There are also legal issues that need to be considered. Intellectual property laws are complex, but as a general principle, employers (not individual employees or work teams) own intellectual property rights unless there are specific arrangements otherwise (Stewart 2013). Profit-sharing policies linked to innovations can provide tangible recognition for employees whose efforts result in new patents, trademarks, designs, copyrights or other commercially valuable inventions. Profit-sharing policies might not be practical in all contexts, but are worth considering, especially in commercial environments. Given the complexity of intellectual property law, organisations seeking to explore these kinds of options should seek legal advice before developing a policy.

In non-commercial environments, other forms of recognition might be more relevant. These can take the form of awards, certificates of merit, letters of commendation or other things that have little or no intrinsic monetary value. The symbolic value of non-financial rewards should not be underestimated, and although they may not in themselves stimulate creativity and innovation, they contribute to a culture in which such contributions are recognised and valued.

Retention is an important factor in nurturing creativity, and policies that offer employees fair, competitive remuneration will help create an environment that is conducive to retention and employee commitment. This should be the fundamental principle underpinning remuneration and reward policies.

Summary

- Creativity and innovation arise through the interaction of organisational structure, culture and HR practices. HR policy is important to creativity and innovation because it underpins HR practices.
- HR policies and practices alone cannot stimulate creativity and innovation. There needs to be alignment between all three sets of factors.
- Research has found that creative people respond positively to work environments where they have autonomy and flexibility.
- Research has also found that a range of HR practices can contribute to organisational creativity and innovation. These include:
  - defining creative requirements in job descriptions and associated documents;
  - providing job security through long-term job tenure;
  - providing frequent performance feedback that is focused on employee development; and
  - providing access to personal and professional development opportunities, as well as cross-functional training and opportunities for job rotation/ mobility.
- The relationship between remuneration and creativity is complex. Mixed research findings have emerged in relation to the effect of incentives, though a common theme is the importance of recognition. Intellectual property law is a significant factor in determining an organisation's approach to recognising and rewarding innovation.

- HR policy areas relevant to creativity and innovation include staffing (recruitment, selection and employment), performance management, training and development, workplace flexibility and remuneration and rewards.

Discussion questions

1. Consider Hamel's view about the importance of purpose (i.e. making a difference). Does this imply that people are more inspired to be creative by the potential to do good in society than by increasing the company's share price or its profits? Is commitment to a cause stronger than commitment to an organisation?
2. Why do you think that job security is important for creativity and innovation?
3. Is it feasible to have one set of HR policies for knowledge workers whose jobs involve generating ideas and another set for employees whose work is more routine and non-creative?
4. Can you train people to be creative? Is creativity in an organisation more about process and technique than it is about inspiration? If so, should organisations invest in creativity training?

References

Beugelsdijk, S. 2008. 'Strategic human resource practices and product innovation'. *Organization Studies* 29(6): 821–47.

Cavagnoli, D. 2011. 'A conceptual framework for innovation: An application to human resource management policies in Australia'. *Innovation Management, Policy and Practice* 13(1): 111–25.

Clegg, S., Kornberger, M. and Rhodes, C. 2005. 'Learning/becoming/organizing'. *Organization* 12(2): 147–67.

Egan, T. M. 2005. 'Factors influencing individual creativity in the workplace: An examination of quantitative empirical research'. *Advances in Developing Human Resources* 7(2): 160–81.

Gibb, S., and Waight, C. 2005. 'Connecting HRD and creativity: From fragmentary insights to strategic significance'. *Advances in Developing Human Resources* 7(2): 271–86.

Hamel, G. 2007. *The Future of Management*. Boston: Harvard Business School Press, pp. 69–121.

Hope Hailey, V. 2001. 'Breaking the mould? Innovation as a strategy for corporate renewal'. *International Journal of Human Resource Management* 12(7): 1126–40.

McLean, L. 2005. 'Organizational culture's influence on creativity and innovation: A review of the literature and implications for human resource development'. *Advances in Developing Human Resources* 7(2): 226–46.

Newell, S., Robertson, M., Scarborough, H. and Swan, J. 2009. *Managing Knowledge Work and Innovation* (2nd edn). Basingstoke: Palgrave MacMillan, pp. 124–43.

Robbins, S., Judge, T., Millett, B. and Waters-Marsh, T. 2008. *Organisational Behaviour* (5th edn). New South Wales: Pearson Prentice Hall, French's Forest, pp. 662–63.

Schaper, M., and Volery, T. 2007. *Entrepreneurship and Small Business* (2nd Pacific Rim edn). Milton: John Wiley and Sons, pp. 54–75.

Searle, R., and Ball, K. 2003. 'Supporting innovation through HR policy: Evidence from the UK'. *Creativity and Innovation Management* 12(1): 50–62.

Stewart, A. 2013. *Stewart's Guide to Employment Law* (4th edn). Leichhardt: Federation Press, pp. 261–63.

Unsworth, K., Wall, T. and Carter, A. 2005. 'Creative requirement: A neglected construct in the study of employee creativity'. *Group and Organization Management* 30(5): 541–60.

Westland, J. C. 2008. *Global Innovation Management: A Strategic Approach*. Basingstoke: Palgrave MacMillan, pp. 291–315.

Chapter 7

POLICY AND ETHICS

In this chapter we examine the role of HR policy in organisational ethics. Most would agree that ethics are important, but because people's fundamental values differ, there is often disagreement about what constitutes ethical behaviour. From an HR policy perspective, there are two ethical dimensions. The first concerns the ethicality of employment practices and the way that individual employees and the workforce in general are managed. The second broader dimension is about the role of policy in promoting and sustaining an ethical business culture. Underpinning these two dimensions are the ethics of the HR profession itself and of individual HR managers and practitioners. Ethics is by nature a complex issue, and it is one of the more challenging aspects of HR policy and of HR practice in general (Figure 7.1).

HR's ethical role

Historically, HR's role as an employee advocate has made it an important player in organisational ethics. As HRM has been redefined as a strategic function, however, that role has become less well defined. There remains a strong view that HR should take a leading role in managing organisational ethics (Harned 2005; Kramar and Martin 2008), but there are other views that point to the dilemmas this can create for HR managers and practitioners attempting to operate as strategic business partners (Ainsworth and Hall 2006). Carey (1999) has proposed that ethics be incorporated into an 'integrity-based' approach to strategy and that, as such, strategic HRM and ethics can coexist, albeit with some tension. Woodd (1997) has observed that although senior management is primarily responsible for organisational ethics, business imperatives can tend to overshadow ethical considerations, creating a need for HR to adopt an ethical stewardship role that effectively balances the two.

Lafer (2005), however, denies that such a balance is possible and suggests that HR ethics is ultimately an unsuccessful attempt to unite two opposing sets of values. While many would dispute Lafer's portrayal of HR ethics as 'distorted, marginal and lifeless', the tension between ethical considerations

Figure 7.1 Dimensions of HR ethics.

and business needs is hard to ignore. Even if we accept that the stewardship role is valid, it can be fraught with dangers and may contribute to the perception of HR practitioners as 'blockers' who are not really attuned to business needs. Winstanley et al. (1996) have also pointed out that assigning ethical responsibility to HR can lead to line management deferring responsibility for ethical issues. This is undesirable because it marginalises ethics as simply an HR issue rather than affirming the role of all managers as upholders of ethical principles and practices. Despite these potential problems, however, HR has adopted (or been assigned) responsibility for ethics in many organisations, particularly the dimension of organisational ethics that is concerned with the treatment of employees.

HR professional ethics

As we have discussed, whatever ethical responsibilities are undertaken by HR in an organisation, they are underpinned by the professional ethics that govern HR practice as well as the personal ethics and values of individual practitioners. Martin and Woldring (2001) have pointed out that, at the level of personal values and interpretation of ethical issues, there are significant individual differences between HR managers. These individual differences can lead to a variety of responses to ethical issues (see Figure 7.2), including doing nothing at all.

While few HR managers or practitioners would admit to adopting positions of complicity or silence on ethical issues, the reality is that they sometimes do. The adoption of one of these positions may be the result of the conflict between being a strategic partner and being responsible for organisational ethics. For instance, an HR manager who has worked hard to be accepted as a genuine

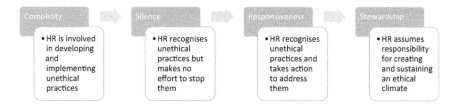

Figure 7.2 Ethical stances and decision-making options.

Adapted from concepts developed by Fisher (2000) and expanded upon by Lowry (2006).

strategic partner and to win a seat at the top table may fear jeopardising that position by not being seen to be a team player. They may, therefore, support executive decisions even when they are ethically questionable and/or in conflict with their personal values.

Scenarios like this can perhaps be explained conceptually by Macklin (2006), who has proposed that HR managers enjoy only 'relative moral autonomy' when it comes to ethical decision-making. This acknowledges that there is sometimes conflict between personal values and organisational values. It also acknowledges that there are constraints on the behaviour of HR managers brought about by their role and the context. For example, an HR manager may have to implement a redundancy programme that he/she had argued passionately against in the boardroom or implement an executive bonus scheme that he/she may consider to be questionable. When faced with dilemmas like these, the purest response would be to resign. Unfortunately, though, not many can afford that luxury.

One way of dealing with ethical conflicts is to base actions and decisions on a professional code of ethics. In Australia, the code of ethics and professional conduct developed and promulgated by the Australian Human Resources Institute (AHRI) outlines nine ethical principles to which its members are expected to adhere (AHRI 2018). These are outlined in Table 7.1 and are similar to the codes of ethics adopted by the Society for HRM in the United States and the Chartered Institute of Personnel and Development in the United Kingdom (and, no doubt, codes in other jurisdictions).

While it is hard to argue with general principles like these, they are open to interpretation. For instance, exactly what is meant by an 'ethical work environment' or 'fair, reasonable and equitable standards of treatment'? These can be interpreted subjectively and will be affected by the context. It could be argued that professional codes of ethics do not really help practitioners to navigate ethically tricky terrain because they tend to be couched in general terms and do not (and arguably, cannot) deal with specific ethical scenarios. Nonetheless,

Table 7.1 AHRI code of ethics and professional conduct

Role	Description
Advancing the profession	Promoting the importance of HRM in the workplace, the business community and society
Leadership	Modelling competent, ethical behaviour; fostering an ethical work environment; fulfilling professional role selflessly
Honesty	Showing honesty, objectiveness and truthfulness in all dealings; not knowingly misleading employer, employees or clients
Integrity	Not promoting self-interest or allowing personal interests to undermine their objectivity, accuracy and independence
Lawfulness	Observing the law; not encouraging, countenancing or assisting unlawful behaviour by employers, employees or clients
Confidentiality	Respecting private or proprietary information; not disclosing confidential information without consent of those concerned unless required by law
Justice	Fostering equal opportunity, non-discrimination; establishing and maintaining fair, reasonable and equitable standards of treatment for all employees
Competence	Maintaining high professional standards; undertaking continuous professional development
Organisational capability	Contributing to and encouraging the development of all employees

Note: AHRI: Australian Human Resources Institute.

they do provide a basic set of principles that practitioners can use as a reference point for their own decisions and behaviours and are useful for that reason.

HR policies have been said to 'define the moral atmosphere within which people work' (Shaw et al. 2009). HR activities, therefore, present plenty of opportunities for unethical practices, especially in areas such as recruitment and selection (Nye 2002). Indeed, staffing practices feature prominently among those issues that cause concern to HR managers, employees and unions, and which have attracted attention in academic and business literature.

A common theme in managerial ethics is the misuse of power. Most of the issues in Table 7.2 can potentially involve some kind of abuse of power. In some cases the resultant unethical behaviour is intentional and calculated, but in some cases it is inadvertent – perhaps the result of ignorance or insensitivity. Inadvertence, however, does not make an unethical practice ethical.

HR decisions, even routine ones, can present opportunities for ethical malpractice, but equally, as Scott (2005) has pointed out, they can also be seen as opportunities to 'do right'. Van Gramberg and Provis (2004) have advocated a

Table 7.2 HR ethical issues in the twenty-first century

Issue	Sub-issues
Discrimination	Attitudes to older workers; parental leave; pay equity; dress codes
Recruitment	DNA testing; psychological testing; use and management of applicants' personal information
Employment practices	Use of contractors; casualisation of the workforce; job security
Whistle-blowing	Public disclosure of wrongdoing; protection of whistle-blowers
Employer vs. employee rights	Right to dismiss; right to strike; right to meaningful work
Remuneration	Differentials between executive and non-executive salaries; incentives and bonuses
Privacy	Monitoring; surveillance; use of employee records
Employee protection	Treatment of employees during mergers and acquisitions; effects of outsourcing

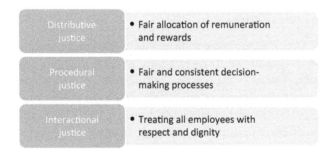

Figure 7.3 Components of organisational justice.

pluralistic approach to decision-making, which strives to achieve the best outcome for all interested parties based on a foundation of fair process. Indeed, fair process is one component of the concept of organisational justice, which is fundamental for framing the ethical treatment of employees (Figure 7.3).

HR policies are the most appropriate vehicles for translating these concepts into practice within organisations. Table 7.3 summarises how HR policies connect with organisational justice principles.

Striving for organisational justice also has business benefits. Frankel et al. (2012) have found that where employees perceive HR policies to be just, their level of identification with the organisation is likely to be higher, and discretionary effort and co-worker support are likely to increase.

Table 7.3 HR policies and organisational justice

Policy area	Organisational justice component(s)
Dress codes	Interactional
Discipline	Procedural
Grievance and dispute resolution	Procedural, interactional
Leave management	Procedural
Attendance management	Procedural
Performance management	Procedural, interactional
Remuneration and rewards	Distributive
Equity and diversity	Interactional
Workplace flexibility	Procedural, interactional
Staffing	Procedural, interactional
Training and development	Procedural
Succession management	Procedural
Health, safety and well-being	Interactional
Privacy	Interactional
Social media	Interactional

Ethical business culture

The principal vehicles for promoting an ethical business culture are organisational codes of conduct or codes of ethics. Because they deal primarily with employee behaviour, they are usually considered to be HR policies, though in some larger organisations they might fall within the purview of a corporate governance unit or similar. Kermis and Kermis (2009) have argued that HR is in a uniquely strong position to influence the development and sustenance of an ethical business culture because it has natural connections with a range of internal and external stakeholders. Indeed, they contend that HR has a responsibility to assume this role.

Yahr et al. (2009) point out that merely having a code of conduct or code of ethics does not guarantee ethical behaviour, and that the effectiveness of these kinds of policies is determined by how well they are designed and implemented as well as the extent to which they are supported by other cultural elements in the organisation. Research has established that employee perceptions of the ethical climate within the organisation will determine their own ethical (or unethical) behaviour (Seligson and Choi 2006; Kermis and Kermis 2009). So, having a code of conduct or ethics that is seen to be ignored or not enforced can be interpreted as an implicit invitation to act unethically. Similarly, where the policy is perceived to be a token policy only (i.e. it is simply a motherhood statement or is couched in such general terms as to be meaningless) it is unlikely to be taken seriously.

An important aspect of demonstrating that organisations take the policy seriously is the way it deals with the reporting of unlawful or unethical behaviour (whistle-blowing). Whistle-blowing can either be internal (reported within the organisation) or external (publicly disclosed). Research by Kassing and Armstrong (2002) has found that within organisations, people are more likely to express dissent about issues related to the fair treatment of employees than about issues connected with ethical business practice, which indicates a general reluctance among employees to involve themselves with contentious issues. Although in Australia and other countries whistle-blowers are now protected by legislation, it is arguable whether or not this legislative protection really encourages people to blow the whistle on their employers' business practices (De Maria 2006). In addition, Miceli and Near (2002) have shown that where an employee reports an issue outside their own area of responsibility, it is less likely to be acted upon. This is perhaps another reason why employees tend to remain silent on broader issues of business practice. Whistle-blowing takes some courage; therefore where an organisation treats the reporting of an incident or practice with disdain, or worse, punishes the whistle-blower, it isn't hard to understand why others might choose not to come forward.

HR policy has an important role to play in supporting an ethical business culture through designing, implementing and managing codes of conduct or ethics and other policies that connect with it (e.g. discipline policy). However, ownership of the issue is not (or should not be) limited to HR. Everyone owns it, and everyone has the responsibility to uphold it. In particular, the leadership group has a crucial role in modelling ethical behaviour and managing ethical issues, including whistle-blowing, appropriately and effectively.

Summary

- HR's role in facilitating organisational ethics has two dimensions: The ethical treatment of employees and the promotion of an ethical business culture. These roles are underpinned by the ethical standards of the HR profession as well as practitioners' own personal values.
- There is considerable debate within the HR profession and among academics in the field about whether or not it is possible for HR to assume responsibility for organisational ethics as well as being a strategic business partner.
- Policies that address the ethical treatment of employees should be based on the principles of organisational justice.
- Policies, such as codes of conduct or ethics, that address the broader culture of the organisation, cannot in themselves influence culture without being modelled on and supported by organisational leaders. Where management

practices and decisions appear to be inconsistent with ethical policies, the policies themselves become ineffective.

Discussion questions

1. Should ethical considerations always take precedence over business considerations?
2. On the whole, are corporate executives really committed to acting ethically for their own sake, or are they more concerned about the damage to corporate image and reputation that might result from public exposure of ethical misconduct within the company?
3. Discuss the strengths and weaknesses of the HR code of ethics and/or professional conduct that applies in your jurisdiction. Is it a reasonable basis for professional practice?
4. Is whistle-blowing always an act of conscience, or is it sometimes an act of spite? Is there an ethical responsibility to protect whistle-blowers even when they are motivated only by a desire to do harm to the organisation?
5. Is it unethical for HR practitioners to continue working in an organisation where the ethical values of the organisation's leaders are at odds with their own values? Is it acceptable to compromise personal values for pragmatic reasons?

References

AHRI. 2018. *Code of Ethics and Professional Conduct*. Melbourne: Australian Human Resources Institute.

Ainsworth, S., and Hall, R. 2006. 'Rethinking HRM: Contemporary practitioner discourse and the tensions between ethics and business partnership'. In G. Hearn and G. Michelson (eds), *Rethinking Work: Time, Space, Discourse*. Sydney: Cambridge University Press, pp. 263–84.

Carey, L. 1999. 'Ethical dimensions of a strategic approach to HRM: An Australian perspective'. *Asia Pacific Journal of Human Resources* 37(3): 53–68.

De Maria, W. 2006. 'Common law, common mistakes? Protecting whistleblowers in Australia, New Zealand, South Africa and the United Kingdom'. *International Journal of Public Sector Management* 19(7): 643–58.

Fisher, C. 2000. 'Human resource managers and quietism'. *Business and Professional Ethics Journal* 19(3/4): 55–72.

Frankel, S., Lloyd, S., Restubog, D. and Bedrall, T. 2012. 'How employee perceptions of HR policy and practice influence discretionary work effort and co-worker assistance: Evidence from two organisations'. *The International Journal of Human Resource Management* 23(20): 4193–210.

Harned, P. 2005. 'When ethics calls the HR helpline'. In M. Losey, S. Meisinger and D. Ulrich (eds), *The Future of Human Resource Management*. Hoboken: John Wiley and Sons, pp. 348–55.

Kassing, J., and Armstrong, T. 2002. 'Someone's going to hear about this: Examining the association between dissent-triggering events and employees' dissent expression'. *Management Communication Quarterly* 16(1): 39–65.

Kermis, G., and Kermis, M. 2009. 'Model for the transition from ethical deficit to a transparent corporate culture: A response to the financial meltdown'. *Journal of Academic and Business Ethics* 2. https://www.aabri.com/manuscripts/09183.pdf.

Kramar, R., and Martin, G. 2008. 'Compliance, ethics and corporate social responsibility'. In *Australian Master Human Resources Guide* (6th edn). North Ryde: CCH Australia, pp. 393–415.

Lafer, G. 2005. 'The critical failure of workplace ethics'. In J. Budd and J. Scoville (eds), *The Ethics of Human Resources and Industrial Relations*. Champaign: Labour and Employment Relations Association, pp. 273–7.

Lowry, L. 2006. 'HR managers as ethical decision-makers: Mapping the terrain'. *Asia Pacific Journal of Human Resources* 44(2): 171–83.

Macklin, R. 2006. 'The moral autonomy of human resource managers'. *Asia Pacific Journal of Human Resources* 44(2): 211–21.

Martin, G., and Woldring, K. 2001. 'Ready for the mantle? Australian human resource managers as stewards of ethics'. *International Journal of Human Resource Management* 12(2): 243–55.

Miceli, M., and Near, J. 2002. 'What makes whistleblowers effective? Three field studies'. *Human Relations* 55(4): 455–79.

Nye, D. 2002. 'The privacy in employment critique: A consideration of some of the arguments for ethical HRM professional practice'. *Business Ethics: A European Review*,11(3): 224–32.

Scott, E. 2005. 'The ethics of human resource management'. In J. Budd and J. Scoville (eds), *The Ethics of Human Resources and Industrial Relations*. Champaign: Labour and Employment Relations Association, pp. 173–202.

Seligson, A., and Choi, L. 2006. *Critical Elements of an Organizational Ethical Culture*. Washington: Ethics Resource Centre.

Shaw, W., Barry, V. and Sansbury, G. 2009. *Moral Issues in Business*. South Melbourne: Cengage, pp. 468–80.

Van Gramberg, B., and Provis, C. 2004. 'Ethics, conflict and human resource managers in the new economy'. Working Paper Series, School of Management, Victoria University of Technology.

Winstanley, D., Woodall, J. and Heery, E. 1996. 'Business ethics and human resource management: Themes and issues', *Personnel Review* 25(6): 5–12.

Woodd, M. 1997. 'Human resource specialists – guardians of ethical conduct?' *Journal of European Industrial Training* 21(3): 110–16.

Yahr, M., Bryan, L. and Schimmel, K. 2009. 'Perceptions of college and university codes of ethics'. *Journal of Academic and Business Ethics* 2. https://www.aabri.com/manuscripts/09282.pdf.

Chapter 8

POLICY, SUSTAINABILITY AND SOCIAL RESPONSIBILITY

Sustainability and corporate social responsibility (CSR) have emerged as major issues in management in recent times. Corporate collapses and the intervention of governments to moderate the environmental, social and economic impacts of those collapses have, for many, underlined the inextricable connection between businesses and the rest of the society. Even so, not everyone agrees that corporations have any responsibility other than to return profit for their shareholders, but that is probably now a minority view.

Sustainable HRM

Sustainability is a concept that grew out of the environmental movement. It connects with concepts such as CSR, ethics, stakeholder management and corporate citizenship. Originally sustainability was about doing no harm (i.e. it was a neutral concept), but today, it is about making organisations successful in the long term by 'doing good'.

According to Clarke (2011), sustainable HRM adopts a holistic view that encourages regeneration and renewal of the workforce. It sees the workforce as an asset that needs to be nurtured rather than cut to save costs. Employee skills and knowledge are valuable and can be tapped by engaging the whole person. Encouraging and supporting learning, development, creativity, opportunity and freedom create an ongoing renewal process.

Sustainable HRM can be seen as the next evolutionary stage of HRM, as Figure 8.1 shows. Strategic HRM aligns HR policies and practices with the achievement of organisational objectives (i.e. its ultimate purposes are economic/financial). Sustainable HRM aligns HR policies and practices with social and human outcomes, as well as organisational outcomes. Sustainable HRM is not a departure from strategic HRM – it is entirely compatible with the desire to contribute positively to organisational performance. However, it adds a further dimension to the way we perceive the role of HRM. As Kramar (2014) has pointed out "It raises the importance of making explicit the moral

Table 8.1 Sustainable and unsustainable HR practices

	Non-sustainable	Sustainable
Staffing	Boom and bust staffing cycles	More stable workforce
Motivation	Focus on extrinsic motivation	Focus on intrinsic motivation
Remuneration	Designed to manage risks and control costs	Designed to realise people's capabilities
Learning	Focus on addressing 'weaknesses'	Focus on developing talents
Performance management	Focus on identifying performance problems	Focus on creating conditions for high performance

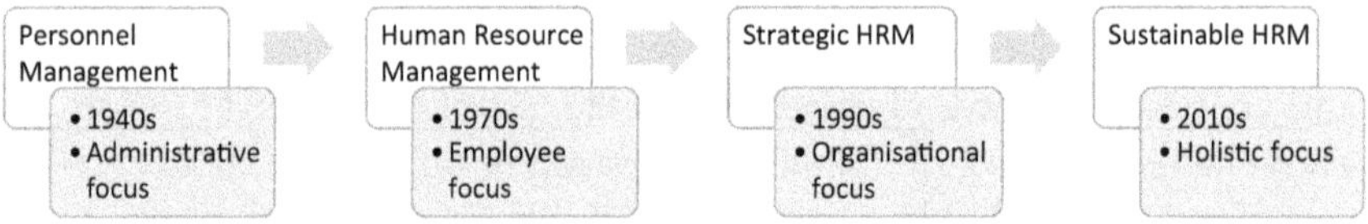

Figure 8.1 Evolution of HRM.

dimensions of HRM policy, the interests that are served by policy and the interconnectedness of internal and external outcomes resulting from these policies."

The kinds of practices outlined in Table 8.1 can be underpinned by policies that prescribe sustainable approaches. For example, staffing policy might emphasise looking for alternatives to downsizing during economic downturns (e.g. wage and salary freezes, suspension of bonuses, reducing hours of work, leave options, flexible work options). Where downsizing is unavoidable, a policy informed by sustainability principles can help to ensure that the process is managed fairly and transparently.

Sustainable HRM can also have an environmental dimension. Indeed, the term 'green HRM' has already been coined to describe HR policies and practices that promote and encourage the sustainable use of resources and the reduction of the organisation's carbon footprint. Such practices could include:

- car-sharing and reducing travel requirements
- virtual work and telecommuting
- recycling programmes
- reducing paper usage (e.g. online pay slips, leave applications, training nomination forms etc.)
- linking bonuses to the achievement of green goals

- designing work spaces for reduced energy usage
- supporting environmental volunteering by employees

A possible organisational benefit of green HRM policies is to enhance attraction, retention and employee engagement, especially among younger people. Despite this, research reveals that, as yet, relatively few organisations actively use HR policies and practices to encourage environmentally responsible behaviour (Zibarras and Coan 2015). Nonetheless, it is a concept that is gaining traction within the broader concept of sustainable HRM.

Corporate social responsibility

It is difficult to define CSR precisely. It is closely related to concepts like business ethics, stakeholder management, sustainability and corporate citizenship, and while its original focus was on reducing the negative social impacts of business activity, it is now more geared towards doing social good (Schwartz and Carroll 2008). Roberts (2003) has contended that while some approaches to CSR are motivated by genuine social concern, others are more about public relations. Indeed, Banerjee (2008) asserts that CSR works more for the benefit of corporations than for society and that CSR strategies and programmes are often limited to scenarios where there are obvious business benefits. Hence, social responsibility is subordinate to profit. While views like these may sound somewhat cynical, they reflect the long-established economic concept of 'enlightened self-interest' – the notion that doing good has benefits for those doing it as well as for those positively affected by it. But while Roberts's view allows for the possibility that organisations might be motivated by something other than commercial gain, Banerjee's view implies that commercial gain is a prerequisite for social action, and hence organisations will only engage in socially responsible practices when they perceive that there is something in it for them.

De La Cruz Deniz-Deniz and De Saa-Perez (2003) distinguish between three conceptual levels of corporate interaction with society (see Figure 8.2). For them, social responsibility is a principle that leads to action that, in turn, leads to social impacts.

HR policy that supports CSR can, therefore, be seen to be socially responsive because it translates principle into reality, which has a positive impact on broader social issues.

Corporate social responsibility and human resource management

The role of HR in CSR is evolving. A 2003 study by the Chartered Institute of Personnel and Development (the peak professional body for HR practitioners in the United Kingdom) found that, at the international level, CSR tended

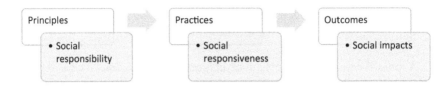

Figure 8.2 Levels of corporate–social interaction.

to focus on issues like adherence to international labour standards and human rights (CIPD 2003). A later study by the Society for Human Resource Management (the equivalent HR professional body in the United States) found that HR was not typically involved in CSR strategy development but was involved in implementation, especially at the level of engaging employees in CSR practices (SHRM 2007). In Australia, 64 per cent of organisations involved HR in CSR programmes in one way or the other. Interestingly, the study also found that the vast majority of organisations (77 per cent in Australia) did not measure their return on investment (ROI) in CSR initiatives. This could indicate that as yet, organisations have not developed the metrics required to assess ROI. It might also indicate that ROI was not the primary motivation for undertaking CSR initiatives, perhaps suggesting that there are some genuinely altruistic motives involved.

Significantly though, the SHRM study focused on HR involvement in the broad range of organisational CSR strategies and programmes but not on how HR policies and practices themselves contribute to CSR. CSR is a broad concept that can include a range of philanthropic and environmental endeavours that are not necessarily related to the organisation's role as an employer. Yet, there is considerable potential for organisations to manage their workforces in ways that contribute positively to a larger social agenda. Broadly speaking, the human resource management contribution to CSR has two levels of focus; these are outlined in Figure 8.3.

It is important to recognise that these two levels of focus do not exist in isolation from one another, and that internally focused policies that have a positive effect on employees can also contribute to a bigger social agenda. In fact, one could argue that initiatives that benefit employees as individuals but do not contribute to a broader social good are not really CSR initiatives at all. Given also that HR is often criticised for being too 'warm and fuzzy', internal focus as an end in itself is likely to fuel further criticism of this kind. CSR is not just about being nice to employees. There are also policies and practices that are purely focused externally. These policies do not necessarily affect current employees but contribute to positive social outcomes by reaching individuals in society who are potential employees. These policies and practices are usually

Figure 8.3 CSR in HR – levels of focus.

related to the way in which the organisation interacts with the labour market. Of course, the best CSR policies and practices are those that have benefits for individuals, organisations and society.

Although the SHRM study showed that in a small percentage of organisations, HR carried primary responsibility for CSR, this is unlikely to ever be the standard model. Indeed, there are good arguments against it. Even so, HR should be a contributor both as a strategist and as an implementer. An important role for HR is to identify those areas of HR policy and practice that will make a substantial contribution to CSR. We discuss policy areas with CSR potential later in this chapter.

Employees as stakeholders

Internally focused approaches to CSR assume that employees are genuine organisational stakeholders whose interests are directly related to the interests of the organisation. Employees are also members of society whose interests extend beyond the workplace. Treating employees as stakeholders, therefore, can be seen to be part of the organisation's commitment to CSR. As we have mentioned, this approach has its critics who see employee-focus as being incompatible with strategic HRM. However, as Brown et al. (2009) have found, most HR practitioners believe that employee well-being is a legitimate strategic issue because it impacts directly on productivity, attraction and retention.

Young and Thyil (2009) have shown that organisational rhetoric that casts employees as stakeholders does not always match reality, and that economic and environmental considerations often outweigh employee issues. As Greenwood and Anderson (2009) have pointed out, there are also inherent dangers in collectively labelling employees as stakeholders. Doing so tends to treat employees as a homogenous group with similar interests, but in reality, workforces are made up of individuals with diverse interests. Nonetheless, in the context of CSR, we need to remember that HR policies and practices that are internally focused also need to connect with broader societal interests and contribute to desirable social outcomes (Figure 8.4).

Figure 8.4 Relationship between employee interests and social outcomes.

CSR is about collective interests rather than individual interests; therefore HR policies and practices with a CSR focus need to address those collective interests. This is not to say that there might not be other benefits to the organisation of addressing individual employee interests, but doing so cannot in itself be considered to be CSR in action.

Organisations as social actors

The concept of CSR is based on the idea that organisations are social actors. This view recognises that organisations exist within a social context and that their actions impact on the societies of which they are a part. Conceptually, CSR is underpinned by the notion of responsible capitalism, which proposes the existence of an unwritten social contract that obliges organisations to act responsibly, recognising their connection with their social context. This connection has long been recognised. Indeed, there is a considerable history of academic interest in the relationship between organisational management and society, although recently that interest seems to have waned in favour of research focusing more on economic issues (Walsh et al. 2003).

Schoemaker et al. (2006) have proposed that genuine CSR stems from values within the organisation and that HR needs to concern itself with values management. This view sees HR and CSR as being interconnected. It also leads to organisational strategy that is driven not just by market factors but by values and the interests of stakeholders, including employees and society. While it is difficult to see the private sector making the transition from market-based to values-based management any time soon, it already exists to a degree within the public and not-for-profit sectors, where the profit motive is largely absent and core business is often concerned with achieving positive social outcomes.

While Schoemaker et al. (2006) present a values case for CSR, Zappala (2004) presents what could be classified as a business case based on the idea that corporate citizenship generates 'mutually reinforcing' benefits. In other words, corporate actions and decisions that have a beneficial effect on society also have a positive effect on employee morale and commitment. As public concern for social and environmental issues increases, and simultaneously, the labour market becomes tighter (as is expected in Australia over the next 20 years), the business case for CSR becomes more compelling. In fact, being a good corporate citizen may become as strong an attraction and retention factor as any HR policy. Of course, this particular business case for CSR is based on enlightened self-interest. It is not values-based as Schoemaker et al. (2006) advocate, and so it might be considered to be less sustainable because, as the labour market becomes less competitive, commitment to CSR may decline. Nonetheless, organisations tend to be far more easily swayed by business arguments than by values arguments, and so labour market conditions might well be the catalyst for organisations to embrace CSR. Proponents of CSR then face the challenge of embedding it in the organisation's culture so that it can survive on its own merits without economically driven stimuli.

Socially responsible HR policy

Staffing policy (recruitment)

Recruitment policy can reflect an organisation's commitment to providing employment opportunities for members of socioeconomically disadvantaged groups such as people with disabilities and indigenous people. Groups like these are substantially over-represented among the ranks of the unemployed, and so providing targeted opportunities can be seen as helping to redress a social imbalance. Indeed, targeting people who are unemployed, regardless of their personal or cultural characteristics, can also be seen as contributing to positive social outcomes. While research suggests that most employers do not consciously discriminate against unemployed jobseekers, most do not target them either (Devins and Hogarth 2005), and unemployed jobseekers tend to fare worse than people seeking to move from one job to another. This is especially true for the longer-term unemployed. Participating in government labour market programmes is often a good way of facilitating this kind of socially responsible recruitment.

Providing entry-level job opportunities for school-leavers, graduates from vocational training institutions or university graduates can also be seen as contributing to a socially desirable outcome. While people entering the workforce are not generally considered to be disadvantaged (unless there are other characteristics that make them so), making the transition from education to work is often difficult because new graduates are competing against people with greater experience. Similarly, providing opportunities for people re-entering the workforce (e.g. people returning to work after raising a family) can also be seen as being socially positive. Indeed, re-entering the workforce can be even more difficult than entering it for the first time.

Where organisations wish to undertake targeted recruitment in the interests of CSR, recruitment policies should specify that commitment. Targeted recruitment policies are particularly suited to scenarios where organisations have regular intakes of new employees. Planned recruitment makes it much easier and more practical to, for instance, quarantine a certain number of positions for applicants with particular characteristics than where recruitment is ad hoc. As such, this approach may not be practical for smaller organisations who only recruit on a replacement basis.

Staffing policy (employment)

Employment policies, too, can support socially worthwhile activities. Policies that support volunteering by employees or participation in the defence reserves are good examples. Such policies would usually allow time off to undertake these kinds of activities and ensure that absences do not disadvantage people's employment status or career advancement.

Parental leave has become a significant social issue in recent years, and there is a considerable groundswell of public support for it. As yet, paid parental leave is not a standard employment condition in Australia, and so going beyond what is legally required and offering it as part of an organisation's employment policy can be seen as meeting a social need. It is also likely to have positive effects on attraction and retention.

The use of contingent workforces has been a topic of much debate in recent times. Staffing policies that favour the use of contingent workers (i.e. casual and non-permanent employees) over permanent workers has been criticised as being socially undesirable because contingent workers have far less job security and fewer entitlements. At a societal level, contingent workers are more vulnerable to economic fluctuations and, because they are less financially secure, are less able to make long-term financial commitments such as mortgages (and less likely to get a mortgage in the first place). Policies that favour permanent forms of employment over contingent employment arrangements can therefore be considered to be socially responsible because employees are not economically and socially marginalised. This is not to suggest that contingent employment should be avoided altogether. After all, some people actually prefer this type of arrangement, and it provides maximum flexibility to businesses. Such a policy is only problematic from a CSR perspective when it becomes the principal form of employment in an organisation.

The practice of offshoring (outsourcing functions to use cheaper overseas workforces) has also been a socially contentious issue. As Holland et al. (2015) have noted, much of the debate has focused on the perceived loss of jobs and skills from the home country. There is also an issue around the potential exploitation of workers in overseas locations (often in developing countries), where employment is less regulated or unregulated and where pay and conditions are well below the standards that would be expected in developed countries. Obviously, exploitation is not socially responsible, though as some companies have pointed out when criticised for the comparatively poor wages and conditions of offshore workforces, these issues need to be seen within the local context. Indeed, some companies claim to pay well above average wages in that particular labour market. It could also be argued that bringing work to developing countries is socially positive because it provides opportunities for employment and training that would not otherwise exist. Hence, at a global level, offshoring can be justified as being socially responsible. This argument counters the argument that sending work offshore is socially detrimental at home – after all, nations with developed economies are already comparatively prosperous; therefore helping a developing nation by providing work oppor-tunities is more laudable than keeping the work at home. It's a nice argument, but not everyone buys it. Organisations embracing CSR need to consider their offshoring policies carefully. If cost rather than a sense of global corporate citizenship is the main driver, claiming offshoring as a legitimate CSR practice has little credibility.

Learning and development policy

As we discussed in Chapter 5, skills shortages are considered to be a major risk for many organisations. The potential for a skills shortage is also a risk for the economy and for society in general, particularly when there is a mis-match between the skills required by business and industry and the skills possessed by jobseekers. Skills shortages combined with chronically high levels of unemployment may seem anomalous, but many developed countries have experienced this phenomenon – to the detriment of both the economy and society. In recent times, as the nature of the psychological contract between employers and employees has moved towards a more transactional model, organisations have been less willing to invest in employee develop-ment because greater employee mobility increases the likelihood that they will not receive an adequate ROI. However, Hall and Lansbury (2006) have pointed out that market approaches to skill development and training do not provide an adequate flow of skills into the labour market. If this is the case, organisations need to make a commitment to training and development that extends beyond their own immediate needs. In short, there is a compelling case for organisations to assume collective responsibility for developing the skills needed by business and industry both for the present and for the future.

Providing entry-level training through traineeships, apprenticeships and graduate programmes is one way that organisations can contribute positively to skills development. Policies that commit the organisation to providing these opportunities can therefore be seen as policies that support CSR. Indeed, this kind of commitment can be seen as being both economically responsible and socially responsible. Similarly, supporting ongoing professional development helps to ensure that skilled employees maintain and enhance their skills and knowledge and are adequately prepared to move into more senior roles, including leadership roles.

Policies like these are good examples of the concept of enlightened self-interest at work. There are obvious benefits to individuals in terms of establishing and developing their own careers, but there are also substantial benefits to organisations – and the economy generally – of having access to a skilled labour market.

Workplace flexibility policy

Work–life balance is among the most discussed issues in society today. With increasing numbers of people seeking to combine work with family responsibilities, or study or other endeavours, or simply to adopt a less stressful lifestyle, the demand for flexible workplaces is increasing. Generational issues impact on this demand too, as a new generation emerges that works to live rather than lives to work and another generation seeks to phase into retirement. Flexible workplace policies that allow for non-standard work patterns can be seen as contributing positively to family life and to a healthier, more balanced society.

Equity and diversity policy

Organisations are microcosms of the societies of which they are part, and so creating fair and equitable workplaces can be seen as aiding social cohesion. Policies that ensure fair treatment and discourage discrimination based on gender, race, ethnicity, disability or other personal characteristics support the type of society in which most people want to live. While affirmative action policies (i.e. policies that seek to redress imbalances or social disadvantage) remain contentious, those organisations that embrace them can be seen as contributing positively to a more equitable society. Similarly, policies that promote diversity can be seen as contributing to increased tolerance and respect for individual or cultural differences both at organisational and societal levels.

Remuneration and rewards policy

One of the biggest social issues for governments is the financial security of retired people. Superannuation is now a compulsory part of remuneration packages for Australian workers, but in most cases, the mandatory employer contribution of 9.5 per cent of salary is not sufficient to provide an adequate retirement income, meaning that a significant number of retirees in the future will be wholly or partly dependent on the government age pension. Given the potentially massive cost of pensions in the future, this presents a dilemma for both government and society. Building a bigger superannuation component into remuneration packages can be seen as a positive response to this problem, as it lessens the likelihood of employees being dependent on the age pension when they retire. The cost to employers can be minimised if additional contributions are treated as part of the overall remuneration package (i.e. employees have an option to convert some of their salary to additional superannuation). Many organisations already do this. Alternatively, allowing employees to salary package personal superannuation contributions pre-tax is also an effective way of encouraging greater retirement savings. Although there is usually a cost to employers in the form of fringe benefits tax, many organisations are prepared to bear the cost in the name of CSR.

Employee safety, health and well-being policy

Public health, whether physical, mental or psychological, is a major social issue. As public health systems struggle to cope with increasing demands and health care costs escalate, governments and the medical professions are placing greater emphasis on preventive measures. Given that many people spend a significant portion of their lives at work, organisations can contribute substantially to this greater social need by enacting policies designed to keep employees safe and healthy. Again, enlightened self-interest can be an important catalyst for these types of policies. Reducing absences caused by injuries or illness, particularly chronic illness, has obvious benefits for every organisation. It also has benefits for society as it contributes to a healthier population, reduces demand on the health system and helps to contain health care costs.

Summary

- Sustainability and CSR span many areas of management and are concerned with the impact of an organisation's business activities on individuals and society. In recent times, the focus has been on how organisations can contribute positively to society rather than simply minimising harm.
- Sustainability and CSR are topical issues and their principles are widely accepted in general society, but not all organisations have accepted that they have any responsibility beyond adhering to the law.

- HR involvement in CSR varies, although in most cases, other areas (e.g. public relations, corporate governance) assume primary responsibility for CSR. HR's role tends to be indirect.
- There is great potential for HR policies to define sustainable and socially responsible people management practices.
- HR practices that embrace sustainability and CSR principles can be internally oriented (focused on employees as legitimate stakeholders) or externally oriented (focused on broader social issues).
- Employee interests are generally linked to societal interests, and so addressing them through HR policies can contribute to CSR.
- HR policies that address sustainability and CSR issues generally also have positive effects on culture and morale and can enhance an organisation's image and its capacity to attract and retain employees.
- HR policy areas that connect with sustainability and CSR include staffing (recruitment and employment), learning and development, workplace flexibility, equity and diversity, remuneration and rewards and employee health, safety and well-being.

Discussion questions

1. Many organisations still take the view that it is not the role of businesses to address social issues; it is the government's role. Do you agree with this view? If so, why? If not, why not?
2. Do organisations have a responsibility to 'do good' regardless of whether there are tangible benefits for them?
3. Should HR be the social conscience of the organisation? What effects might this role have on the status of HR? Is it compatible with being a strategic business partner?
4. Do the ethics and values of the HR profession require that practitioners embrace the principles of sustainability and CSR in HR policies, regardless of whether the organisation is committed to them?

References

Banerjee, S. 2008. 'Corporate social responsibility: The good, the bad and the ugly'. *Critical Sociology* 34(1): 51–79.

Brown, M., Metz, I., Cregan, C. and Kulik, C. 2009. 'Irreconcilable differences? Strategic human resource management and employee wellbeing'. *Asia Pacific Journal of Human Resources* 47(3): 270–94.

CIPD. 2003. *Corporate Social Responsibility and HR's Role: A Guide*. London: Chartered Institute of Personnel and Development.

Clarke, M. 2011. *Readings in HRM and Sustainability*. Prahran: Tilde University Press.

De La Cruz Deniz-Deniz, M., and De Saa-Perez, P. 2003. 'A resource-based view of corporate responsiveness towards employees'. *Organization Studies* 24(2): 299–319.

Devins, D., and Hogarth, T. 2005. 'Employing the unemployed: Some case study evidence on the role and practice of employers'. *Urban Studies* 42(2): 245–56.

Greenwood, M., and Anderson, E. 2009. 'I used to be an employee but now I am a stakeholder: Implications of labelling employees as stakeholders'. *Asia Pacific Journal of Human Resources* 47(2): 186–200.

Hall, R., and Lansbury, R. 2006. 'Skills in Australia: Towards workforce development and sustainable skill ecosystems'. *Journal of Industrial Relations* 48(5): 575–92.

Holland, P., Sheehan, C., Donohue, R., Pyman, A. and Allen. B. 2015. *Contemporary Issues and Challenges in HRM* (3rd edn). Prahran: Tilde University Press, pp. 40–56.

Kramar, R. 2014. 'Beyond strategic human resource management: Is sustainable human resource management the next approach?' *The International Journal of Human Resource Management* 25(8): 1069–89.

Roberts, J. 2003. 'The manufacture of corporate social responsibility: Constructing corporate sensibility'. *Organization* 10(2): 249–65.

Schwartz, M., and Carroll, A. 2008. 'Integrating and unifying competing and complementary frameworks: The search for a common core in the business and society field'. *Business and Society* 47(2): 148–86.

Schoemaker, M., Nijhof, A. and Jonker, J. 2006. 'Human value management: The influence of the contemporary developments of corporate social responsibility (CSR) and social capital (SC) on human resource management (HRM)'. *Contribution for the Proceedings of the 10th Annual Conference of the Reputation Institute*. New York City, May.

SHRM. 2007. *Corporate Social Responsibility: United States, Australia, India, China, Canada, Mexico and Brazil: A Pilot Study*. Alexandria, VA: Society for Human Resource Management.

Walsh, J., Weber, K. and Margolis, J. 2003. 'Social issues and management: Our lost cause found'. *Journal of Management* 29(6): 859–81.

Young, S., and Thyil, V. 2009. 'Governance, employees and CSR: Integration is the key to unlocking value'. *Asia Pacific Journal of Human Resources* 47(2): 167–85.

Zappala, G. 2004. 'Corporate citizenship and human resource management: A new tool or a missed opportunity?' *Asia Pacific Journal of Human Resources* 42(2): 185–201.

Zibarras, L., and Coan, P. 2015. 'HRM practices used to promote pro-environmental behaviour: A UK survey'. *The International Journal of Human Resource Management* 26(16): 2121–42.

Part II

POLICY PROCESSES

Chapter 9

POLICY NEEDS IDENTIFICATION

The policy needs identification process is the first stage of a cycle of activity that represents a systematic approach to policymaking. The cyclical nature of the process emphasises the fact that HR policies are dynamic and should not be allowed to become dated or irrelevant. Policymaking should be an ongoing process, recognising that organisations and business environments change constantly (Figure 9.1).

Policy needs inputs

As discussed in Part I, HR policy is impacted by many issues and connects with a range of management and organisational factors both within the sphere of human resource management and outside it. All of these factors need to be taken into account when identifying policy needs. While it is difficult to deny the logic of this kind of approach, the reality in many organisations is that HR policies are developed in a reactive way that is sometimes entirely divorced from larger organisational planning processes. As we discuss later in this chapter, on occasion it is necessary to develop policy reactively, but this should not be the basis for all policymaking. Indeed, it should be the exception rather than the rule (Figure 9.2).

Critical incidents

Critical incidents are events that highlight the need for a new policy or for an existing policy to be amended. Given that the nature of critical incidents tends to be negative, an immediate policy response is usually required. There is almost no limit to the kinds of crises that might befall an organisation; therefore despite even the best risk management plans, there will inevitably arise at some point issues that were unforseen and that need to be addressed urgently. Some of these include:

- an adverse finding in a court or industrial tribunal
- an adverse media report about employment practices

Figure 9.1 The policy cycle.

Figure 9.2 Policy needs inputs model.

- a workplace injury or death, or a close call
- a criminal act or instance of misconduct
- a workplace conflict or dispute

Adverse findings in a court or industrial tribunal can relate to issues like unfair or unlawful dismissal, breaches of industrial agreements, unfair or unethical treatment of an employee or the awarding of compensation to an employee due to workplace-related ill health or disability. Such findings indicate error on the part of a person or persons within the organisation and therefore hold the organisation liable. Obviously, none of these kinds of outcomes are desirable for any organisation. One incident of this type is too many, and so the most appropriate response is to take steps to ensure that it doesn't happen again.

Similarly, adverse media reports can be very damaging to an organisation's reputation and its attractiveness to prospective employees, customers or investors. Media reports can focus on almost any aspect of human resource management deemed to be in the public interest. In recent times, the management of redundancy programmes has provided much grist for the media mill. Outsourcing policies can also be the focus of media attention, particularly when they result in job losses. Indeed, any employment practice has the potential to draw public attention to an organisation. The issue of executive remuneration is perhaps the most contentious HR issue to have attracted media attention in recent years, and this is a good example of how media coverage can put an HR issue into the public domain. In Australia, for example, the amount of media attention focused on this issue led to the setting up of a federal government enquiry. While it is true that some media reports are sensationalised or biased, others highlight legitimate public concerns that need to be addressed, and be seen to be addressed, in order to minimise or counteract the damage.

Workplace deaths or serious injuries almost always find their way into the media. They also result in formal investigations by government agencies charged with responsibility for occupational health and safety, and there can be harsh consequences for the organisation if it is found to have been negligent or deficient in its management practices.

Employee misconduct can encompass many different acts, including harassment, bullying, misuse of employer resources, divulging commercially confidential information, fraud and embezzlement. The way these kinds of incidents are dealt with can reflect as much on the organisation as the acts themselves.

The same can be said for workplace conflicts and disputes. Inevitably, there will be conflicts and disputes within organisations. Some of these will be business related, for example, a dispute between managers over resources. Others will be interpersonal disputes caused by any number of things, including personality clashes. Most workplace disputes will be relatively minor, but some will be more serious. Where these disagreements lead to unpleasant incidents such as assaults or ill-treatment, the effects on morale, productivity and team cohesion can be devastating.

In many cases, policy is an effective (though not the only) vehicle for responding to these kinds of incidents. Having comprehensive policies to guide decision-making in areas such as employee health, safety and well-being, discipline, termination, redundancy, remuneration, conflict and dispute resolution and employee conduct demonstrates an organisation's commitment to ensuring that critical incidents are treated with appropriate gravity. It should be noted, however, that the mere existence of policies does not guarantee immunity from repeat incidents. The successful implementation and management of those policies is what will make the difference – these issues are discussed in subsequent chapters.

Table 9.1 HR policy areas affected by legislation

Legislation type	HR policies affected
Industrial relations	Remuneration
	Discipline and termination
	Leave management
	Attendance management
Occupational safety and health	Employee health, safety and well-being
	Workplace flexibility
	Dress code
Anti-discrimination and fair treatment	Equity and diversity
	Staffing
	Performance management
	Grievance management
	Code of conduct
	Employee privacy

Legislation

As we discussed in Chapter 2, HR policy is framed by a complex web of legal factors, including legislation. Compliance with relevant legislation is, therefore, a priority for HR policymakers. Legislative requirements vary from state to state and change regularly. It is beyond the scope of this book to list every piece of Federal and state legislation applicable to workplaces, but it is useful to focus on the broad areas of HR that can be affected (Table 9.1).

Clearly, policies that contravene legislative requirements are not valid, and so the needs identification process should incorporate a review of relevant legislation. Given that most HR practitioners are not lawyers, it is prudent to seek professional advice on legal matters. Many larger organisations retain a law firm to provide exactly this kind of advice. Employer organisations like chambers of commerce and industry can also provide guidance on legal compliance matters.

Business plans

HR practitioners should always be aware of their organisations' business plans, and should preferably be involved in developing them. Business plans may highlight the need for new HR policies or for revisions to existing ones. Business strategies that have HR policy implications include those relating to

- mergers and acquisitions
- opening new branches or outlets

- new projects coming on stream
- closing branches or discontinuing projects
- adding new product lines or services, or discontinuing them
- outsourcing of functions

All of these strategic actions have staffing and employment implications; therefore the needs identification process should anticipate the kinds of HR issues that will need to be dealt with when the strategies are enacted. These might include redundancies, relocations or recruitment issues. Business expansion may mean that new types of occupations and new kinds of workers become part of the organisation, which may require additional or revised policies in areas such as dress codes, performance management, employee development, safety or remuneration. The danger of not doing this is that there will be a mismatch between existing policies and the new circumstances, or policy gaps. These can lead to the kinds of critical incidents discussed earlier.

Risk management plans

As we discussed in Part I, HR policy connects strongly with organisational risk management processes. Logically, therefore, an organisation's risk management plan should be a key reference document for HR policymakers during the needs identification process. HR policies should certainly address those risks identified as high level and preferably the medium-level risks too. In the absence of an organisation-wide risk management plan, HR should undertake a separate HR risk assessment process. Obviously it is preferable for HR risks to be seen in a broader context, but the reality is that some organisations do not undertake any formal risk management process. Circumstances like these offer HR an opportunity to lead the way and to demonstrate the kind of business focus that is consistent with being a strategic business partner.

Consultation

The nature of HR policy means that there are many stakeholders. Indeed, as employees, everyone in the organisation has an interest in the types of HR policies that are developed and implemented. As we discussed in the opening chapter, it is important for HR to address any perceptions that it is divorced from operational reality or that HR policy is merely a bureaucratic imposition. Consultation during the needs analysis process is one effective way of helping to break down negative perceptions like these, and so it should be an integral part of a structured approach to needs identification. Organisational stakeholders include executive and line management as well as employees at

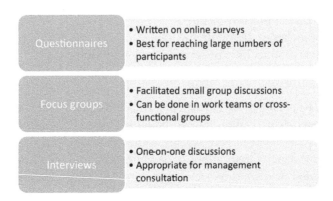

Figure 9.3 Consultation methodologies.

all levels. Depending on the industry and the degree of workforce unionisation, unions may also be important stakeholders. Each of these groups will have different perceptions and different needs and wants.

Consultation can be a long, arduous process, and so it should be undertaken with full commitment. It can sometimes be viewed sceptically by management and employees, especially if there is a history of token consultation. A superficial consultation process can actually do more harm than good. There are several different consultation methodologies which are outlined in Figure 9.3.

Each methodology has its advantages and disadvantages. The choice of methodologies will depend very much on the context. Usually a combination of methodologies works best, with collective methods like questionnaires and focus groups for employees and interviews for managers or specialised stakeholders like union representatives. Whichever methodologies are used, the process needs to be structured rather than being a free-for-all. It is useful in most cases to begin by putting something on the table for discussion – a draft policy, a list of policy options or at least some broad discussion points. Background information should also be provided for participants, including data from business plans and risk management plans, so that everyone understands the kinds of business issues that the policies need to address.

Consideration should also be given to the choice of person to conduct the consultations. An HR practitioner who is coordinating the needs identification process is one option. This has the advantage of directness – people can provide input to the actual person who is responsible for the process and who is likely to be developing and writing the policy. This will foster confidence for participants that their messages are getting through to the right person. Having the HR manager conduct the consultation process is also an option. This has the advantage of credibility – people will be more confident that their input is reaching a person with decision-making power. It is also an option to split consultative responsibilities. For example, a practitioner (or practitioners) might do the consultations with employees, while the HR manager might undertake the management and/or union consultations. Decisions about who should be involved need to take account of two things: The nature, structure and culture of the organisation and the capacity of people in HR to successfully manage the process. This is particularly true where focus groups are being used. Focus group facilitators require suitable skills to ensure the discussion does not degenerate into unruliness or stray from the point at hand. Although it could be argued that these are essential skills for anyone working in HR, the reality is that not everyone has them.

A third option is to have an external person conduct the process. This has two potential advantages. First, a suitable choice will ensure that a person with appropriate facilitation skills is engaged. Second, the fact that the person doing the consultations is independent may mean that people are more confident about the integrity of the process (no political agendas) and are more open in expressing their views. The main disadvantage of using external consultants is the cost, although it might well be considered a good investment if it enhances the quality of the consultation process and the information that comes from it.

One possible downside to consultation is that the act of soliciting people's views may raise expectations. Realistically, it will almost never be possible to incorporate everyone's policy needs and wants; therefore it is possible that some people may feel somewhat let down if their particular input is not incorporated into the final policy. This is not unique to HR policy consultations but is an inherent danger in any kind of consultative process. It is not possible to totally guard against this. It is, however, possible and advisable to flag this reality at the beginning of the process without conveying an impression of tokenism. A genuine consultative process will try to address all the issues raised and reconcile the different needs and wants expressed by different parties – this is an essential part of the policy development process which we examine in the next chapter.

Summary

- Policy needs identification is the first stage in the policy cycle and lays the foundation for policy development.
- Policy needs are shaped by a range of factors, including critical incidents, legislation, business plans, risk management plans and consultation outcomes.
- The needs identification process represents a good opportunity for HR to demonstrate their credentials as strategic business partners.

- It is also an opportunity for HR to address any negative perceptions of their policy role by connecting HR practitioners to organisational stakeholders and providing forums where the rationale for policies can be explained and discussed.

Learning activity – case study 9.1

A critical incident

Lewis is the CEO of the Unlimited Pizza Company, a gourmet pizza business which has experienced rapid growth in the five years since it was established. The company has a corporate office which is staffed by a handful of people. There is no HR specialist, and there are no HR-specific policies in place. The payroll is managed by the company accountant. There are 20 outlets across the metropolitan area. Each outlet has a manager who handles all day-to-day management issues, including employment. There are now more than two hundred employees, many of whom are employed on casual contracts.

Recently an issue arose which caused the company some angst and resulted in a good deal of negative publicity. An employee who was an overseas student made a complaint through the union, claiming that he had been underpaid for the entire two-year duration of his employment. A court case ensued, which found that the employee had been underpaid. It subsequently emerged that everyone in that outlet had been underpaid and that the manager had routinely falsified his employment records to show that people worked fewer hours than they actually had. The media picked up the story, and Lewis had to respond publicly as the CEO. One common question that was put to him was: "How will you ensure that this doesn't happen again?"

The manager responsible was dismissed. An audit of the other 19 outlets showed that there were no similar issues and that all other employees were being paid correctly.

Discussion questions

1. Is the development of an HR policy (or policies) an appropriate response to this critical incident?
2. If so, what kinds of policies might help to ensure that the incident is not repeated?

3. Given that the incident arose as a result of the actions of one rogue manager, is a policy response really needed? If so, why. If not, why not?
4. Should Lewis consider employing an HR specialist?

Learning activity – case study 9.2

Needs identification in a growing business

Alex started his web design business seven years ago, operating from home. The business has been a great success and has grown significantly. Alex now employs nearly a hundred people and is finding that managing the workforce is becoming more and more complex. He decides to ask a consultant to help him put some proper HR systems in place. He subsequently engages Georgia after a recommendation from a business colleague.

The company has a diverse workforce. About half his people are aged 30–50, and many of these have families. Most of the other half are younger than 30, and most of these are singles or couples without children.

When Georgia asks Alex what workforce issues are impacting the business, he lists the following:

- Creativity is the soul of the business, and so it is important to maintain a culture that supports creativity and innovation.
- Turnover of younger employees is starting to become an issue.
- Competition for skilled people is increasing, and it is sometimes difficult to find suitable people when the need arises.
- Some of his more mature employees are experiencing difficulty balancing work and family life.

Discussion questions

1. What kinds of HR policies might be useful to address the workforce issues the business is facing?
2. Given the size and maturity of the business, is it better to have lots of policies or just a few key ones?
3. Outline the kind of consultative process that Georgia should use as part of the needs identification process. Who should she talk to? What sorts of questions should she ask?

Chapter 10

POLICY DEVELOPMENT

Policy development is the process of translating the data gathered in the policy needs identification process into coherent policy documents. The development process can be said to include two distinct stages: the shaping stage and the writing stage. Policy shaping is essentially a cognitive process – the thinking stage that precedes the writing of the policy document itself. Figure 10.1 shows how the shaping process occurs.

Data analysis

Once the needs identification process has been completed, there will be a large amount of data from different sources that need to be considered. The objective of the analysis stage is to make sense of all this information and to develop a clear picture of the organisation and its needs and wants. As we have discussed in Chapter 2, policy is influenced by internal and external factors, and so contextual information also needs to be considered at this point. Depending on the organisation's existing systems and processes, there may also be other data available that can become part of the analysis process. These could include workforce data drawn from the organisation's HR information system and/or qualitative data from employee perception surveys or similar organisational development initiatives. If available, these kinds of data are valuable to policy developers.

Classifying the various pieces of data is a good way to bring some order and structure to the process. Table 10.1 shows how this might be done. Once classified, it should be possible to identify the themes emerging within each category.

As we discussed in Chapter 3, HR policy needs to facilitate the organisation's HR and business strategies, and so this needs to be a primary consideration. However, this is not always a simple matter. As we also discussed in Chapter 3, HR policy is not solely about strategy. It is also about ethics, corporate social responsibility and organisational culture, and so there is potential for strategic imperatives to conflict with other aspects of HRM. This is especially

Table 10.1 Data classification

Data classification	Method
Contextual data	Legislative and regulatory requirements
	Labour market information
	Government policies
	Industrial relations climate
Business data	Strategic plans
	Operational plans
	HR strategies
	Risk management plans
	Financial plans
Workforce data	Turnover
	Absence rates
	Injury rates
	Salary and employee on-costs
	Expenditure on training and development
	Performance appraisal outcomes
	Demographics
Employee issues	Cultural perceptions
	Quality of work life feedback
	Grievances

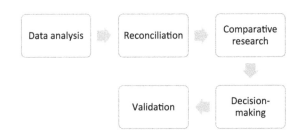

Figure 10.1 Policy shaping.

true during periods of economic downturn, where financial constraints may mean that cost control is a powerful driving force. These are the kinds of issues that need to be reconciled before decisions are made about the shape of HR policies.

Reconciliation

Inevitably, some competing priorities will emerge from the data analysis process. Adverse economic conditions may lead to strategies with unpleasant HR consequences, such as downsizing, wage restraint or outsourcing of non-core functions. Ideally, of course, HR would have had input to the strategic planning process, although the reality is that this is not always the case. In organisations where strategic decisions are handed down as faits accompli without HR input, HR is obliged to act on them. Attempting to block legitimate business strategies would not be appropriate and would undermine the strategic business partner role. However, HR does have a responsibility to operationalise those strategies through policy in a way that does not compromise the organisation's legal or ethical position and minimises the negative effects on organisational culture. Indeed, situations like these can be seen as opportunities for HR to demonstrate its value by steering the organisation safely through potentially treacherous waters.

Comparative research

This stage is about identifying good practice. Many organisations post their HR policies on the internet, so using an internet search engine can often turn up dozens of example policies from a range of different organisations worldwide. These examples can provide useful guidance to HR policymakers, both in terms of content and presentation.

Of course, there are many more organisations whose HR policies are not in the public domain. Indeed, in commercial environments, some organisations see their HR policies as potential sources of competitive advantage, and so they are treated with the same level of confidentiality as information about business processes and other management practices. However, in non-competitive environments like the public and not-for-profit sectors, there are often HR practitioner networks that facilitate communication and information sharing. These networks can be useful vehicles for accessing policies from similar organisations.

While comparative research is potentially a labour saving tool, simply adopting another organisation's policies is neither advisable nor professional. All HR policies need to be tailored to the specific needs and culture of the organisation; therefore policymakers should resist the temptation to 'borrow' others' policies lock, stock and barrel.

Decision-making

The decision-making stage is where the specific policy provisions are formulated. In most cases, policymakers have a range of policy options (which we discuss in Part III). The different options reflect all the factors we have discussed so far, and the decisions about which options are appropriate are essentially the result of balancing all of those factors. This begs the question of whether or not all factors are equally important. Proponents of strategic HRM might argue that strategic imperatives override all other factors. This implies that strategy is HR's primary concern, but as we have already observed, there are other concerns that should also be part of the equation.

Another important aspect of the decision-making process is the balancing of short- and long-term needs. Staffing, employee development, remuneration and leave management policies, for instance, can all be affected by short-term economic factors. But if the policies adopted in these areas are too severe, even temporarily, they could have undesirable longer-term consequences that hinder the organisation's capacity to recover quickly when the economic situation improves. The decision-making process underlines the importance of business awareness for HR practitioners, who need to understand the business consequences of policy decisions, as well as their impact on employees. The ability to effectively sell policy proposals is a vital skill for HR policy practitioners. This can only be achieved if HR has credibility with all levels of management.

Validation

The final step in the policy shaping process involves validating the policy decisions before creating the policy document. This is essentially a second consultation process, though it need not be as formal or structured as the consultations undertaken during the needs identification process. The validation stage allows policymakers to gauge stakeholder responses to policy proposals and to pave the way for formal endorsement once the policy has been finalised. At this point, there is no final policy document; therefore the process is very much about discussing the possible shape of the policy with relevant people, including senior managers, line managers and employees. Much of this can happen on a one-to-one basis although where a consultative committee exists, this is obviously a good forum for these kinds of discussions.

While the validation step might be time consuming, especially in a large organisation, it can actually save time in the long run by pre-empting issues or objections and addressing them before the policy document is submitted for endorsement. One of the biggest advantages of the validation process is that it is non-confrontational; therefore potentially contentious aspects of the policy can be discussed as possibilities rather than as final decisions in an atmosphere of cooperation. Effective validation can also minimise the likelihood of the policy being resisted or disregarded once it is implemented, because key stakeholders are more likely to understand the rationale and will feel that their particular issues and concerns have been listened to.

Table 10.2 Design principles

Principle	Description
Brevity	Policy documents should be concise. In most cases, one to four pages is an ideal length (not including procedures)
Visual impact	Policy documents that are dense blocks of writing are more difficult to read and less likely to be read. The use of white space improves the document's appearance and impact
Sectionalisation	Dividing the policy document into distinct sections and subsections with headings makes it easier to identify relevant information and aids visual impact
Paragraph numbering	Numbering makes it possible to refer to specific sections when invoking the policy for decision-making

Table 10.3 Policy document structure

Element	Description
Policy statement	A brief statement of intent and rationale
Scope	Who is covered by the policy
Definitions	Key terms used in the policy
Policy details	The requirements or conditions of the policy
Links	Other related policies
Endorsement details	Name and date
Contact person	Name and contact details of HR person who can give advice on the interpretation and use of the policy

Policy document design

There is no standard format for policy documents. However, there are several design principles that should be applied to policy documents regardless of the design detail. The overall objective of policy document design is to maximise the likelihood that people will actually read the document properly, rather than just skimming over it or not reading it at all. Simplicity is the key to user friendliness. Table 10.2 summarises these principles.

The policy document should be more than just a statement of the policy's provisions or conditions. It should also include relevant background information, including the reasoning behind it, as well as information that helps people interpret the policy and/or seek advice about it. Whatever structure is used, all policies should be structurally consistent. Table 10.3 is a guide to document structure.

Writing style and language

The audience for policy documents includes everyone in the organisation, and so the writing style and language need to be as inclusive as possible. Policy documents should be written in plain English and should not sound like legal documents or use obscure or specialised language or jargon.

They should also be explicit. Almost any piece of writing is open to interpretation – policy documents should allow as little scope as possible for different interpretations. The meaning should be crystal clear. Draft policies should be proof-read and tested for user-friendliness and clarity.

Policy shortcuts

A range of templates and 'off-the-shelf' policies are available commercially. The quality varies. Costs also vary. Packages of policies are also available. Products like these are, by nature, generic, and so they are unlikely to capture the nuances of individual organisations. In addition, many of them emanate from overseas, especially the United States, where the legal and regulatory contexts are different, and so these are generally unsuitable for use in Australian organisations. It is also common for these products to be sold sight unseen, because making the detail available to potential buyers would defeat the purpose of selling them commercially. Consequently, there is an element of risk involved.

As we have already observed, HR policies should ideally be tailored for the organisation; therefore the use of generic policies is not advisable. However, they can be a useful starting point for policy writers, especially inexperienced ones. For the purpose of comparative research, generic policies can be useful in competitive environments where policy sharing is not possible, or where comparable policies are not accessible in the public domain.

As we have seen in this chapter, the policy development process, when undertaken systematically, can be quite resource intensive. The reality is that in some organisations the HR team is very small, and so using consultants for this type of work might be a necessity. Thus, some organisations outsource policy development. While this is preferable to using generic policies, care should be taken that the final product is in fact organisation specific, rather than a disguised 'off-the-shelf' policy. The downside, of course, is cost.

Decisions about using these kinds of products and services should take account of costs, quality, time and the level of policy skills within the organisation.

Summary

- The policy development process incorporates two distinct stages: policy shaping and policy writing.
- The *policy shaping process* is about interpretation of the data from the needs analysis process, reconciling competing needs and wants, undertaking comparative research, making decisions about the content of the policy and validating those decisions through further consultation. It is perhaps the most important stage in the policy development process.
- The *policy writing process* should begin with sound design principles and emphasise clarity of expression. Policy documents should use a simple format with relevant headings and be written in plain English that is accessible to everyone in the organisation.
- Policy shortcuts can be convenient but are generally not as effective as developing policies in-house. Nonetheless, generic policies and templates can serve as useful references, and policy consultants can free up scarce resources in small HR teams.

Learning activity – case study 10.1

Reconciling redundancy policy

Delectable Smallgoods is a manufacturing company with 400 employees, mostly process workers. The company has been hit hard by the economic downturn, and the recent business planning process has resulted in a decision to lay off 20 per cent of the workforce, about 80 people. The decision was taken with regret by the management as it has never laid off workers before and has always strived to maintain a stable and loyal workforce. Most of the affected workers are union members, and management has already canvassed the redundancy issue with union representatives. Obviously, the union is unhappy with the prospect of seeing so many of its members lose their jobs. Because the company has never enacted a redundancy programme before, there is no redundancy policy in place.

Discussion questions

Explore the issues you would need to reconcile in developing a redundancy policy for the company. In particular, you should consider the following questions:

1. Who are the stakeholders whose interests you would need to consider?
2. What legal and ethical issues would you need to consider?
3. What sorts of issues does the policy need to cover?

Learning activity – case study 10.2

One policy, three interpretations

Wordsmith's is a retail bookseller with several stores across the metropolitan area. Each store employs full-time and part-time staff. Many of the part-time employees are students, and business fluctuates seasonally (e.g. very busy in the Christmas/New Year period, quiet during the winter months). It is common for employees to leave and be re-employed at a later time according to these seasonal fluctuations and their own schedules. One of the provisions of the company's staffing policy relates to the recognition of prior service. It states:

> Staff whose employment is terminated and who are subsequently re-employed will not have their prior service taken into account for purposes of accruing leave or other entitlements.

A new HR manager has recently been appointed, and as a result of a grievance lodged by an employee in one store, she discovered that the policy was being interpreted differently in that store than in the others. The manager of the store from where the grievance had come had interpreted the policy as applying to any former employee regardless of the circumstances of their leaving. Other store managers were interpreting the policy as applying only to people who were dismissed, not to employees who had left of their own accord or who had been employed on a temporary basis in the first place. In addition, another store manager was interpreting the policy as applying only to prior service at that store, not at any of the others.

Your task

1. Why do you think this policy provision exists?
2. Rewrite the policy provision to reflect its rationale and to eliminate any ambiguity in its wording.

Appendix: Example policy document structure

1. POLICY STATEMENT
2. SCOPE
3. DEFINITIONS
4. POLICY DETAILS
    4.1 Subheading
        4.1.1
        4.1.2
    4.2 Subheading
        4.2.1
        4.2.2
        4.2.3
    4.3 Subheading
        4.3.1
        4.3.2
    4.4 Subheading
        4.4.1
        4.4.2
        4.4.3
        4.4.4
5. LINKS
6. ENDORSEMENT DETAILS
7. CONTACT

Chapter 11

POLICY IMPLEMENTATION

The effectiveness of the policy implementation process is the major factor determining the extent to which a policy is understood and followed within an organisation. Unfortunately, it is a process that is not well carried out in some organisations. If the policy is not communicated effectively or embedded in the day-to-day management practices of the organisation, there is a good chance that it will not be followed. Perhaps even more worryingly, poor implementation may lead to the policy being followed correctly by some, incorrectly by others and not at all by yet others. This kind of inconsistency is a recipe for managerial disaster and reflects very poorly on HR. To be perceived as a bureaucrat is bad enough; to be perceived as a bureaucratic bungler is even worse.

Problems like these can be avoided by following a systematic implementation process, as outlined in Figure 11.1.

The approval process

All HR policies require executive endorsement before they can be implemented. In some cases the CEO is the authorised person whereas in other cases it may be another senior executive, perhaps a corporate services director or similar position holder. In some organisations, policies need to be endorsed by an executive committee before being officially signed off by the CEO. Endorsement processes will vary from organisation to organisation. However, regardless of the process or the person or persons responsible for endorsing the policy, the principles that should be followed are the same.

As we have already discussed, some of the groundwork for executive approval can be done during the needs identification and development stages in the form of formal or informal consultation. Nonetheless, even where senior management has been consulted as part of those processes, they may not necessarily be aware of the input from other stakeholders. In some cases, the final shape of the policy will match what senior management expected, but in other cases there will be differences because other factors and views were also taken into account during the development stage.

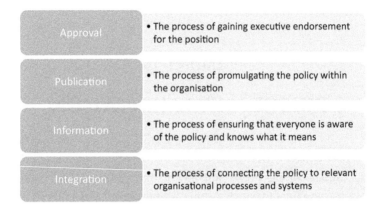

Figure 11.1 Steps in the policy implementation process.

Whatever the circumstances, HR must construct a compelling business case for the policy. The best vehicle for this is usually a policy proposal document that can be circulated among relevant decision-makers and discussed in an appropriate forum such as a monthly executive committee meeting. The proposal should include:

- the rationale for the policy
- an explanation of how it connects with broader organisational issues, for example, strategic direction, risk management
- if it is a new policy, the factors driving the need for it
- if it is a revised policy, the factors driving the need for change
- its operational impact
- the benefits to the organisation of implementing the policy
- the costs/risks of not having the policy

The proposal should always be accompanied by a draft policy document.

Effective needs identification and development processes will maximise the chance that the proposal will be endorsed, but this should never be taken for granted. Sometimes, especially where committees are involved, discussions might result in new issues coming to light, or an individual who opposes the policy might sway other decision-makers during the course of the meeting. The upshot of non-approval could either be that the policy requires amendment or that it is rejected outright. Usually, where amendment is recommended by decision-makers, it is because there is an issue with a particular aspect of the policy. If the proposal is rejected altogether, it normally indicates that decision-makers are unconvinced by the whole idea, and that they do not believe that the policy is necessary or adds anything useful. Where this occurs, it can indicate that the groundwork has not been done properly.

Nonetheless, a rejection may not necessarily be the end of the road. At this point, HR needs to make a judgement about whether the policy proposal is worth pursuing. This might depend on a range of factors, including organisational politics and the nature of the relationship between HR and senior management. Obviously, where HR is perceived as a genuine business partner, there is a better chance that the pursuit of the issue will be worth the effort.

In some cases, an individual HR practitioner may be particularly passionate about a policy proposal, perhaps one that deals with an ethical or equity issue. Passion is a two-edged sword, however. On the one hand, it can be very persuasive; on the other hand, it can be perceived as being irrational.

Where HR decides to pursue a rejected policy, this is best done informally, by talking to decision-makers one-on-one in order to understand the rationale for the rejection. Such a process may compensate for a lack of consultation in the needs identification and development stages (better late than never!) and could provide an opportunity for decision-makers to have their concerns allayed and to modify their views. Alternatively, it might clarify the shortcomings of the proposal and serve as a lesson for the HR practitioner concerned.

The publication process

Once the policy has been endorsed it can be made public. Increasingly, electronic publication is the preferred mode of promulgating and storing policies, though many organisations retain a traditional hard copy policy manual too. The fundamental principle of publication is that HR policies need to be accessible to everyone. Information technology has made this far easier than it once was although there are still potential pitfalls.

In the past, it was common for HR policy manuals to sit on a shelf in the HR department. Not surprisingly, it was rare for managers or employees to venture into the HR department to check a policy detail. Consequently, the manual tended to be read mainly by HR people – and sometimes not even by them. Unfortunately, in some contemporary organisations, the electronic equivalent of this situation has resulted from HR policies being buried among complex matrices of folders within organisations' information systems. People will soon lose patience if they have to search several levels of electronic folders to find the information they are looking for.

Organisations with well-designed intranet systems are in a good position to publish HR policies in a way that makes them easily accessible. Often, intranets include an employee information page where people can access many different information sources with a single mouse click. This is an ideal place for HR policies.

As we have observed previously, some organisations choose to publish their HR policies more widely, usually via their public websites. This might be a strategic decision – part of an organisation's efforts to attract high quality job applicants. Policies in areas like staffing, employee health and well-being, learning and development, workplace flexibility, remuneration and equity/ diversity might well be seen as potential attractors. Indeed, they may have been designed for that specific purpose. The principal objective of publishing HR policies outside the organisation is to paint as full a picture as possible of what life as an employee might be like. These policies could be seen as complementing an organisation's published vision and mission statements and as part of the public image it projects. The downside of this kind of publication is that competitors can see it as well, and so one organisation's good ideas might be copied by others competing in the same labour market, thereby negating any competitive advantage. The decision to publish or not publish HR policies outside the organisation needs to consider these kinds of factors and should not be made unilaterally by HR. Input from marketing, public relations and other relevant areas of the organisation should also be taken into account.

The information process

The action of publishing a policy does not, in itself, ensure that people are aware of it or know how to apply it appropriately. The publication of new or revised policies needs to be supported by an information giving process. Broadly speaking, information strategies can be classified as being either passive or active.

Passive information strategies alone are unlikely to be very effective. The objective of the information process is to ensure that everyone in the organisation is alerted to a policy's existence and purpose, and so HR needs to take an active role in the information process rather than relying exclusively on passive methods. The best results come from using a combination of passive and active strategies.

Active information strategies involve face-to-face contact with managers and employees. In larger organisations, briefing sessions for managers and employees are a good way to reach people. Sessions like these are efficient because they inform a substantial number of people at one time. The downside of this approach is that participants must stop work to attend. This may result in operational difficulties, especially where front line customer service staff are involved. However, if the sessions are kept short and sharp and scheduled to

Figure 11.2 Passive and active information strategies.

enable work areas to retain some staff at all times, most operational concerns can be allayed.

Alternatively, HR representatives can attend regular team and/or management meetings to brief managers and employees on the policy. This approach has the advantage of not imposing on the regular routines of work areas.

While this type of information strategy is more time-consuming for HR, it is far more effective than a passive strategy and has the added advantage of raising HR's profile by increasing visibility and interaction with employees at all levels. At the end of the day, an active information strategy will make it much more difficult for people to claim ignorance or lack of understanding of the policy, increase the likelihood that the policy will be correctly applied and decrease the likelihood of issues like inconsistent interpretation arising later (Figure 11.2).

The integration process

This is perhaps the most important part of the policy implementation process, yet it is the one most often neglected in practice. Integration involves connecting the policy to organisational systems and processes. Doing this embeds it in day-to-day operational activity and makes it part of the way the organisation does business.

The connections made will depend on the type of policy, but could include the kinds of systems and processes shown in Figure 11.3.

For example, information about an organisation's new performance management policy could be included in induction programmes to ensure that new employees understand how their performance will be assessed and how performance data will be used. The requirement to carry out performance

Figure 11.3 Policy integration options.

appraisals in accordance with the policy could be built into managerial job descriptions as well as being a part of the criteria by which each manager's performance is appraised. Building appropriate training and information about the policy into management development programmes would underpin these requirements. The importance of the policy and its connection with other measures of business performance would be underlined by including completion rates for appraisals as part of the organisation's matrix of performance measures.

Failure to integrate policies will diminish their importance and relevance and imply that HR policy is divorced from operational reality. This tends to promote the perception that HR policy is nothing more than bureaucratic imposition.

HR policies also need to be integrated with one another. In many cases, the reality is that policies evolve, and so they tend to be developed and implemented at different times for different reasons. This is especially true where policies are amended or created as a result of a critical incident. A sound policy development process should take into account the impact a new or amended policy will have on existing policies. However, re-checking as part of the implementation process is a good way to make doubly sure that all HR policies fit together in a coherent way.

Summary

- Policy implementation is a four-stage process encompassing approval, publication, information and integration.
- The approval process can be aided by appropriate consultation with decision-makers during the policy development stage. Approval blockages can be addressed through further consultation.
- Electronic publication is the preferred option for new or amended policies, intranets being particularly effective. Policies need to be accessible to everyone in the organisation and not buried deep within complex information systems.
- Publication should always be backed by an information giving process. Active information strategies like information sessions and participation in team and/or management meetings are effective ways of ensuring that everyone is appropriately informed. Reliance on passive information strategies alone will be far less effective and may lead to the policy being ignored, misinterpreted or incorrectly applied.
- Policies need to be integrated with existing organisational processes and systems such as training and induction programmes, management development programmes, performance appraisal criteria and organisational measurement criteria. They also need to be integrated with each other to ensure consistency and coherence.

Learning activity – case study 11.1

Dealing with rejection

Marcus is an HR adviser with a government agency that is responsible for delivering a range of social services and assistance payments to people in distress. As a result of recent changes to government policy, some of these services and payments have been withdrawn or reduced, affecting a large number of the agency's clients. In a discussion with the agency's call centre manager, Marcus has discovered that these changes have resulted in a sharp increase in the number of abusive and threatening calls from clients expressing their anger and frustration over the policy changes. Not surprisingly, stress levels among call centre staff have increased markedly. Some staff members have been so distressed by the verbal abuse and threats they have received that they have been unable to continue working. Absence rates are rising and morale is declining.

After discussing with the call centre manager and several staff members possible ways to address the situation, Marcus has prepared a proposal for the establishment of a peer support programme as part of the agency's employee health, safety and well-being policy. Under the proposal, a team of call centre staff would be trained to provide emotional support to colleagues in the immediate aftermath of an unpleasant incident, helping them to regain their composure and return to their work stations as quickly as possible. The training would also enable peer supporters to recognise symptoms of deeper distress that might require professional support such as counselling.

Given the urgency of the matter and his desire to have the proposal endorsed at the monthly executive committee meeting (due the following week), Marcus prepared his proposal very quickly, emphasising the rising stress levels and declining morale in the call centre. To his surprise, the proposal was rejected as being too costly and an overreaction to what was considered to be a temporary situation. The HR director has advised him to reassess the situation but, recognising Marcus's strong commitment to the proposal, has also indicated that if he wishes to pursue it further, he can do so.

Discussion questions

1. How might Marcus have increased the chances of having his policy proposal approved by the executive? Are there additional arguments he could have included in his business case?
2. Did the urgency of the situation warrant Marcus's abbreviated approach to the policy development process?
3. Should Marcus accept the executive committee's decision and look for another solution, or should he pursue it further?
4. If he pursues it, what would be the best strategy?

Learning activity – case study 11.2

Integrating a new policy

Rockwell Resources is a mining company with around four hundred employees. It has operations in several remote locations and a city-based head office. An amended learning and development policy has just been endorsed which includes new provisions for studies assistance.

Under the new provisions, employees undertaking relevant tertiary studies are entitled to up to 40 hours of paid study leave per semester.

This can be used for attending classes, working on assignments or preparing for exams. The entitlement is subject to operational requirements and must be approved by the employee's manager.

Discussion questions

1. What processes and systems would the new policy provisions need to be integrated with?
2. What other HR policy areas might be impacted by the new provisions?

Chapter 12

POLICY REVIEW

Policy review is the final stage of the policy cycle. Its fundamental purpose is to ensure that existing policies are still relevant. A systematic review process helps to ensure that HR policies are living documents that retain their currency and usefulness as circumstances and organisational needs change.

Timing and frequency of the review process

Logic suggests that the formal review process should dovetail with the business planning process. This helps to ensure that organisational priorities and strategic objectives are the principal drivers for policy reform. However, policies should be capable of review and amendment at any time, not just during a designated review period. As we have already discussed, critical incidents or changes in the business environment may require an immediate policy response. So, in practice, the review process is ongoing. Nonetheless, a formal review period ensures that every policy is subjected to regular scrutiny, not just those that are obviously affected by significant events or changes.

The frequency of the formal review process depends on several factors, including the nature of the organisation, the number of policies and the volatility (or stability) of the environment. An organisation with a relatively small number of policies might review them annually. A larger organisation with a more comprehensive policy portfolio may conduct formal reviews every two or three years. The longer the period between reviews, the higher the likelihood that issues will arise, and so more frequent reviews might seem preferable. However, a comprehensive review process can be quite resource-intensive, and so decisions about their frequency need to take account of operational considerations and resource availability. In many ways, the review process is similar to the needs identification process. The difference is that the review process relates to existing policies. It makes sense, therefore, for the review process and the needs identification process to take place simultaneously. Streamlining the two processes in this way makes both more efficient and helps to guard against delays. It also lessens the demands made on stakeholders, which helps HR to

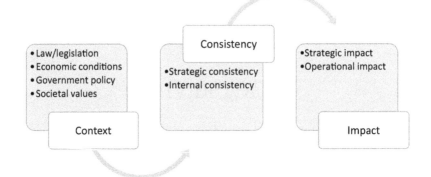

Figure 12.1 Policy review process.

avoid being perceived as organisational bureaucrats focused more on carrying out processes than actually contributing meaningfully to the business.

Dimensions of policy review

Broadly speaking, the review process can be said to have three dimensions as shown in Figure 12.1.

Context

As we discussed in Chapter 2, HR policy is affected by a range of contextual factors, including:

- law/legislation
- economic conditions
- government policy
- societal values

While significant contextual changes are likely to be addressed immediately and appropriate policy changes made, not all changes are dramatic in nature. Indeed, it could be argued that many changes are incremental and, therefore, small. However, over time, the magnitude of changes like these could be quite large. Failure to recognise relatively small incremental changes could result in a crisis point being reached where it becomes obvious that existing policy is no longer appropriate. This might manifest itself as a critical incident.

This is particularly true where societal values are concerned. Shifts in public opinion can evolve over time. Organisations need to be sensitive to these shifts and to whether policy is slipping out of sync with prevailing values and opinions. The executive remuneration issue is a good example of how some organisations have failed to recognise a growing public concern (or at least failed to take it seriously). In Australia, public disquiet about the seemingly disproportionate rises in executive remuneration levels in comparison to non-executive remuneration had been building for several years, fuelled by widespread media coverage. Despite this, only few top-end organisations (those paying the highest executive salaries and bonuses) changed their remuneration policies. As a result, executive remuneration became the subject of a government enquiry and a public and political debate about the need for some kind of regulatory regime – a consequence that most businesses would have found highly undesirable. In this case, government recognised the shift in values and responded to it. It could be argued that if more organisations had recognised that the social landscape was changing and had responded accordingly, they would not have had to publicly defend their remuneration policies. Neither would they have had to deal with the negative PR that arose from their reluctance to change their policies.

Economic and labour market conditions impact directly on staffing policies, remuneration policies and a range of other policy areas that affect the organisation's capacity to attract and retain people. A booming economy and a buoyant labour market might lead to policies geared towards attraction, retention and development. However, an economic downturn will require those policies to be reviewed and perhaps discontinued or suspended in favour of policies more geared towards controlling wage costs and other employee-related expenditure.

The complexity and fluidity of the legal framework also provides fertile ground for policy review. Significant legislative change is usually well publicised within the professional HR community, and so most organisations are able to recognise and respond to it. However, case law decisions are usually less well publicised. New case law decisions may signal a subtle shift in the prevailing interpretation of legal principles. Such shifts could affect areas like discipline and equity policies, dress codes or codes of conduct.

Similarly, major government policy changes are likely to be well publicised especially in the period immediately after a new federal or state government has been elected. Changes of government often signal ideological shifts that lead to significant policy reform. However, this is not to suggest that policies only change when governments change. Governments respond to changing economic and social issues constantly, and so policy changes can happen at any time. In many cases, these are more policy adjustments than radical policy changes, and they may be implemented without much fanfare. Nonetheless, adjustments to government policy can have an impact on organisational policy, especially in areas like staffing, remuneration, safety, privacy and training.

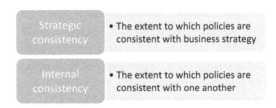

Figure 12.2 Policy consistency.

To ensure that organisations are aware of these kinds of contextual changes and their possible implications for policy, the formal policy review process should begin with an environmental scan. Information sources could include:

- professional associations
- employer support organisations, for example, chambers of commerce and industry
- employment law specialists
- business networks
- business publications
- media digests
- customer reference groups

Consistency

Reviewing policy consistency is about ensuring that policies continue to perform the role that they were originally intended for. There are two aspects of consistency that need to be assessed (Figure 12.2).

Assessing strategic consistency is about reviewing business strategies and the HR strategies that emerge from them. Remembering that policy's strategic role is to transform HR strategies from theory to practice, any policy that runs counter to strategic objectives obviously needs attention. For example, in a buoyant labour market, a recruitment policy that requires formal advertising of all vacant positions may work against the strategic objective of labour market competitiveness because it doesn't allow the organisation the flexibility it needs to recruit people using quicker methods.

Internal consistency is also important because of the degree of interconnectedness between different aspects of HRM and, therefore, between HR policies. Policies obviously need to be compatible with one another – this is why the integration process is so important during policy development. However, a flawed or missing integration process or subsequent amendments to policies

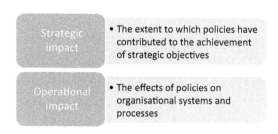

Figure 12.3 Policy impact.

may cause them to diverge and become mutually inconsistent. So the review process should include a compatibility analysis to identify any inconsistencies that have not been recognised previously.

Impact

The final stage of the review process concerns the effect that the policies have had in the organisation. There are two aspects to this, as illustrated in Figure 12.3.

Strategic impact analysis requires measurement of HR outcomes in strategically important areas. These will vary according to the needs of the organisation. Table 12.1 shows how HR policies might affect significant HR outcomes of the type likely to feature as part of an organisation's strategic HR objectives.

The main issue with HR measurement, of course, is the fact that outcomes are generally affected by a range of factors. It is, therefore, difficult to make direct causal links between policies and outcomes. In addition, as Table 12.1 shows, some policies might contribute to several different outcomes, making the connection between policies and outcomes even more complex. However, issues like these should not prevent analysis of the possible connections between policies and outcomes. Other factors that might affect outcomes need to be taken into account and judgements made about the extent to which they might have influenced outcomes. For example, the introduction of an attendance management policy might not necessarily lead to an immediate reduction in absence rates. This might be because of an increase in legitimate absences caused by seasonal factors such as the weather, or by the impact of a contagious illness that might be sweeping the community. However, analysis of absence data might reveal that, even though overall absence rates might not have changed or even increased, absences have declined on Mondays and Fridays (the days most associated with illegitimate absences). This would, therefore, indicate that the policy has had a positive impact, although it is

Table 12.1 Strategic impact measures

Policies	HR outcomes
Attendance management	Reduced absence rates
Leave management	Reduced leave liability
Safety	Reduced time lost through injury
	Reduced number of workers' compensation claims
	Reduced industrial disputation
Equity	Reduced number of grievances
	Reduced turnover
Workplace flexibility	Reduced turnover
Staffing	Reduced vacancy filling times
	Reduced recruitment costs
	Increased numbers of job applicants
	Reduced turnover
Code of conduct	Reduced number of disciplinary actions due to misconduct
Employee development	Increased number of internal promotions
Remuneration and rewards	Reduced turnover
	Increased numbers of job applicants
	Reduced industrial disputation

impossible to quantify that impact exactly. Conversely, if there were no significant changes and no identifiable mitigating factors, one could logically conclude that the policy had not had the desired effect.

Qualitative information gathered from employees and management might also help to determine the presence or absence of mitigating factors. In addition, it is the key to determining the operational impact of policies. Some organisations convene a policy review group to help them assess operational impact. Such a group might be made up of a cross-section of people from different parts of the organisation and from different occupational groups. Alternatively, separate cross-sectional groups might be set up for management and employees, recognising that the issues might be different for each. This kind of feedback helps to pinpoint any unforeseen issues that might arise from the implementation of policies, such as instances where a policy is impacting on operational efficiency or effectiveness in an undesirable way. In smaller organisations, a less formal approach (such as an HR representative meeting with key people on a one-to-one basis) can be equally effective. As we have already observed in our discussion of the needs analysis process, consultation is also a good way of breaking down any real or perceived barriers between HR and the rest of the organisation.

The fundamental principle of policy review is that no HR policy should be considered to be set in concrete indefinitely. While some policies (i.e. those more geared towards compliance issues) might undergo relatively little change over time, other more strategically oriented policies might change frequently. A formal policy review process ensures that every policy is subject to regular scrutiny and its effectiveness assessed. The reality is that some policies will inevitably outlive their usefulness and will need to be discarded or significantly amended. The ultimate outcome of policy review is that every policy is a living document and that organisations' policy portfolios are dynamic.

Summary

- Policy review is an ongoing process and should not be limited solely to designated policy review periods.
- Notwithstanding this, formal review processes ensure a systematic and proactive approach to maintaining and improving policies. The review process should dovetail with business planning processes and can be combined with the policy needs identification process for efficiency.
- Reviews should assess three policy dimensions: context, consistency (strategic and internal) and impact (strategic and operational).
- Though it is sometimes difficult to quantify policy impact precisely, analysis of workforce data, qualitative data and mitigating factors can be effective for assessing the effectiveness of policies.

Learning activity – case study 12.1

Understanding contextual change

GreenFoods is a large supermarket chain with stores throughout the metropolitan area and in the larger regional centres. Its staffing policy has traditionally been to maintain a small core workforce of permanent full-time staff (mainly managers and supervisors) with the majority of employees being contingent workers employed on a casual basis, allowing the company maximum workforce flexibility. This has been considered by management to be essential given the nature of the industry and the high turnover of staff.

Recently there has been some media attention given to contingent employment practices like the one adopted by GreenFoods. The media coverage has focused on the negative social effects of the employment insecurity and unreliable income experienced by contingent workers.

Various politicians have also weighed into the debate, some supporting the negative views being put by the media, others supporting employers' needs for maximum efficiency and flexibility in a competitive marketplace. Although GreenFoods has not been named in the media thus far, the company's HR manager is concerned that the issue is potentially damaging to its reputation and may lead to employee unrest.

Discussion questions

1. Is the recent media coverage a signal of changing social attitudes on the issue, or is it merely the 'flavour of the month'?
2. How could GreenFoods determine whether it's an issue of genuine concern among its own employees?
3. What would be the advantages and disadvantages of modifying the company's staffing policy to lessen the reliance on contingent workers and increase the proportion of permanent employees?
4. What should the HR manager do?

Learning activity – case study 12.2

Operational impact and risk

Erica is an HR adviser with Foresight Finance, a large national company providing financial services to individuals and businesses. She is managing a policy review process, the first that has been undertaken since the company's HR policies were revamped two years previously. To assess operational impact, Erica has convened a review group made up of a range of people at all levels in the organisation.

There has been some strong feedback from managers about the company's performance management and termination policies, which they believe are making it difficult to deal effectively with underperforming employees. Essentially, managers believe that the policies are too bureaucratic and that dismissing an employee because of poor performance is almost impossible because of the policy requirements. The policies require a period of active performance management (close supervision, additional training and monitoring of output and work quality) for a minimum period of three months before an employee can be dismissed for poor performance. Feedback indicates that, rather than embark on such a protracted process, managers are not addressing performance issues at all or are trying to offload underperforming employees to other departments.

The original rationale for the policies was to protect the organisation from unfair dismissal litigation and to ensure that underperformance issues were managed transparently. Erica believes that the rationale remains valid, though she accepts that the process is somewhat demanding. Operational level employees participating in the review group have expressed the view that the policies are useful for protecting employee rights and that, in some cases at least, management opposition simply reflects the fact that managers would rather get rid of a problem than try to solve it.

Discussion questions

1. What are the implications for the company of the managers not addressing performance issues or seeking to transfer employees whose performance is problematic?
2. Are the managers' concerns legitimate? What are some of the possible operational impacts of following the current policy requirements?
3. Does operational efficiency override the risk of litigation?
4. Should Erica amend the policy? If so, why and what changes should be made? If not, why not?

Chapter 13

MANAGING POLICY ISSUES

In the preceding chapters we have discussed the stages of the policy cycle from needs identification to review. However, the HR policy function is not simply a series of actions undertaken routinely. At every stage of the cycle and between them, policies need to be actively managed. Policy management is primarily about ensuring that policies are properly utilised and adhered to and that any problems or blockages are dealt with effectively. Broadly speaking, policy issues can be classified into three main types (Figure 13.1).

Role duality

As we discussed in Chapter 1, there are two aspects of HR policy. The compliance aspects ensure that legal and regulatory requirements are met while the strategic aspects facilitate change and contribute to the organisation achieving its strategic business objectives. There is a fundamental tension between these policy aspects. Compliance policies can be perceived as being restrictive and, therefore, detrimental to efficiency and the achievement of business objectives. These are the kinds of policies that often lead to HR being labelled as bureaucratic and concerned only with enforcing rules. To complicate matters further, most policies embody both compliance and strategic aspects. The compliance aspects of policies can have the effect of limiting their potential strategic impact or at least being perceived that way. Nonetheless, compliance policies are necessary because the labour market is highly regulated. Consequently, strategic objectives need to be achieved within that regulatory framework. Table 13.1 summarises the nature of the major HR policy areas in relation to compliance and strategy.

In addition, as we have previously discussed, policies also need to be consistent with common law principles and case law decisions. Policy management can thus be seen to be something of a balancing act between what is required by laws and regulations and what the organisation needs to be successful.

The key to managing the tension between compliance and strategy is communication. This is one reason why the implementation process is so

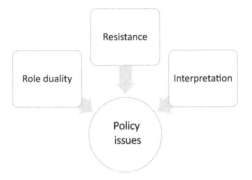

Figure 13.1 Types of policy issues.

important. Done properly, policy implementation raises awareness of both the compliance requirements and the strategic intents of HR policies. Nonetheless, even where there has been a thorough implementation process, circumstances will inevitably arise where HR needs to restate the rationale for certain policies. Ideally, HR practitioners operating as strategic business partners will have ongoing relationships with managers and employees. The closer those relationships, the more likely it is that compliance aspects can be reiterated effectively.

It can be difficult to explain policies in terms that are purely strategic. Strategic objectives such the enhancement of organisational culture, attraction, retention and long-term workforce planning can seem rather nebulous to line managers who are focused on operational realities. Indeed, they can often be dismissed as being theoretical or 'warm and fuzzy'. One of the most convincing ways to justify policies is to emphasise their risk management function. No organisation wants to be subjected to litigation, prosecution or public censure. This is obvious to everyone; therefore even if the strategic objectives of policies seem vague and hard to define in concrete terms, the risks and consequences of non-compliance are usually self-evident.

Balancing the dual roles of policy police and strategic business partner is perhaps HR's most challenging task. However, effective communication and good relationships can make the job easier.

Resistance

One of the possible consequences of the tension between operational reality and policy requirements (whether compliance-based or strategic) is resistance. Resistance can take one of two forms.

Active resistance needs to be addressed directly through dialogue with the complainant/s. HR needs to listen to the issues and consider legitimate

Table 13.1 Compliance and strategic aspects of HR policy

Policy area	Compliance aspects	Strategic aspects
Dress codes	Health and safety regulations Anti-discrimination legislation	Enhancement of corporate image
Codes of conduct/ethics	Criminal code Anti-discrimination legislation	Enhancement of organisational culture Attraction Retention
Grievance and dispute resolution	Anti-discrimination legislation	Enhancement of organisational culture
Discipline and termination	Industrial relations legislation	Productivity
Leave management	Employment awards and agreements	Management of leave liability Productivity
Attendance management	Employment awards and agreements	Management of absence rates Productivity
Performance management		Alignment with business objectives Productivity
Remuneration and rewards	Industrial relations legislation Employment awards and agreements	Attraction Retention Labour market competitiveness
Equity and diversity	Anti-discrimination legislation	Enhancement of organisational culture Attraction Retention
Workplace flexibility	Employment awards and agreements	Attraction Retention Productivity
Staffing	Anti-discrimination legislation Skilled migration policy Employment awards and agreements	Attraction Retention Labour market competitiveness
Employee development and training	Occupational health and safety legislation Certification and licensing requirements	Attraction Retention Workforce planning
Succession management	Anti-discrimination legislation	Workforce planning
Employee health, safety and well-being	Occupational health and safety legislation	Attraction Retention Productivity Reduction of workers' compensation costs
Employee privacy	Privacy legislation	Productivity

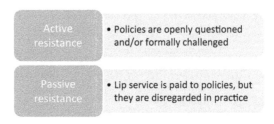

Figure 13.2 Types of policy resistance.

operational concerns, and policies should be reviewed in the light of this two-way dialogue. As we have already observed, no policy should be set in concrete indefinitely, and even if there are aspects of a policy which are non-negotiable for compliance reasons, there is usually some scope for movement if the policy is having unforeseen and undesirable side effects.

It is important to determine the extent of the opposition. Widespread opposition generally means that there are, in fact, genuine operational issues underlying the opposition.

Managing passive resistance is more difficult, but the same principles apply. Once alerted to the issue, HR first needs to attempt to resolve it informally through dialogue with the relevant person. It is important to discover whether the person is unaware of the policy or whether they have an issue with it. If there is an issue of concern, the nature of that issue needs to be explored. Passive resistance is less likely to be widespread than active resistance. Often it is just one person. If this is the case, there is perhaps less justification for amending the policy, although the potential for amendment should be assessed on the merits of the objections rather than on the number of opponents. The likelihood is, however, that the person resisting the policy will need to modify their behaviour accordingly.

If non-compliance continues, it becomes a performance/disciplinary issue that needs to be managed appropriately, usually by the person's own manager rather than by HR. Of course, this is not the preferred outcome. It is far better to resolve issues like these through dialogue and negotiation rather than by enforcement. However, if there are no legitimate reasons for changing a policy, every employee is obliged to observe it regardless of whether or not they agree with it.

Interpretation

As we discussed in Chapter 11, it is important to pay careful attention to the wording of policy documents to eliminate as much as possible the potential for them to be misinterpreted. In reality, some existing policy documents within an organisation may be loosely worded or ambiguous in their meaning, and this can lead to different interpretations. Sometimes these misinterpretations can persist for years and the original intent of the policy may be lost as a result. This is obviously a scenario that HR policymakers would want to avoid.

Equally undesirable is a scenario where different parts of the organisation interpret the same policy differently. These differences can also persist over time, especially where workplaces are geographically dispersed and don't interact very much. A similar danger arises where HR is devolved to specific workplaces or business units. HR practitioners operating in isolation from one another might also interpret the same policy differently, and inconsistencies might arise as a result. In theory, this shouldn't happen because one would expect that HR professionals in a devolved environment would maintain regular communication with their colleagues in other parts of the organisation. However, the reality is that maintaining this effective communication is sometimes easier in theory than in practice.

Where questions arise as to the correct interpretation of policies, HR is usually the final arbiter. Having developed the policies, HR should know the rationale behind them, their compliance functions and/or their strategic intents. This is why each policy document should include the name of the appropriate contact person in HR. This is often the person who originally wrote the policy, although with staff movements, it isn't always possible to maintain this connection with the original author.

Perhaps the most salient issue in interpreting policy is that the interpretation should be consistent with the words themselves. This is true even where it becomes evident that the wording is flawed or the original intention has not been conveyed effectively. Indeed, policy interpretation rulings by HR can be contentious if they are not fully understood or where HR appears to be invoking provisions that are not specifically included in the policy. This might result in a grievance, especially where the policy concerns employee entitlements or issues of fairness and equity. Given that organisational policies are considered to be part of the employment contract, making policy rulings based on what the policy should have said rather than on what it actually says could have unpleasant legal implications too.

Uncertainty about the correct interpretation of a policy is generally an indicator that precision is lacking and that the wording of the policy needs to be revised. Even so, given the vagaries of the English language, even the most carefully crafted policy can be interpreted differently by different people. HR's role as interpreter and arbiter, therefore, remains central to the policy function.

Summary

- Policy management is an ongoing process of overcoming problems and blockages and ensuring a consistent approach.

- The need to balance compliance with strategy, and HR's dual role as policy police and strategic business partner, can create tension. However, that tension can be lessened where effective information and integration processes are carried out when policies are first implemented. Positive ongoing relationships between HR and the rest of the business also help to ameliorate this tension.

- Resistance to policies can either be active or passive. In either case, dialogue with complainant/s is the key to resolution. Where policies impact negatively on operations, HR needs to do whatever possible to reduce or eliminate the ill-effects without compromising the policy.

- Interpretation issues can arise because of imprecise wording or lack of detail in policy documents. HR usually has the final word on interpretation issues, but they need to take care that their interpretations reflect the actual wording of the policy rather than what might have been intended originally but not successfully conveyed.

- Policies that are misinterpreted or that generate regular enquiries about their meaning should be reviewed and rewritten to improve their clarity and to reduce the potential for future problems.

Learning activity – case study 13.1

Dealing with resistance

Kate works in HR for a large law firm in the central business district. Recently, she developed and implemented a workplace flexibility policy that includes provisions for home-based work. The firm's partners have strongly supported the policy and have indicated that they see it as an important part of a longer-term strategy to become an employer of choice.

About three months after the policy was implemented, Kate received a complaint from one of the paralegals in the firm's corporate law division. She was aggrieved that she had not been allowed to access the home-based work provision of the policy because the head of the division, Alex, would not approve it. Further investigations by Kate revealed that no one in that division had been allowed to access any of the policy's flexibility provisions – Alex had refused every application. This had caused some resentment among the division's employees – lawyers, paralegals and administrative staff alike.

Kate subsequently emailed Alex to set up a meeting to discuss the issue, but she received a rather curt reply. He said that while flexibility was fine in theory, it was not appropriate for a corporate law practice, and since the policy allowed for division heads to approve or not approve applications based on operational requirements, he was merely exercising his managerial right. He also said that he saw no need for a meeting to discuss the issue.

Discussion questions

1. What might be some of the reasons behind Alex's refusal to allow his staff to take advantage of the flexibility policy?
2. Given that Alex is exercising a legitimate managerial right under the policy, should Kate pursue it?
3. If she did decide to pursue the matter with Alex, what arguments could she use to try to change his view?
4. What are the consequences of Alex's division being the only one not to allow flexible work arrangements?
5. How should Kate respond to Alex's email?

Learning activity – case study 13.2

A question of interpretation

Kevin works as an IT support officer for a large financial institution in Melbourne, Australia. He also participates in the sport of hurling, a traditional Irish game similar to hockey. Hurling is very much a minor sport in Australia, played only in Sydney, Melbourne and Perth, mostly by Irish expatriates. Recently the GAA (Ireland's Gaelic sports body) invited a representative team from Australia to visit Ireland for a series of games against Irish club teams. An Australian team has been selected from participants in the three cities where hurling is played, based on ability and the capacity of players to fund their own air fares. Kevin is one of those selected.

Although the self-funding requirement has stretched Kevin's finances, he has committed to it on the basis that his company has an international sporting leave provision as part of its staffing policy. The policy states:

> Employees who are selected to represent Australia in sport, whether as an individual or as part of a national team, are entitled to up to two weeks paid leave per annum to enable them to compete, subject to the operational requirements of the employee's work unit.

Kevin duly applied for leave under the provisions of this policy, outlining all the details of the team and the trip, including an official letter from the Gaelic Football and Hurling Association of Australasia confirming his membership of the Australian team. The application was supported by Kevin's manager, but his plans were thrown into confusion when he was advised by HR that his application had not been approved. Kevin was shocked by this and asked HR for an explanation. HR agreed to provide the rationale for the decision in writing. The following is what Kevin received:

The application under the international sporting leave policy was rejected for the following reasons:

1. The fact that team members come from only three states casts doubt on whether or not the team is a national team.
2. The fact that team members are required to fund their own travel costs also casts doubt on the status of the team as a bona fide national team.
3. The team will be competing against club teams in Ireland, not the Irish national team or national teams from other countries.
4. Approval of the application would not be consistent with the spirit of the policy, which is to support employees who are selected to represent Australia in significant international sporting events such as world championships or Olympic Games.

Without paid leave, Kevin's ability to fund his trip is doubtful. Not surprisingly, he is quite upset at the outcome and is considering instigating a grievance over HR's interpretation of the policy.

Discussion questions

1. Should Kevin challenge HR's interpretation of the policy? If so, what should his argument be?
2. Is HR's interpretation reasonable in the circumstances?
3. Should the policy be amended? If so, how would you change it to make it clearer?

Part III

POLICY APPLICATIONS

Chapter 14

CODES OF CONDUCT

A code of conduct is a policy which outlines acceptable standards of behaviour in the workplace and acceptable business and professional practices. Policies like these perform several functions as outlined in Figure 14.1.

Put simply, codes of conduct spell out the rules that apply to how employees deal with one another and customers and clients, and how business should be conducted within the organisation. Effective codes of conduct help to ensure that organisations operate within the law and that everyone in the organisation acts in accordance with accepted social standards and expectations. In a sense, an organisation defines itself through its code of conduct. Its code also helps to shape the way that the organisation is perceived by potential future employees, investors and the community at large. There are several dimensions to workplace conduct. Not all organisations will include every dimension in their code – the types of behaviours included and the specific behavioural guidelines that apply will vary according to the nature of the organisation and its business. Nevertheless, it could be argued that codes of conduct should be as comprehensive as possible.

Ethics and integrity

This is a fundamental dimension. Almost all organisations have (or should have) clear ethical guidelines that are relevant to their particular context. In fact many organisations choose to have a separate code of ethics rather than incorporating ethical dimensions into their code of conduct. This emphasises the level of importance placed on ethics by the organisation. In addition, some industry and professional associations develop codes of ethics to which their members commit. The existence of an industry or professional code of ethics should not deter organisations from having their own organisation-specific code, though of course, organisational codes need to be consistent with the prevailing industry or professional codes.

Most codes of ethics prescribe qualities such as diligence, duty of care and honesty in business dealings. Provisions like these are consistent with

Figure 14.1 Rationale for codes of conduct.

the common law principles governing the employer–employee relationship, requiring employees at all levels to apply themselves conscientiously to their work. In a similar vein, respect for statute law is sometimes also built into codes of ethics, recognising that society and business are both regulated by such laws. This kind of requirement implies that it is incumbent upon everyone to be aware of the legal and/or regulatory framework that surrounds them. While most people have a good general understanding of laws that apply in society (e.g. the criminal code), sometimes industry-related laws and regulations are less well understood, especially where they are complex. Indeed, some industries (financial services, for example) have extremely complex regulatory regimes. In countries like Australia, New Zealand and the United Kingdom, public sector regulatory frameworks stem from the traditions of the Westminster system of government which emphasises the independence of the public service from the political side of government. Including respect for law in a code of ethics helps to draw attention to the fact that every employee is subject to applicable statutes and regulations.

Ethical conduct may also include acting in the public interest. This is one way in which organisations can express their commitment to corporate social responsibility. Of course, defining public interest is difficult, and interpretations will vary. It could, in fact, be argued that including public interest provisions in a code of ethics is merely symbolic. Nonetheless, their inclusion still has value if it contributes to a culture of social responsibility.

One of the more complex issues relating to ethics and integrity is the question of accepting gifts and hospitality. Many businesses give and receive gifts or hospitality as part of the relationship-building process with clients, suppliers and other stakeholders. This is an accepted part of business. But how much is too much? When does relationship-building cross the line and become bribery or inducement? While few would have a problem with an employee accepting a lunch invitation from a client or supplier or a bottle of wine at Christmas, accepting a valuable gift like a car might be viewed in a very different way.

One way that organisations address this issue in their codes of ethics is to define the limits in dollar terms. In some public sector jurisdictions, for example, it is common for ethical guidelines to limit the monetary value of hospitality that can be accepted, and for gifts to be declared and, in some cases, relinquished to the custody of the organisation. Anything worth more than the limit must be refused. Admittedly, the public sector is probably more sensitive to issues like these than the private sector, but the principles are essentially the same whichever sector one works in. Most codes of ethics preclude the acceptance of any amount of cash. The monetary limit for acceptance of gifts or hospitality needs to be considered and set according to industry norms and societal expectations. Such limits also need to be revised regularly in line with movements in the consumer price index or changes in industry or societal standards. Of course the issue works both ways, and so codes of ethics should also include provisions governing the giving of gifts and hospitality by employees.

Interpersonal relationships

Most codes of conduct will include some provisions relating to the way employees interact with one another and with clients, customers, suppliers and other stakeholders. The most basic of these provisions relates to the need to treat people with respect. Most codes of conduct, therefore, include provisions prohibiting violence, bullying, intimidation, harassment and other obviously dysfunctional behaviours whether verbal or physical. Cyber bullying is an issue that has emerged in recent years; it is advisable to include provisions that relate specifically to this kind of behaviour too.

Discrimination on the basis of race, religion, gender, age, disability, sexuality or other personal characteristics should also be specifically prohibited in codes of conduct. This needs to be consistent with whatever anti-discrimination legislation applies. Policies covering other aspects of people management such as staffing should also embody anti-discriminatory practices. These types of policies tend to relate mainly to organisational decision-making rather than to day-to-day interactions. The code of conduct is the appropriate policy to ensure that anti-discrimination principles are embraced in all aspects of organisational life, not just decision-making.

In organisations where employees deal directly with members of the public, incidents sometimes occur where employees are abused or threatened by customers or clients. Whatever the context, employees should not have to tolerate this kind of treatment, and their rights should be enshrined in policy. Policies dealing with these kinds of issues will usually allow employees to terminate contact with an abusive or threatening customer or client. Incidents involving threats or abuse should also be documented in case they become the subject of a customer complaint.

The issue of intimate relationships in the workplace is obviously very sensitive. Some organisations have policies relating to personal relationships between co-workers, recognising that it is inevitable that these will occur from time to time. While it would not be appropriate or practical to try to prohibit intimate relationships between employees, some organisations have policies preventing couples from working alongside one another or having a supervisory relationship at work. Policies like these are obviously more workable in larger organisations where there is scope for people to be transferred to other departments or other locations. Some organisations, either by choice or by necessity, do not impose policies relating to colleagues and personal relationships. Ultimately, the organisation needs to decide on the appropriate balance between employee rights, the interests of the business and practicality.

The issue of intimate relationships between employees and other stakeholders also needs to be considered. This is particularly relevant where there is a duty of care such as in educational institutions or organisations providing medical/health services, counselling or other services to clients who might be vulnerable. In these kinds of organisations, intimate relationships with clients are clearly unethical and should be explicitly prohibited in the organisations' codes of conduct.

Tobacco, alcohol and drugs

Most workplaces today are smoke-free, and where this is not specifically prohibited by public health or occupational health and safety legislation (as it is in hotels and restaurants), the organisation should include a non-smoking requirement in its code of conduct. This might apply not only to smoking in offices or other business premises, but also in company vehicles. Many organisations allow employees who smoke to do so outdoors and away from the immediate workplace. In some cases, this is permissible only during designated breaks, although organisations allow employees to take additional smoke breaks outside designated break times. Where this is allowed, the policy needs to make clear whether or not smokers are required to clock off while taking a smoke break.

Clearly, the use of alcohol and recreational drugs is not appropriate in workplaces, and codes of conduct should explicitly prohibit such behaviour. In some organisations, however, policy does allow for alcohol consumption on work premises outside working hours, usually in the context of social activities arranged by or approved by the organisation. It is advisable too that policies prohibit employees attending the workplace while under the influence of alcohol or recreational drugs regardless of where those substances were consumed. This is particularly important for safety reasons where employees operate machinery, drive vehicles, work at heights or perform medical procedures. This prohibition is also important if employees deal directly with customers or clients.

Conflicts of interest

Conflicts of interest occur where decisions give an unfair advantage to decision-makers or people associated with decision-makers, or where a perception of unfair advantage may result. This may relate to decisions concerning remuneration, job appointments, promotions, the awarding of contracts to suppliers or service providers, or other management decisions. The conflict might occur due to the presence of a family or personal connection and/or a financial gain. Examples of potential conflicts of interest could include cases

- where an employee is involved in a job appointment or selection decision and a family member or friend is one of the applicants
- where a manager is responsible for making a remuneration decision such as a salary increase or bonus payment for an employee who is a family member or friend
- where a manager responsible for awarding contracts has a financial interest in one of the companies being considered, or where a relative or friend is the proprietor of one of the companies or has a financial interest

Situations like this will occur from time to time. In such circumstances the code of conduct should require that employees declare their conflict of interest and exclude themselves from the decision-making process. This is a fundamental business ethics principle.

Confidentiality and protection of information

Common law requires that employees protect the interests of their employers. This includes a requirement that commercially sensitive information be protected and not disclosed to competitors. The code of conduct should reflect this important and fundamental requirement.

The code may also include provisions relating to dealing with outside organisations such as the media, lobbyists or other interest groups. This is particularly relevant in the public sector where disclosure of confidential public policy decisions or matters under consideration may be construed as being inappropriate or even corrupt. Some organisations have strict policies concerning who can talk to the media or to other groups seeking to influence decisions. Where these provisions exist, they usually designate specific people or the holders of specific positions as the authorised representatives of the organisation.

Some organisations may also have policies concerning the disclosure of information about customers or clients, especially financial or personal information. These types of policy provisions usually prevent employees from releasing information to unauthorised parties outside the organisation in the interests of protecting commercially confidential information or the customer or client's privacy.

External employment and other activities

Some organisations require that employees inform their employers it they wish to undertake a second job or conduct private business activities. In some cases they will be required to seek formal clearance. This is to remove the possibility of a conflict of interest. Obviously, it would not be appropriate for employees to use their positions or their employers' intellectual property for their own personal gain. Nor would it be appropriate for employees to enter into competition with their employers. Requiring employees to disclose details of other paid employment or business activities is legitimate and should be included in the code of conduct.

Similarly, involvement in other activities such as board and committee memberships may also be of legitimate concern to employers, particularly where they are paid positions. In most cases, though, external board and committee work is voluntary, and most organisations would have no problem with it. Indeed, an employer will often encourage active participation in professional associations or community-based groups as this reflects positively on the entire organisation.

Party political activities and political activism through lobby groups or similar organisations may cause employers some angst, but care needs to be taken in considering whether or not codes of conduct should require employees to disclose such activities. In most cases, it should be adequate to require employees to declare any external activities that may create a conflict of interest or impact on their ability to undertake their duties. Insisting that employees disclose details of private activities may be seen as intrusive, and attempting to specifically prohibit certain kinds of activities or involvement with certain groups may impinge on employee rights to freedom of association.

Use of employer's resources

Most codes of conduct will include provisions relating to the use of the organisation's resources. Obviously these resources are provided to enable employees to carry out their duties effectively rather than for personal use, although some organisations do allow employees private use of some resources as a 'perk'.

Some organisations, for instance, allow employees to have custody of company vehicles. In cases like these, the code of conduct should make clear the extent to which employees can use those vehicles. In some cases, company vehicles can only be used outside normal working hours for travel to and from work. In other cases, organisations may allow the custodian to use the vehicle for private purposes outside working hours. If this is the case, there may be limits placed on the extent of usage that is allowed (usually expressed in terms of kilometres travelled), and these should be outlined in the code of conduct. Provisions like these would not usually apply where the employee's vehicle is provided as part of their remuneration package.

Many employees have custody of corporate credit cards, and clearly policies and guidelines are needed to govern their use. In addition, stringent financial accountability processes must exist to prevent their misuse. While it could be argued that issues relating to corporate credit cards are more financial policies than HR policies, reiterating those financial policies in a code of conduct is a good way to reinforce the message.

Similarly, usage of computers and email facilities could be seen as being within the purview of IT policy rather than HR policy. However, as these kinds of policies relate to employee behaviour, it could equally be argued that they have a legitimate place in an organisation's code of conduct. Most organisations tolerate the use of IT equipment for personal business such as web browsing and email in the same way as they tolerate employees making personal phone calls. However, inappropriate use such as accessing pornography or other suspect websites and downloading offensive or illegal material is not tolerated. These kinds of prohibitions should be spelt out in policy. Where the organisation chooses to treat the use of IT facilities as an HR issue, the code of conduct is the appropriate vehicle for doing this.

One of the most prevalent forms of communication technology today is the mobile phone. Many organisations provide mobiles for business purposes, and often employees are permitted to use their mobiles as their personal phones too. With mobile phones having increasing capacity to access all kinds of online services and products, some organisations may wish to place limits on how the employer-provided mobile can be used and/or the expenditure that can be incurred on calls and other activities that are not work related. If so, the code of conduct may be an appropriate place for those policies to be articulated.

Employee conduct outside the workplace

Logic would suggest that codes of conduct should apply only to employee conduct at work. However, some employers may have a legitimate concern about the way employees conduct themselves outside the work environment too. In most cases, it would be inappropriate for codes of conduct to attempt to regulate employee behaviour outside the work environment, but there are some notable exceptions. For example, in circumstances where a person is easily identifiable as an employee of a particular organisation because they are wearing a uniform or corporate attire, it could be argued that misbehaviour outside the work environment might tarnish the organisation's image. It might, therefore, be deemed appropriate for codes of conduct to apply where employees are wearing such clothing, even when they are not on duty. This could be a legally complex issue; therefore before enacting policies that extend beyond the work environment, it would be advisable to seek legal advice.

Similarly, in industries like the media or sport, where an employee may have a high public profile, misconduct outside the workplace may be seen as bringing the organisation into disrepute. Indeed, in recent times there have been several cases involving prominent sportspeople where their employers have taken disciplinary action because of inappropriate off-field behaviour. Within that environment, there seems to be general acceptance that codes of conduct can legitimately apply more broadly than is the norm. This is the exception rather than the rule, however.

Reporting breaches of the code

All employees have an ethical responsibility to uphold the code of conduct and to report any breaches of the code. This duty should be made clear within the code. Turning a blind eye should not be an option. It is also incumbent on the employer to protect employees who report breaches from recrimination. This may include provisions for protecting the identity of whistle-blowers. This does not necessarily mean allowing employees to make anonymous reports, as this may encourage malicious reports driven more by personal ill-feeling than by ethical considerations. Nonetheless, employees should feel that they can make legitimate reports in confidence. Processes for reporting breaches should be outlined in the code. Usually, HR is the appropriate department for dealing with alleged breaches.

Table 14.1 Code of conduct policy linkages

Policy	Linkage
Discipline policy	Defines consequences of breaches of the code of conduct
Grievance policy	Describes action that can result from breaches of the code, especially in relation to interpersonal and conflict-of-interest issues
Equity policy	Code of conduct reinforces and supports anti-discrimination provisions
Performance management policy	Performance criteria should reflect code of conduct requirements
Financial policies	Code of conduct may reinforce financial management requirements (e.g. corporate credit card usage)
IT policies	Code of conduct may reinforce IT policies (e.g. internet and email usage)

Where breaches are criminal in nature, there is a legal obligation for employees to report them, and this, too, should be outlined in the code of conduct.

Policy linkages

Codes of conduct link with several other policy areas as shown in Table 14.1.

Summary

- Codes of conduct help to promote a positive, ethical workplace culture that embodies socially responsible behaviour and helps to manage risks that result from misconduct.
- Codes may cover a range of different areas of employee behaviour depending on the nature of the organisation. These can include:
  - ethics and integrity
  - interpersonal relationships
  - tobacco, alcohol and drugs
  - conflicts of interest
  - confidentiality and the protection of information
  - use of employer's resources.
- Codes of conduct would not normally cover employee behaviour outside the work environment. Exceptions may be considered in relation to periods where employees may be wearing uniforms or other corporate clothing or

where employees have a high public profile that associates them with their employer.

- Codes should incorporate requirements for employees to report breaches, especially where those breaches involve illegal activity. Confidentiality provisions should apply to protect the identities of employees who report breaches.

Learning activity – case study 14.1

Public interest or conflict of interest?

Kate is an HR policy officer with the Department of Public Health, which operates a network of public hospitals and health services as well as undertaking public health research and planning for future health service needs. It is a very large organisation, employing more than twenty thousand people, and has facilities all over the state.

A recent independent audit revealed that a significant number of clinical employees had accepted gifts from pharmaceutical companies who sold drugs to the Department for use in its facilities. The total annual value of these pharmaceutical purchases was more than $250 million. The gifts included electronic equipment such as iPads as well as travel to overseas medical conferences. It appeared that the practice of receiving gifts had been going on for some years and had become an accepted part of the culture of the organisation.

When these findings were made public, there was an outcry from within government and from the general public. In response, the department's CEO expressed some concern about people receiving gifts such as iPads, but he defended the practice of accepting travel and accommodation to attend conferences on the grounds that it was essential that clinicians stayed up-to-date with the latest developments in their fields, and that the department's budget did not allow for funding of travel to overseas conferences. It was, therefore, in the public interest to allow these trips to continue. He also pointed out that while clinicians often made recommendations for drug purchases, the final decisions were made by the department's procurement division, not by the clinicians who were accepting the gifts.

Amid the public debate over the issue, Kate has been asked by the department's HR director to review the code of conduct with specific reference to the acceptance of gifts and hospitality. The current code of conduct requires employees to:

- behave honestly and with integrity in the course of their employment
- act with care and diligence
- treat everyone with respect and courtesy and without harassment
- comply with all applicable laws
- comply with any lawful and reasonable direction given by someone who has authority to give the direction
- maintain appropriate confidentiality in dealings related to departmental business or the treatment of patients
- disclose, and take reasonable steps to avoid, any conflict of interest (real or apparent) in connection with their employment
- use departmental resources in a proper manner
- not provide false or misleading information in response to a request for information that is made for official purposes
- not make improper use of inside information or the employee's duties, status, power or authority in order to gain, or seek to gain, a benefit or advantage for the employee or for any other person
- at all times behave in a way that upholds the values, integrity and good reputation of the department

Discussion questions

1. Which provisions of the current code relate to accepting gifts and hospitality? Are those provisions detailed enough?
2. If purchasing decisions are not made by clinicians, is there really a conflict of interest at all? Does it matter that there may be a perception of conflict, even if no real conflict exists?
3. Given that the Department is a government agency operating with taxpayer funds, should it be more sensitive to potential conflicts of interest than a private company?
4. What changes should Kate recommend to the existing code?

Learning activity – case study 14.2

Managing workplace relationships

Simon is the HR manager for a large accounting firm. He has recently become aware of rumours concerning one of the firm's partners, Robert, who, it is said, is having an affair with his secretary. He is married, and the secretary is considerably younger than he is. From what he has been able to gather, there are mixed feelings about it among employees and other managers. Some think it's amusing, others think it's inappropriate and morally questionable. Simon is concerned about the rumours, especially as Robert is responsible for his secretary's performance appraisal and for determining her salary.

The company has a code of conduct, but there are no provisions relating to intimate relationships in the workplace. While Simon accepts that workplace relationships are inevitable, he believes that this is problematic where the people involved have a supervisor–subordinate relationship because of the potential for bias in decision-making. He believes that the secretary should be transferred to another position to remove the potential for bias.

Discussion questions

1. Is it reasonable for the firm to require employees engaged in a relationship not to have a supervisor–subordinate relationship?
2. Should Simon amend the existing code of conduct to include this provision?
3. Given that the rumoured affair is covert, would changing the policy really change anything in this case?
4. Is it really any of the company's business?
5. Is it Simon's responsibility to broach the issue with Robert?

Chapter 15

DRESS CODES

Many organisations have policies governing the way employees dress and present themselves. There are several reasons for having such policies. In industrial environments such as manufacturing, mining and construction, dress codes are primarily for promoting safety. In medical, personal services, food processing or food handling environments, hygiene is the primary driver for dress codes. In industries like these, dress policy provisions are as much for the protection of customers as for employees. From a risk management perspective, such policies can also help to protect the organisation from costly litigation. In commerce, government, retailing, hospitality or any business environment where customer service is a priority, dress codes are usually implemented to enhance corporate image and to convey an appropriate sense of professionalism (Figure 15.1).

While case law supports an employer's right to impose dress codes for legitimate reasons, the imposition of unreasonable or discriminatory dress codes can be problematic. Some of the possible pitfalls are explored in this chapter. This area of policy is one where societal values and standards come into play. Attitudes to certain aspects of dress and personal presentation tend to change over time; therefore what is considered reasonable and fair may also change. This is perhaps the biggest issue that needs to be taken into account when formulating dress and presentation policy, and it is a compelling reason to review dress codes regularly.

Safety

Dress codes that relate to safety are usually governed by legislative requirements. Most jurisdictions have comprehensive occupational health and safety legislation, with regulations that are highly prescriptive. This type of legislation and its attendant regulations can run to hundreds of pages, with specific requirements being laid down for specific industries. Policymakers need to refer to these when formulating or reviewing policy. In some cases, organisations may include the legislative requirements in their occupational health and safety policies rather than covering them as part of a dress code – obviously, there is a strong connection between the two. It matters little which policy covers these legislative and regulatory requirements, as long as they are covered.

Figure 15.1 Dress code rationale, by industry.

While it is beyond the scope of this book to explore in detail the relevant legislation in different jurisdictions, there are common themes that are worth outlining. The main dress requirement in most legislation concerns the provision and wearing of personal protective clothing and accessories such as overalls, gloves, hard hats, protective eyewear, earmuffs, safety belts and safety boots. It is usually required that employers provide such essential safety clothing free of charge and that they be replaced as needed without cost to the employee. It is generally the employee's responsibility to ensure that protective clothing and equipment is maintained in serviceable condition.

Hygiene

Dress codes for hygiene may also connect with occupational health and safety legislation, though not in all cases. Regardless of legislative requirements, however, organisations involved in work where cleanliness and protection from infection are important should have policies addressing the wearing of appropriate clothing.

The specific requirements of dress codes for hygiene will vary according to the industry. They might include the mandatory wearing of aprons, gloves or hair nets or, in some environments, the prohibition of certain types of clothing or accessories. Jewellery, for example, may be considered a potential hazard for occupations involving medical treatment, personal services or working with food. This is because jewellery items might become detached. No restaurant customer wants to find someone's earring in their meal!

Corporate image

Most organisations want to project a professional image; thus corporate dress codes are common. But while it is difficult to argue against dress codes that are imposed for safety or hygiene reasons, corporate dress codes are not intrinsic to job requirements and can be contentious if they impose conditions that seem unnecessary or onerous. Although it is quite legitimate for organisations to apply dress codes to enhance corporate image, policymakers need to ensure that the policy requirements do not simply reflect one view of what is considered to be appropriate professional attire. Corporate dress codes are sometimes driven by boards of directors or senior management, whose ideas may be seen by others as conservative or outdated. Unpopular dress codes can cause minor rebellions, such as employees protesting against a requirement to wear ties by wearing ties with outrageous designs or colour schemes which are actually less professional-looking than wearing no tie at all. Protests like this, while humorous, can be difficult to manage.

Some dress codes include requirements for employees to wear uniforms or corporate clothing which includes the company logo or other identifying features. These kinds of requirements are generally well accepted by employees, especially where the clothing items are provided free or at a discounted price. Some organisations also pay for dry cleaning of uniforms and corporate attire. When considering a policy like this, organisations should also analyse whether corporate attire should be mandatory or optional. A mandatory requirement may be more problematic where it is being introduced for the first time. Making the requirement voluntary but providing the corporate wardrobe free or at reduced cost can be an effective way of encouraging people to participate without appearing to be too authoritarian.

Some corporate policies venture into areas such as personal grooming and other aspects of personal presentation such as tattoos and piercings. These are all potentially contentious areas because attitudes to them can vary significantly. There is a danger in attempting to address issues like these that the policy will be subjective, perhaps reflecting the fact that some people simply don't like certain hairstyles, beards, nose studs or tattoos. As mentioned earlier in this chapter, societal values and standards are relevant to issues like these. For example, tattoos and body jewellery are far more prevalent today than they were ten years ago, and 'designer stubble' is considered fashionable by many males. Policies that attempt to preclude practices like these may be seen as an unwarranted intrusion on personal rights unless there is a compelling rationale supporting them. Issues concerning fashion are often generational, and policymakers need to take account of generational differences in setting the parameters of dress and personal presentation policies. Effective corporate dress codes should not prevent people from dressing and presenting themselves fashionably.

Equity issues

It is important that dress codes not prevent employees from wearing clothing with cultural or religious significance such as Muslim hijabs or Sikh turbans.

Dress codes that do not respect cultural or religious differences are unlikely to withstand legal scrutiny if challenged. An adverse finding in a court or industrial tribunal on such a matter is also likely to attract media attention and would reflect poorly on the organisation.

Dress codes that discriminate on the basis of gender are also problematic. For example, an organisation whose policy prevents women from wearing trousers or men from wearing earrings will almost certainly be seen as discriminatory by a court or tribunal. Traditionally accepted gender-specific dress and presentation requirements can also be interpreted as discriminatory, such as requiring men to wear ties but not women, or prescribing a certain hair length for men but not for women. To avoid problems like these, dress codes should outline requirements without reference to gender.

Free dress days

Free dress days are common in the corporate environment. These are often linked to charitable causes (e.g. people make a donation to a charity to be allowed to wear casual clothing to work). Some organisations make it a regular weekly occurrence (e.g. every Friday) and see it as part of a culture that promotes better employee morale. While it might seem anomalous to have a policy governing free dress days, some organisations have found it necessary because some employees have taken their 'casualness' a bit too far by coming to work scantily clad or wearing clothing or accessories which are at the extreme end of fashion trends. There may also be exclusions from free dress days that need to be spelled out in the policy. For instance, it may not be deemed appropriate for front-line customer service staff to dress casually (although most organisations don't have a problem with this). It may also be inappropriate for employees to dress casually if they are representing the organisation at an external event or function on that day or visiting clients' workplaces. Having a free dress policy is quite legitimate, provided it observes the same principles as for regular dress policies.

Policy content

Dress codes should include the following:

- rationale for the policy, including any legislative or regulatory requirements
- specific descriptions of acceptable dress standards, taking account of the equity issues that have been discussed
- specific descriptions of unacceptable dress standards, also taking account of equity issues

- requirements for uniforms or corporate attire, including purchase/owner-ship and cleaning arrangements and whether or not compliance with the policy is mandatory or voluntary
- provisions relating to free dress days, if applicable
- consequences of non-compliance (linked to discipline policy)

Summary

- Dress codes help to ensure employee safety and hygiene while also contrib-uting to a positive public image for the organisation.
- Protective clothing and equipment should be provided by the employer and maintained by the employee.
- Case law generally supports an employer's right to impose a dress code provided that it is not discriminatory.
- Good dress codes balance organisational need with employee rights and should not prevent employees from presenting themselves fashionably.

Learning activity – case study 15.1

The cost of looking sharp

Chic Apparel is a fashion company with an extensive network of retail outlets that employ more than three hundred people. The company's dress code requires its retail sales staff to wear the company's own labels at work and to update their wardrobes when new season fashions are released.

Chic is a top-end fashion label, and its clothes and shoes are expensive. Its sales staff receive modest salaries. Even though the company allows staff to purchase the clothing and footwear at a substantial discount (50–60 per cent), the frequency with which employees are required to update their wardrobes means that some employees are spending more than 30 per cent of their gross salaries on clothes and shoes. The company also polices the code strictly.

Recently the union representing sales staff has approached manage-ment requesting a meeting to discuss the policy. Their view is that the policy disadvantages employees financially and is unfair.

Discussion questions

1. What would be the company's rationale for the dress code?
2. Is it reasonable for the company to require its employees to wear its clothing exclusively while at work?

3. Is it reasonable for the company to require employees to wear new season fashions only?
4. Is the discount reasonable?
5. How might the company address the union's and its employees' concerns?

Learning activity – case study 15.2

A big problem

Stewart works for a government agency in an administrative role. He occasionally deals with members of the public, but most of the time his work is away from public areas of the office. Stewart is a very large man, standing nearly 2 metres tall and weighing 140 kilograms, and as a result, he has great difficulty finding clothes that fit well and look smart. He cannot afford to have clothes tailor-made or shop at specialist clothing stores, and so he has to find off-the-shelf clothes as best he can. Consequently, he often looks somewhat scruffy because he can't keep his shirt tucked in and his trousers are often too short.

Stewart recently applied for a promotion to a position that involved much more public contact. His application was unsuccessful, and he sought feedback from the selection panel. He was told that one of the reasons for his application being unsuccessful was that his appearance was not consistent with the agency's dress code for public contact positions, which required employees to 'maintain a neat, professional appearance'. Stewart was upset by this, feeling that the dress code unfairly discriminated against him because of his size. He resolved to discuss the matter with HR before deciding whether to take any further action.

Discussion questions

1. Does Stewart have a case? Does the code unfairly discriminate against him?
2. Is the term 'neat, professional appearance' suitable as part of a dress code? Is it objective enough? Is it precise enough?
3. How should HR respond to Stewart's situation?

Chapter 16

DISCIPLINE POLICY

Discipline policies provide the framework for dealing with misconduct or unacceptable behaviour. Usually, minor infringements are dealt with informally as part of the day-to-day supervisory process. Formal disciplinary processes come into play only when the nature of the action is relatively serious. When dealing with these kinds of issues, consistency and transparency are the guiding principles. Poorly conducted or unfair disciplinary processes can lead to unpleasant outcomes, including industrial action and litigation, and so it is important that organisations get it right. The processes and outcomes must be both fair and, importantly, seen to be fair. Figure 16.1 shows the kind of structured process around which discipline policy should be built.

Incidents

Disciplinary action may arise from a range of dysfunctional behaviours, the most common of which would include:

- habitual poor attendance or timekeeping
- inappropriate behaviour towards others, including harassment, intimidation, bullying or assault
- breaches of the organisation's policies or code of conduct
- unethical behaviour
- dishonesty
- negligence

It is important to note that a discipline policy should not apply to poor performance. This is a performance management issue that should be dealt with according to the organisation's performance management policy, not through discipline policy.

Figure 16.1 Components of the disciplinary process.

Discipline policy might be invoked in relation to a variety of incidents, including:

- a grievance lodged by another employee
- a complaint from a customer or client
- an unpleasant workplace incident
- the day-to-day supervisory process
- auditing or other governance processes
- whistle-blowing

Less common, but equally compelling, are circumstances where employee misconduct becomes public through a media report or public statement by an aggrieved party. Obviously, most organisations would prefer that disciplinary issues be dealt with in-house and without external scrutiny. Nonetheless, whether or not the issue is in the public domain should not make a difference to the way it is dealt with – discipline policies should be designed with a view to be applied regardless of the level of external scrutiny. Additionally, organisations need to be accountable for their disciplinary policies and processes because there is always the possibility that a disgruntled employee who has been formally disciplined may seek review or redress through an external body or through legal proceedings.

Investigation

Discipline policy should require that incidents be investigated by an independent person to determine whether or not disciplinary action is warranted. In many cases, this investigation is an HR function. Sometimes, however, an external investigator will be engaged. This might be preferable if the alleged incident is particularly serious. The discipline policy should also ensure that organisational justice principles are followed, particularly in relation to procedural justice. To this end, the policy needs to make specific mention of:

- the need to formally advise an employee that he/she is the subject of a disciplinary investigation and the precise nature of the misconduct that has been reported or alleged
- the right of the employee to respond to any allegations made against him/her before any conclusion is reached

Often, the investigation will include an interview with the employee concerned. Where this occurs, the policy needs to support the employee's right to be represented or to have an observer present. Often a union representative will take this role, but it can be anyone the employee nominates.

The policy should also make clear that where the investigation suggests that a criminal act may have occurred, the matter will be reported to the appropriate authorities, that is, the police. Internal investigations would usually cease once the matter has been referred to a law enforcement agency.

The question of whether or not the employee should be suspended while the investigation takes place depends on the nature of the alleged behaviour. It would be hard to justify suspending an employee because of pending disciplinary action for poor attendance, for instance, but suspension might well be considered seriously if the incident was related to inappropriate workplace behaviour (such as an assault or allegation of sexual harassment) or where negligence or dishonesty have been alleged. The policy needs to allow for suspension based on the circumstances. It should also nominate the decision-maker. Suspension can either be with pay or without pay – again, the decision needs to be based on the circumstances, and the policy should allow for both options. It should also allow employees who are suspended without pay to access any accrued leave entitlements during their suspension.

In all cases, but especially where a suspension has occurred, the policy should specify that the investigation be carried out promptly.

Documentation

Because of the high level of transparency and accountability that is necessary when dealing with disciplinary issues, the policy needs to emphasise the importance of documenting every aspect of each case. This might include:

- documentary evidence of the alleged misconduct, for example, a supervisor's report, copy of customer complaint or statement from an aggrieved party
- copy of witness statements or other testimonial evidence
- copies of relevant operational documents (e.g. attendance sheets, leave applications, work records)
- documentation of the investigation process followed

- copies of all correspondence with the employee being investigated
- copies of any written responses or submissions by the employee being investigated
- documentation of any verbal communication with the employee being investigated or with witnesses, complainants or others associated with the case
- records of any advice received from external sources (e.g. legal advice)
- records of interviews carried out as part of the investigation
- a record of the outcome, including details of counselling and disciplinary action taken

The policy also needs to specify how long the records need to be retained. There may be legislation relating to document retention, especially in the public sector, and so policymakers need to check this.

Decision

Once the investigation has been conducted and the documentation gathered, a decision has to be made about the case. The policy should specify who the decision-maker is (i.e. the occupant of a specific position). That person should not be the same person who has undertaken the investigation, but rather someone with authority in the organisation who is able to review the information gathered during the investigation stage and the documentation. Normally the person undertaking the investigation, whether internal or external, will make a recommendation to the decision-maker based on their assessment of the situation. The decision-maker can either accept or reject that recommendation.

Feedback

Where the investigation does not support the allegations and no further action is necessary, the employee needs to be informed of this fact. This notification should be made in writing and the document retained as part of the record of proceedings. One possible outcome of a finding that the employee has no case to answer is that the employee feels resentful that the issue was pursued in the first place. This may have negative consequences if not managed appropriately. In these circumstances it may be advisable for the employee to be counselled, with the aim of him/her gaining an understanding of why the allegations were made and how similar circumstances could be avoided in future. One policy option would be to require an appropriate person, perhaps a senior manager or the HR manager, to have this conversation with the employee at the conclusion of the process.

The offending employee should also receive appropriate counselling where the alleged misconduct is confirmed by the investigation. The purpose of the counselling will depend on the nature of the misconduct and the action being taken. In cases concerning poor attendance or timekeeping, for example, the required standard should be made clear, and the counselling interview could focus on strategies for overcoming the problem. In more serious cases, the counselling interview might be used to advise the employee of the disciplinary action that is to be taken. The discipline policy should specify that the counselling interview occurs at the conclusion of the investigatory process and must outline the issues that need to be broached. It should also specify the person or position responsible for undertaking the interview. These kinds of interviews can be challenging and sometimes unpleasant; thus few people in the organisation would volunteer to do them. However, an employee who has been subject to a disciplinary investigation must not be left wondering about the outcome or be unclear about the consequences. The policy should commit the organisation to appropriate follow-up in every case.

Action

In cases where the alleged misconduct is confirmed by the investigation, disciplinary action needs to be taken. This action should be commensurate with the seriousness of the offence. It would not be appropriate for the policy to try to define specific actions for specific offences as each case needs to be treated on its merits. However, it is useful to outline the range of possible disciplinary actions in the policy, without linking them to specific offences. Figure 16.2 summarises some of the more common disciplinary actions that can be undertaken by organisations. This is not an exhaustive list, but it covers the vast majority of disciplinary cases in most organisations.

Levying financial penalties (i.e. fines) on employees for disciplinary reasons can be problematic. While it is true that this is common practice in some industries such as professional sport, it would not be appropriate for most organisations.

Appeals

Discipline policies should always include provisions for affected employees to appeal if they do not believe that the process or the outcome is fair. Figure 16.3 outlines a typical appeal process.

Generally, the process begins with a request for the original decision-maker (ODM) to reconsider the decision. If the issue remains unresolved, internal reviews are usually carried out by a senior person within the organisation,

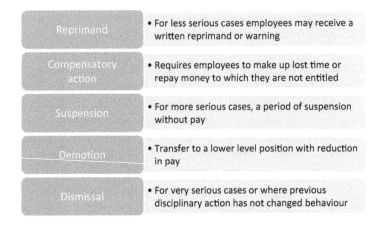

Figure 16.2 Summary of disciplinary actions.

Figure 16.3 Typical disciplinary appeal process.

possibly the CEO. If there is still no resolution, the final stage of the process involves appealing to an independent body outside the organisation. Depending on the nature of the appeal and the industry, external reviews can be carried out by a court or an independent appeals tribunal. Appeals, especially external appeals, are obviously to be avoided if possible because they can be costly and resource-intensive. In addition, the upholding of an appeal can reflect badly on the organisation. A comprehensive discipline policy reduces the likelihood of appeals by ensuring that disciplinary matters are handled fairly and equitably. In cases where disciplinary actions are subjected to external scrutiny, the existence of a discipline policy and the organisation's adherence to it will increase the likelihood of the process and outcome being found to be valid.

Policy linkages

Discipline policy links to several other HR policies and should be consistent with them. Policies with connections to discipline policy include:

- code of conduct
- dress code
- occupational health and safety policy
- staffing policy
- attendance management policy
- grievance policy

Summary

- Discipline policies should deal with instances of employee misconduct rather than performance issues. Performance issues should be dealt with under the organisation's performance management policy.
- Policies should prescribe a systematic process that includes investigation, documentation, counselling and action.
- The investigation should be characterised by open communication and appropriate attention to both employer and employee rights.
- Discipline policies should require that all cases be comprehensively documented.
- Regardless of the outcome of the investigation, the employee concerned should receive counselling. This should include full explanation of the reasons for the employee's actions being deemed inappropriate, explanation of the process and outcome, and discussion of measures to prevent recurrence of the unacceptable behaviour.
- Disciplinary action should be commensurate with the severity of the offence. Policies should outline the range of possible actions.
- Policies should always allow for the affected employee to appeal if he/she is dissatisfied with the process or the outcome.

Learning activity – case study 16.1

Developing a discipline policy

Metallica Pty Ltd manufactures metal components for construction (roof trusses, door and window frames etc.). It employs about 80 staff made up of a small managerial/administrative team and about 70 production staff (mostly metal trades and assembly workers). The workforce has a mixed age profile, with more young people joining the company in recent times. Of the production workers, 80 per cent are male and 90 per cent are union members. The relationship between the union and management is okay but could be more cooperative. Turnover is relatively low but has started to increase.

Recently a disciplinary issue arose that was not handled particularly well, and it has caused some friction between management and workers (and their union delegate). The issue concerned a production worker who took some of the company's equipment home on the weekend to use on a private project. He had not sought permission to do this, and the production manager was furious when he discovered what had happened. He gave the worker a robust verbal dressing-down, including the use of several expletives, and assigned him to the heaviest, dirtiest work in the plant for the rest of the week as a punishment.

The employee was unhappy with the treatment he received and complained to his union representative. Specifically, his complaints were:

- He did not know that using company equipment on weekends was not allowed. Other workers had told him that they had done it themselves and no one seemed to mind.
- The production manager had just exploded – shouting, swearing and verbally abusing him in front of other workers. He had not given the worker a chance to respond or put forward his side of the story.
- The punishment was humiliating and inappropriate given that the worker had an exemplary record up to that point, and he had returned the equipment promptly and in good condition.

The union and the worker's colleagues are quite upset, and the union representative has indicated that industrial action might be taken if the matter is not handled satisfactorily from here on. The manager concerned has acknowledged that it could have been handled better but has also pointed out that he didn't really know how the company wanted disciplinary issues handled or what he should or shouldn't do. The company has no discipline policy.

The CEO has counselled the production manager about his intemperate behaviour and language. He has also confirmed that the worker's unauthorised use of the company's equipment was not acceptable. However, he has instructed that the worker return to his normal duties. He has indicated to the union that he will have a formal discipline policy developed immediately to ensure that future disciplinary issues are handled better. The union is happy with this outcome.

Susan is Metallica's HR coordinator. The CEO has asked her to develop the new policy as a matter of priority.

Discussion questions

1. Outline a process for developing the policy.
2. Given that the need for the policy has arisen as a result of a critical incident, what issues and sensitivities does Susan need to consider during the policy development process?
3. Outline the main provisions that Susan should recommend for the policy. Are they any different from the policy provisions you might develop in a different context, say a government agency or a law firm?

Source: Fazey, M. 2017. *Cases in HR Practice and Strategy* (3rd edn). Prahran: Mirabel Publishing, pp. 127–29. Used with permission.

Learning activity – case study 16.2

Applying discipline policy

Jack is the HR manager for a large local government authority. He has been contacted by an auditor in the authority's finance branch who has discovered an anomaly in one manager's corporate credit card statement. It appears that the manager, who is responsible for the parks and gardens branch, has used his corporate credit card to purchase building materials consistent with a home renovation project. The auditor has contacted the vendor (not one of the authority's approved suppliers) and confirmed that the materials purchased were for a pergola and were delivered to the manager's home address. The total value of the purchases was $2,000.

The auditor has stated that he believes there is clear evidence that the manager has breached the authority's financial policies by using his corporate credit card inappropriately and that disciplinary action needs to be taken. The authority has a comprehensive discipline policy in place, and Jack is responsible for its application. After reviewing the evidence, Jack concludes that there is a prima facie case for the discipline policy to be invoked. The manager concerned has been with the authority for five years and has a good record in both performance and conduct.

Discussion questions

1. Outline the steps that Jack should take to instigate the discipline process.
2. Who should investigate the case?

3. Should the manager be suspended while the disciplinary investigation is undertaken?
4. What documentation should be assembled in this case?
5. If the case against the manager is confirmed by the investigation, what disciplinary action would be appropriate?

Chapter 17

GRIEVANCE AND DISPUTE RESOLUTION POLICY

Within any group of people, there will inevitably be disagreements and disputes. While this is not bad in itself, disputes and disagreements can be problematic if not resolved quickly and effectively, and this is the primary reason that organisations have grievance and dispute resolution policies. Unresolved grievances can result in workplace disharmony, reduced productivity, reduced team cohesion, increased absenteeism and even litigation. Grievance and dispute resolution policy is about managing those risks. The benefits of effective dispute resolution are self-evident: better morale, increased retention and the creation and maintenance of an organisational culture that values fairness and recognises the rights of employees at all levels to be heard.

Types of grievances

Grievances can result from any number of scenarios, and it would be impossible to define every possible grievance in a policy document. Broadly speaking, however, grievances can be classified into three main types: policy disputes (grievances against the organisation), decision disputes (grievances against management) and interpersonal disputes (grievances between individuals). Figure 17.1 shows some of the more common types of grievances in each of these categories. Some organisations also have grievance policies for customers and other stakeholders. While the principles of these types of policies are the same as for internal grievance policies, they are outside the scope of this book.

Policy principles

Grievance policies should be underpinned by guiding principles that recognise employee and employer rights and embody natural justice. Figure 17.2 outlines those principles.

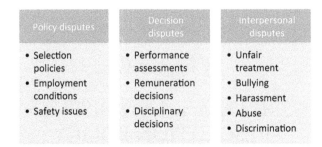

Figure 17.1 Types of grievances and disputes.

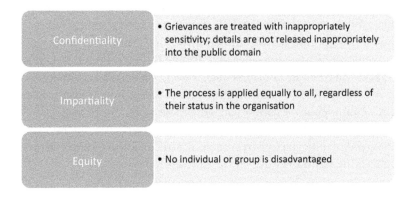

Figure 17.2 Guiding principles.

It is important that grievance policies be procedurally fair and be seen to be fair. Indeed, the same broad principles apply to grievance and dispute resolution policies as apply to discipline policies.

Policies should, therefore, ensure that:

• employees who are the subject of a complaint are informed of this fact and have a right to respond to the complaint
• employees are entitled to representation during the process
• grievances are dealt with promptly

Those lodging grievances should also be protected from victimisation either by the person being complained about or by anyone else. Grievance policy should make clear that attempting to persuade the complainant to withdraw their grievance through intimidation or threats is unacceptable and will result in disciplinary action.

The right to appeal is also a fundamental principle that needs to be enshrined in the grievance policy. As discussed in Chapter 16, appeal rights usually encompass both internal and external review options. These same options should be open to those appealing against the outcome of grievances.

Roles and responsibilities

Grievance policy should define clear roles and responsibilities. Grievances and disputes are often not easy to handle; therefore the policy should guard against people passing the buck to avoid getting involved in what might be a delicate or unpleasant process.

Clearly HR has a central role to play in grievance and dispute resolution, as policymakers and managers and also as coordinators of the process. It is not HR's role to resolve each grievance or dispute, but the policy should define exactly who (or what position in the organisation) is responsible, or whether these tasks are best carried out by an external party. One of HR's key responsibilities is to determine to whom the grievance needs to be referred. In some organisations, a senior manager is designated as grievance resolution officer, and it is his/her role to arbitrate on grievances. In other organisations, a grievance committee considers each case. However, where the grievance is serious (e.g. a complaint of sexual harassment) it may be appropriate to refer the matter to an appropriate external body immediately.

Some large organisations have designated grievance officers who provide advice and information to employees who are aggrieved and considering their options. Grievance officers are not responsible for the process itself; they merely advise colleagues about their rights and responsibilities, the provisions of the policy and how the process will be managed. Grievance officers are usually not HR officers. They tend to be people from a range of positions and locations throughout the organisation who are seen not to have a vested interest in the process. They are usually volunteers and receive specific training to enable them to carry out their advisory role. In smaller organisations, nomination of specific grievance officers may not be feasible and HR should assume the advisory role.

Resolution and accountability

Grievance policies should also outline the process for resolving issues. This process will vary according to the nature of the grievance and the organisation, but broadly speaking, resolution processes will typically have three stages.

The policy document needs to outline this process in broad terms. Typically, policies allow for an initial attempt to resolve the grievance informally with

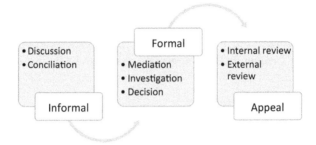

Figure 17.3 Grievance resolution process.

escalation to more formal processes if this is unsuccessful. Some policy documents incorporate a detailed process diagram outlining the different steps, although it could be argued that these kinds of diagrams are procedures rather than part of the policy. It could also be argued that each grievance should be treated according to its particular circumstances and that including detailed process diagrams either as part of the policy or as a separate procedure document is not helpful because it tends to imply a one-size-fits-all approach. A degree of judgement will always be necessary when determining how best to handle a grievance, and as has already been discussed, HR should assume that role. An aggrieved employee is more likely to feel that the issue has been properly dealt with if the process is tailored to the particular complaint rather than simply having a standard procedure applied to it. Clearly, quick resolution is in everyone's interests, and so the policy needs to be geared towards achieving this by the most appropriate and effective method (Figure 17.3).

Grievance processes should be fully documented with the basis for decisions or actions made clear. Grievance policy should, therefore, include provisions requiring each case to be documented. Each decision should be capable of being reviewed by an external body if required.

Vexatious grievances

A grievance which has no basis or is trivial in nature can be said to be vexatious. These kinds of grievances arise from time to time and need to be dealt with. Grievance policy, therefore, should include provisions covering the management of vexatious grievances.

In most cases, vexatious grievances arise either as an expression of a disgruntled individual's anger and frustration, or as the result of a personal conflict. Disgruntled employees sometimes become serial grievance-lodgers. Dealing with these issues can be time-consuming and ultimately pointless, and so the policy needs to allow scope for a grievance to be deemed vexatious and be dismissed. These sorts of provisions should also require the organisation to advise the complainant that the grievance has been deemed vexatious and provide the reasons for that decision. Where the grievance is the result of a personal conflict, the intent may be to discredit a particular individual or to simply make trouble for them. Both these scenarios are symptoms of deeper issues that need to be addressed outside the grievance process.

While vexatious grievances are annoying, care needs to be taken not to be too hasty in judging them as such. One of the dangers of not treating a grievance with appropriate gravity is that the complainant will take their complaint to an external body. If it turns out that the grievance was legitimate and that the organisation had wrongly deemed it to be vexatious, the consequences could be damaging to the organisation. Of course, a vexatious complainant may take their complaint to an external body anyway. If this happens, the issue is really out of the organisation's hands, although it is likely to have to justify its inaction. Having specific policy provisions relating to vexatious grievances will help with that process and reduce the likelihood of the organisation being found to have treated the case inappropriately.

Summary

- Grievance policy can be seen as a risk management policy because it helps to avoid the negative consequences of unresolved conflict.
- Grievances usually fall into one of three categories: policy disputes (grievances against the organisation), decision disputes (grievances against management) and interpersonal disputes (grievances between individuals).
- Grievance policy should be underpinned by the principles of confidentiality, impartiality and equity and embody procedural fairness principles in the same way as discipline policy.
- Roles and responsibilities need to be clearly defined in the policy. Specific roles will vary from organisation to organisation. HR has a key role as policymaker, policy manager and coordinator of the process.
- Policies should allow for an escalating resolution process that is fully documented and capable of external review.
- Provisions covering vexatious grievances should also be included.

Learning activity – case study 17.1

Reviewing grievance policy roles and responsibilities

Radley's Merchant Bank has a staff of around three hundred, all operating from the company's office in the central business district. Veronica is the HR manager, and during her two years in the role, she has taken great care to ensure that all of the company's HR policies are reviewed and updated regularly. One of the last policies to be reviewed is the grievance and dispute resolution policy. The policy is quite basic, and it outlines a process whereby the CEO is the arbiter of all grievances. Veronica suspects that the policy was developed when the company was much smaller, but given how busy the CEO is these days, she doubts whether it would be practical to continue this way – for a start, it would compromise the speed with which grievances could be dealt with.

Consequently, Veronica has developed a proposal for a revised policy in which a five-person grievance committee made up of representatives from the executive, line management and HR would deal with grievances and make decisions. When the revised policy was put forward for endorsement, however, it was opposed by several of the company's executive committee members as being too resource-costly. The CEO made it very clear that he did not want the decision-making role and did not have the time to do it justice in any case. A counterproposal emerged that Veronica herself should be the decision-maker. This was endorsed by the committee. When told of the decision, Veronica simply shook her head and went back to her office to begin work on developing a new proposal.

Discussion questions

1. Was Veronica's original proposal too resource-costly?
2. Why was she unhappy with the executive committee's recommendation? What problems might there be if the HR manager were the arbiter of all grievances?
3. What other alternatives are there for who has jurisdiction over grievance outcomes?
4. What should Veronica do now?

Learning activity – case study 17.2

The reluctant harassment victim

Ryan is the HR coordinator for an analytical laboratory that employs a hundred or so scientists, technicians and support staff. Recently, he was contacted by a young laboratory assistant, Emily, about a possible grievance case. Ryan asked Emily to come and see him, which she did.

Emily told him that she was being 'hassled' by one of the technicians in her section; she refused to name the person. She claimed that he had tried on several occasions to arrange a date with her and that she had refused. By the end, she was quite annoyed and had told him to 'piss off'. Since then, he had been verbally abusing her (quietly so no one else could hear) and deliberately bumping into her quite forcefully when they passed each other (again, taking care that no one else was around to see it).

Ryan advised that she definitely had grounds for a grievance and outlined the process for her. Emily expressed concern that if she lodged a formal grievance, the situation would become even more intolerable. She wanted the situation resolved but didn't want to go through a formal process because it would draw attention to her and be embarrassing. She also said that if her grievance resulted in disciplinary action against the male colleague, this might have repercussions for her too and she feared being victimised by other male employees who might take their mate's side. 'Can't you just transfer him to another section? Or transfer me?' she asked.

Discussion questions

1. Is Emily right? Would a formal grievance process just make things worse? If so, what is the point of having a grievance policy?
2. Can a grievance policy actually provide real protection against victimisation?
3. Given that Ryan has been told about the situation (albeit informally), does he now have an obligation to pursue the issue regardless of Emily's wishes?
4. What might be the consequences of leaving this issue unresolved?

Source: Fazey, M. 2017. *Cases in HR Practice and Strategy* (3rd edn). Prahran: Mirabel Publishing, pp. 130–31. Used with permission.

Chapter 18

ATTENDANCE MANAGEMENT POLICY

Absenteeism is a perennial problem in many organisations. In Australia, for example, taking 'sickies' (i.e. taking days off without a legitimate reason) has become a cultural norm, even to the point of being regarded by some as a 'great Australian tradition'. The costs of illegitimate absences, both to organisations and to the economy, are significant, yet many organisations tacitly support a culture of absenteeism by accepting it as inevitable, not managing it actively and even budgeting for it.

Attendance management policies challenge that tacit acceptance by making a clear statement about what is acceptable and what is not and by underpinning management strategies and practices designed to minimise illegitimate absences. Attendance management policies also address issues like tardiness and poor timekeeping.

It is important to remember that employees are entitled to paid leave for legitimate absences; therefore attendance management policies need to acknowledge this and not discourage people from using their leave entitlements legitimately. All employment awards and agreements allow a certain number of days for sick leave or personal leave, and industrial relations legislation prescribes these kinds of leave as minimum entitlements. Therefore, attendance management policies need to be consistent with whatever is prescribed by legislation and by the prevailing award or industrial agreement.

Understanding absenteeism

Managing absenteeism effectively depends on organisations understanding it. There are two aspects to this. First, organisations need to be aware of the quantum and pattern of absenteeism. This obviously requires data to be gathered and reported on. Analysing these data allows organisations to benchmark their absence rates against norms in their industry and to identify whether there are variations between absence rates in different parts of the organisation or between different occupational or demographic groups. The second aspect is about understanding the reasons for employees being absent. Table 18.1 summarises the more common reasons.

Table 18.1 Reasons for workplace absences

Legitimate reasons	Illegitimate reasons
Illness	Low morale/commitment
Injury	Low job satisfaction
Family responsibilities	Work pressures
Emergencies	Workplace conflict
	Lack of accountability for absence
	Lack of attendance management policies
	Lack of active management of absenteeism

Illegitimate absences are often caused by organisational issues. In circumstances like these, simply having an attendance management policy will not in itself remedy the problem. Indeed, it could be seen as treating the symptom rather than the cause. Attendance management policies need to be seen as part of a broader solution that includes addressing cultural and management issues within the organisation.

Presenteeism

In recent years, the concept of presenteeism has emerged as a growing issue. Presenteeism occurs when employees attend the workplace when they are unwell or injured. In many cases, minor ailments or ongoing medical conditions are the cause. In other cases, emotional or psychological states impact negatively on the person's well-being. Work effectiveness and productivity are negatively affected by presenteeism. In addition, whatever the underlying cause of the person's malaise, continuing to attend work may worsen it and delay recovery.

Employees may continue to attend work when unwell for a variety of reasons, including a strong work ethic and commitment to the organisation. While attitudes like this are laudable, presenteeism is actually detrimental both to the individual and to the organisation. Employees may also fear being labelled as fragile or vulnerable if they take time off, and that such a perception might affect their status or career prospects.

Attendance management policies need to deter presenteeism. This means balancing the pressures to attend with the well-being of the individual and the interests of the organisation. Attendance management policies that are too harsh may have the effect of encouraging presenteeism. If this is the case, the policy is flawed.

Roles and responsibilities

Attendance management policies need to assign specific responsibilities for monitoring and managing absences. Including this kind of information in a policy document sends a clear message to everyone that absenteeism is important enough to be scrutinised and reported on as part of the organisation's ongoing management practices.

Monitoring is best done by HR. Ideally, HR departments should be collecting, collating and analysing absence data on an ongoing basis and reporting it as part of the regular organisational performance measurement process. Line managers need to be advised of any anomalies or apparent trouble spots so that action can be taken.

Line managers have a central role to play in attendance management, and this should be made clear in the policy. This responsibility extends beyond ensuring that leave applications are submitted and that unscheduled absences are covered operationally. The policy should assign responsibility to line managers for actively managing absences through prevention and accountability measures.

Long-term absences also need to be managed. In most cases, longer periods of absence are legitimate and caused by serious illness or injury or an ongoing domestic situation such as caring for a seriously ill relative. These kinds of absences are probably best covered by a leave management policy than an attendance management policy. Where the absence has resulted in a worker's compensation claim, this needs to be managed in accordance with the organisation's workplace health, safety and well-being policy.

Prevention and accountability

As has been discussed, absenteeism can be the result of organisational issues that impact negatively on employees' levels of job satisfaction, commitment or morale, or because of the pressures of the job itself. The policy should acknowledge this and affirm the organisation's commitment to creating a positive work environment. Other HR policies such as grievance and dispute resolution, workplace health, safety and well-being, performance management and workplace flexibility can all contribute to creating a positive and supportive culture that encourages attendance – these connections should be outlined in the organisation's attendance management policy.

Specifying attendance requirements in the policy is also a useful measure for preventing tardiness or poor timekeeping, especially in organisations that deal directly with the public or where there are specific reasons for employees being on duty at certain times of the day. Notwithstanding flexible work arrangements, attendance management policies need to define the core hours applicable to the business. This might include provisions requiring employees to be in attendance before a certain time in the morning and/or the earliest time that employees can leave at the end of the day (usually corresponding with the hours that the business is open to the public).

Many organisations require employees to formally record their attendance using manual or electronic time sheets. Where this is a requirement, the onus is on employees to record their attendance accurately, but the policy should also require supervisors to sign off the time sheets. In addition, some organisations audit time sheets periodically. This is usually an HR function and is done to detect anomalies or irregularities that might require attention or explanation.

Attendance management policy should also specify employees' obligations to notify their supervisor if they will not be attending due to illness or other unforeseen circumstances. The usual requirement is for employees to advise supervisors by direct contact before a certain time in the morning. Some organisations specify that the contact has to be by phone rather than by email or text message. Some also specify that the employee must actually speak to the supervisor rather than leave a message with someone else. These kinds of provisions are designed to promote personal accountability and are perhaps best applied in organisations where absenteeism is a particular problem. In organisations with a strong attendance culture, they may be seen as unnecessarily strict, implying lack of trust. In setting the policy requirements for notification of unscheduled absences, policymakers need to make a judgement about how strict the policy should be.

A common policy provision is a requirement for employees to provide medical certificates where they have taken time off due to illness or injury. In most cases, the requirement for a medical certificate applies for absences of more than two consecutive days, though some organisations impose even more stringent requirements such as requiring medical certificates for all absences due to illness, including single-day absences. Whether or not this is reasonable is debatable. The reality is that people often don't go to the doctor every time they are feeling unwell, and in many cases, the illness passes after a day or two. The rationale for such a strict policy is usually based on preventing malingering, but imposing too strict a requirement for medical confirmation might actually do more harm than good if it causes stress or inconvenience to those who are genuinely but not seriously ill. Whatever the policy requirement for providing medical certificates, organisations should avoid requiring employees to divulge details of the nature of their illness, unless there are occupational health and safety implications. Most people would consider medical issues to be private. Attendance management policies, therefore, need to balance accountability with basic rights to privacy. There is no justification for unnecessary prying into an employee's medical status.

After an unscheduled absence, it is common for employees to return to work and simply resume their duties without follow-up action. A useful active management practice is to require supervisors to follow up unscheduled absences when the employee returns to work. Where the employee is returning after illness or injury, this is to ensure that the employee has recovered and to enquire about any work restrictions that might be necessary, or the necessity for further absences for medical appointments or ongoing treatment. Where an employee is returning after an absence caused by family responsibilities or an emergency, the purpose of the follow-up is to enquire whether the situation has been resolved and whether or not there are likely to be further absences. In both cases, it may be necessary to take steps to clear backlogs of work, and this should be discussed and planned with the employee. Again, respect for privacy needs to be a consideration when following up absences. Follow-ups should not be inquisitions. Rather, they should emphasise employee welfare and operational management issues. The message to employees should be that the organisation is actively managing absences. A desirable consequence of a follow-up policy is that it will have a deterrent effect on illegitimate absences.

Rewards and incentives

Another approach to attendance management is to actively encourage attendance by offering rewards and incentives for good attendance. This might be in the form of an attendance bonus, payable annually to employees who have not had any unscheduled absences in the previous year. The rationale for attendance bonuses is to deter illegitimate absences. However, they may also have the undesirable effect of discouraging people from taking legitimate leave, resulting in people coming to work when sick or injured, or taking other forms of leave (e.g. annual leave or flexitime leave) instead of sick leave or personal leave. This might be addressed to some degree by specifying that the bonus is payable to those who have not taken any uncertified leave (i.e. without a medical certificate or other documentary evidence), but this might still disadvantage people who have a legitimate reason for being absent. Alternatively, the policy might allow a certain number of unscheduled absences, with the bonus being payable to those who have taken less than a certain number of days off. However, this might not deter illegitimate absences strongly enough and may even tacitly condone them by implying that it is acceptable up to a certain point. The size of the bonus is also an issue that needs to be considered. Too small an amount may not have the desired effect. Too large an amount may exacerbate the inequities described above, or may not be financially sustainable. Non-financial incentives could also be considered, though the same equity issues would exist.

While rewards and incentives might be effective in the short term, their long-term viability is questionable. They are perhaps best applied as a short-term culture change policy in organisations grappling with chronically high levels of absenteeism.

Disciplinary measures

Attendance management policies should outline the consequences of unacceptable attendance. They should specify that the provisions of the organisation's discipline policy will be invoked for breaches of attendance policy. Such breaches might include:

- making false claims (e.g. claiming sick leave when not sick)
- not notifying supervisors of unscheduled absences
- failing to provide certification where it is required
- habitual tardiness or poor timekeeping
- falsifying attendance records such as time sheets

Penalties for breaches of attendance policies typically include reprimand, docking of pay, requiring certification for all absences for a specified period or, in serious cases, suspension or dismissal.

As discussed in Chapter 16, disciplinary action needs to embody natural justice principles and penalties should be commensurate with the offence.

Summary

- Attendance management policies should be designed to minimise illegitimate absences while respecting employees' rights to use sick leave and personal leave entitlements responsibly.
- Policies should be supported by management practices that actively manage attendance issues and by ongoing monitoring and analysis of absence data.
- Accountability measures such as recording of attendance, notifying supervisors of unscheduled absences, providing medical certification and supervisor follow-up should be included in the policy. But these measures should respect employee privacy and not disadvantage employees who may have ongoing medical or family issues.
- Rewards and incentives such as attendance bonuses can be effective for changing attendance cultures but may also have equity and sustainability issues.

- Attendance management policies need to clearly spell out unacceptable attendance practices and the consequences of policy breaches (with appropriate reference to discipline policies).

Learning activity – case study 18.1

Creating an attendance culture

Helen is an HR adviser for a major bank. The bank's call centre is one of her clients. It is experiencing high rates of absenteeism, and recently there have been instances of people being absent and not calling to advise that they wouldn't be in. The call centre manager believes that firmer management is required but is hampered by the fact that there is no attendance management policy.

The call centre has 60 staff, predominantly in the 18–30 age bracket. Staff members come from a variety of backgrounds, including retail sales, clerical and hospitality. All are employed under the bank's collective agreement. Salaries are quite low. Standard call centre management practices apply (e.g. monitoring of calls, regular performance feedback, high levels of quality control).

Helen has been assigned the task of developing an attendance management policy for the call centre.

Discussion questions

1. What research would Helen need to do during the policy development process?
2. What factors may be contributing to the high levels of absenteeism?
3. Discuss the policy options that might be effective in reducing absenteeism in the call centre.
4. Identify the best options. Outline your reasons for choosing those options.

Learning activity – case study 18.2

Phoning it in

Steve works in HR for a finance company. The company has an attendance management policy that requires employees to phone in before 8:30 a.m. to advise if they are not coming in. The policy also requires that they speak to their supervisor directly. The policy specifically precludes people notifying their absence by email or text message, or leaving a voicemail message, or a message with another employee.

Recently, Steve undertook a review of the policy along with a number of other HR policies. As part of the review he sought input from employees at all levels through focus groups. The policy provisions relating to calling in sick were widely criticised by the focus groups. Younger employees were particularly opposed to it on the grounds that electronic communication was very much the norm for them, and there was no point in requiring people to phone in.

Discussion questions

1. What would be the rationale for requiring people to phone in and speak directly to their supervisor?
2. Is that rationale valid today?
3. Are there any issues around allowing people to notify absences using electronic communication?
4. Should Steve amend the policy? If so, what should the amended requirements be?

Chapter 19

LEAVE MANAGEMENT POLICY

Leave management policy is primarily about controlling the level of leave liability being carried by an organisation. Leave liability is the amount of paid leave that has been accrued by employees but not taken. Excessive levels of leave liability are undesirable both from a financial management perspective and from a workforce management perspective. While there are many forms of leave available to employees, liability issues arise only in relation to forms of leave that are cumulative in nature, notably annual leave and long service leave. Non-cumulative leave such as bereavement leave does not present a liability problem because any unused leave does not carry over to the next year. Leave management policies ensure that employees take their leave entitlements within a reasonable time frame, thereby reducing financial liability, improving operational management and helping to maintain employee well-being (Figure 19.1).

Reasons for excessive leave accrual

Some studies have shown that as much as a third of the workforce do not take their leave entitlements in any one year. Broadly speaking, the reasons for this can be divided into two categories as Table 19.1 shows.

Organisational reasons tend to revolve around short-term operational considerations such as not having the capacity to release employees because of increased business levels or not having adequate relief arrangements in place. Skills and/or labour shortages can also have an impact on an organisation's capacity to let employees take leave because of the unavailability of suitably skilled replacements either within the organisation or on the short-term job market. Organisational reasons tend to be more pronounced in smaller organisations. Larger organisations are likely to have greater financial and staffing capacity to cover absences; however, in circumstances where budgets and staffing allocations are devolved to individual business units, the capacity to cover staff absences may be no greater than in a small organisation.

In many cases, employees themselves choose not to take leave when it accrues. This may stem from dedication to their work or to the organisation,

Table 19.1 Reasons for leave accrual

Organisational reasons	Personal reasons
High workload levels	High commitment levels
No internal relief staffing arrangements	Financial buffer in case of job loss
Cost of temporary replacement staff	Saving for longer leave next year
Skills shortages	Saving leave for lump-sum payout on retirement
Labour shortages	

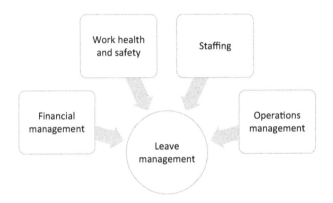

Figure 19.1 Leave management policy connections.

or it may be a deliberate strategy. For some employees, having a lot of leave owing is a bit like having money in the bank – it provides a sense of security knowing that it is there 'just in case'. Other employees see little point in 'wasting' leave when they have no specific plans for it. This is especially true for long service leave.

Certain occupational and demographic groups tend to be more likely to accrue excessive levels of untaken leave. These include men, older employees, long-serving employees, higher income earners and people in leadership and managerial positions.

Consequences of excessive leave accrual

Failing to control leave liability can have negative medium- and long-term consequences for organisations and employees. Where organisational issues prevent the release of staff for extended periods, any subsequent bursts of leave-taking may cause considerable pressure on budgets and staffing allocations. Similarly, during periods of economic downturn, the cost of redundancy programmes can be increased significantly because of the need to pay out all accrued leave entitlements to those who are leaving. Not allowing people to take leave because of operational pressures can also have a negative effect on morale, commitment levels and productivity.

Where employees themselves choose not to take leave, issues such as stress, burnout and declining work quality may take their toll. Increases in workplace accidents and injuries, increased levels of sickness and unscheduled absences and higher levels of workplace conflict can all result from a workforce that is insufficiently rested. Indeed, leave management can be seen as an integral part of work/life balance strategies that are designed to enhance employee well-being and job performance.

Policy options

As with most areas of HR policy, the options for dealing with leave management issues should take account of the nature of the organisation and its business as well as the requirements of industrial legislation, awards and employment agreements. In broad terms, policy options can be classified as either compliance measures or flexibility measures. Often, a combination of compliance and flexibility measures will provide the right mix of 'carrot and stick' to effectively manage leave liability without causing employee unrest or industrial disputation.

Compliance options would usually revolve around requirements for employees to take leave within a certain period of accruing it. For example, employees may be required to take annual or long service leave within a year of it falling due. Including provisions that allow employees to defer leave-taking beyond the specified time limit for a specific reason injects some flexibility into the arrangement, although such provisions need to be managed within the spirit of the policy (i.e. not simply used as a way of not enforcing it). Specifying maximum amounts of leave that can be accrued will have a similar effect. This might require that employees accrue no more than two years' worth of annual leave entitlement (usually 40 days). A further option might be to require employees who have accrued more than 20 days of leave to negotiate a plan with their managers to clear the excess. For options like these to be successful, leave accruals need to be routinely monitored by HR. In addition, line managers need to commit by observing the requirements of the policy. This means balancing policy requirements with operational requirements.

Flexibility options are usually designed to encourage employees to clear their leave accruals by giving them the opportunity and incentive to do so. A fundamental flexibility option might be to allow people to take small amounts of annual leave at operationally convenient times rather than having to take it as a block. This way, employees can take a few days leave or even a single day at different times according to their needs. The result is that relief arrangements and costs are minimised because managing the absent employee's workload is easier, and there is less need for a temporary replacement. Similar provisions might also be applied to long service leave. It may, in fact, be a more attractive option for employees to take long service leave in small chunks rather than as one three-month period. This could allow people to spread their long service leave over a period of years, perhaps giving them an additional one or two weeks of leave a year while retaining a certain amount of leave 'in the bank'. This has less of an immediate effect on liability, and so it may not be a viable option where an organisation is trying to make substantial leave liability reductions. However, once liability has reached an acceptable level, it could be a sustainable option.

Cash-out options allow employees to have some or all of their leave accrual paid out rather than having to take it. While this is effective for reducing liability, it needs to be considered carefully. From an employee well-being perspective, it would be unwise in the longer term to allow employees to habitually cash out their leave accruals without actually taking a break. For this reason, it is preferable for cash-out policies to place some restrictions on how much leave can be cashed or how often employees can use the cash-out option. A further issue to consider is that using cash-out options may affect an employee's tax liability by pushing them into a higher marginal tax bracket. These sorts of implications need to be made clear in the policy, perhaps including a requirement for HR to calculate the possible effects and advise the employee before payment is approved.

Taking accrued leave on half pay can act as a leave-taking incentive for people who wish to extend their leave entitlements. Under this kind of arrangement, an employee can take twice the normal amount of leave on half pay. Half pay options can be applied to both annual leave and long service leave and have the advantage of reducing leave costs while offering greater flexibility to employees.

Purchased leave options may also encourage employees to take leave more regularly. These types of options usually require employees to sacrifice a percentage of their salaries in exchange for additional leave. Two common purchased leave models involve employees sacrificing approximately 8 per cent of their salaries for an extra four weeks of annual leave, or sacrificing 20 per cent of their salaries in exchange for a year's leave every five years. Options such as these can have operational implications, of course, and should be considered carefully before being implemented. Where an organisation is actively encouraging work–life balance or attempting to change the leave-taking culture, they may be effective options.

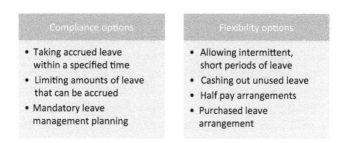

Compliance options	Flexibility options
• Taking accrued leave within a specified time • Limiting amounts of leave that can be accrued • Mandatory leave management planning	• Allowing intermittent, short periods of leave • Cashing out unused leave • Half pay arrangements • Purchased leave arrangement

Figure 19.2 Leave management policy options.

Flexibility options may also enhance attraction and retention and reduce the level of unscheduled absences; thus they should be considered in this light as well as for their potential to contribute to leave management (Figure 19.2).

Leave restrictions

As has been mentioned, it is necessary to balance leave-taking with operational needs. In some organisations, there may be genuine reasons why leave needs to be restricted at certain times. This will usually be due to seasonal factors affecting the business. For instance, retailers may need to restrict absences during the busy period leading up to Christmas, and accounting firms may need to do so in the period around the end of the financial year. Leave management policies need to include these kinds of restrictions if they are relevant to the business. Restrictions should apply primarily to annual leave, not to forms of leave that are not voluntary (e.g. sick/personal leave, bereavement leave). Applying restrictions to long service leave may also be problematic because of the fact that long service leave can involve a lengthy absence from the workplace. However, where an organisation's leave management policy allows the taking of long service leave in smaller chunks, restrictions could reasonably be applied to periods of four weeks or less.

Leave of absence

A leave of absence is an extended period of unpaid leave. People take leaves of absence for a variety of reasons usually connected with their lives outside work. Leave management policies should include provisions for managing this type of leave.

From a management perspective, a leave of absence can be problematic because it usually requires the absent employee to be replaced while they are away, but it also requires them to be accommodated when they return. For this reason, some organisations require people taking a leave of absence to become 'unattached'. This means, that while they remain an employee of the organisation, they are not guaranteed a return to their original job. Much can change during an extended absence; therefore provisions like this allow employers to assess the organisation's needs at the time the employee returns and to deploy him/her according to prevailing conditions and organisational structures.

While unpaid leave does not contribute directly to overall leave liability, allowing an employee to take a leave of absence while they have paid leave owing is not ideal. For this reason, some organisations require all paid leave entitlements to be exhausted before a leave of absence can be approved.

Summary

- Leave management policies underpin the effective management of leave liability and connect with financial management, operations management, occupational health and safety and staffing issues.
- Excessive leave stockpiling can be caused by a range of organisational issues as well as by deliberate employee strategies.
- Where there is a culture of people not taking leave when it accrues, there can be negative consequences for budgets, staffing allocations, employee well-being and productivity.
- Policy options can encompass both compliance measures that require employees to take leave rather than accruing it indefinitely, and flexibility measures that provide incentive and opportunity for people to take leave regularly.
- Leave management policies should also specify any restrictions that might apply to leave-taking because of operational issues such as seasonal workload fluctuations and should include provisions for managing leaves of absence.

Learning activity – case study 19.1

Managing a dual leave culture

Martin is the HR manager at a large private hospital. He has been there for about six months. Recently, the hospital's finance manager drew Martin's attention to the large leave liability that was currently being carried, expressing concern that it seemed to be steadily rising and was getting to the point of being unsustainable. Martin's examination of leave records indicated that while clinical and support staff seemed to be taking leave regularly, members of the management team were not. In fact, some senior managers appeared not to have taken any leave for three years, and several others had taken only a week or two during the same period. Several managers had also accrued long service leave which had not been taken.

The hospital's management team are all employed under common law contracts that specify an entitlement of four weeks' annual leave and three months' long service leave after ten years. However, there is no specific leave management policy. Martin has concluded that the hospital needs one.

Discussion questions

1. What might be some of the reasons that managers do not take their leave entitlements?
2. Does Martin need to find out more about the reasons? If so, how should he do it?
3. What kinds of policy options might be effective in reducing leave liability and encouraging a culture of more regular leave-taking among managers?
4. Given that there seem to be no leave liability problems with clinical and support staff, would it be appropriate to develop a policy just for managerial staff, or different policies for different employee groups? Or should there be a single policy for everyone?

Learning activity – case study 19.2

Managing a leave of absence request

George is a 49-year-old medical laboratory technician in a large private hospital. His work involves analysing blood and tissue samples for diagnostic purposes. He is one of a team of technicians who do this work. George has been doing the job for 12 years and is the most experienced member of the team. He is seen by his colleagues as a great source of information, advice and corporate knowledge. However, over the past year or so, George has felt somewhat restless and bored. He has done everything that is possible to do in his current role, and there is very little challenge left. It has become routine and not very interesting. There are no higher level technical positions in the hospital's organisational structure, only management roles. In any case, George isn't really interested in management and isn't motivated by making more money. The idea of climbing the corporate ladder doesn't excite him at all.

George's declining motivation hasn't gone unnoticed. At his recent performance appraisal interview, George's manager, Keith, raised the issue with him, and George conceded that he was feeling pretty stale and unmotivated after 12 years of doing the same work. He also said that he and his wife were considering spending some time in the United States, where their daughter was living with her American partner and asked whether it would be possible to take an extended leave of absence, probably 12 months.

Keith is inclined to approve George's request and has sought advice from the HR department about it. HR has informed him that there is currently no policy covering leaves of absence. However, the HR manager is sympathetic to Keith's situation and undertakes to develop a policy that would allow George to take up to 12 months of unpaid leave.

Discussion questions

1. What management issues might arise when allowing an employee to take an extended leave of absence?
2. Should all employees be able to apply for a leave of absence, or should there be some eligibility criteria? If so, what should those criteria be?
3. Should there be minimum and/or maximum periods for leaves of absence. If so, what should they be?
4. What if George takes the leave, but then wants to return early? Should the policy allow for this?
5. Should the organisation stay in touch with George during his absence? If so, whose responsibility should this be?

Chapter 20

PERFORMANCE MANAGEMENT POLICY

Performance management (PM) is one of the more problematic areas of HRM. Research has shown that employees generally do not believe they get enough day-to-day performance feedback and that formal performance appraisal processes are frequently not done well or not done at all. There are many reasons for this, including:

- Many managers find the feedback process difficult and daunting, and they lack the confidence and skills to tackle it.
- The process is seen to be a bureaucratic imposition.
- There are often no linkages between performance appraisal and other HR processes, and so it is perceived to be a meaningless exercise.
- Performance appraisal systems are too complex and not well understood.
- The system is not actively driven by HR, and not reviewed frequently enough.
- There are no consequences for managers who do not undertake the process with their employees.

While most people and organisations can see the logic of having a PM system, it is difficult to translate that theoretical support into practice. Even in organisations where PM processes are carried out, there is potential for conflict and even litigation if employees are dissatisfied with the process or the outcome, especially where appraisal outcomes influence remuneration or promotion decisions. Hence, PM is something of a minefield.

While not a panacea for these kinds of issues, a PM policy can certainly help to create an environment where PM is more likely to be carried out and carried out well, and where the system is actively managed. The major reasons for having a PM policy are:

- to ensure a consistent approach to PM
- to ensure procedural fairness and natural justice
- to inform employees about how their performance will be assessed
- to outline the possible outcomes of the process.
- to show the links between PM and other HR processes and functions

Figure 20.1 Performance management – strategic linkages.

Performance management is one policy area that encompasses both compliance elements and strategic elements. While there are no legislative requirements for organisations to undertake formal performance appraisals, the fact that an organisation requires that the process take place gives it its compliance focus. As already observed, performance appraisals can lead to conflict or litigation if not conducted fairly. A PM policy that prescribes a legally and ethically defensible process can minimise the likelihood of conflicts and litigation. It can also protect the organisation from adverse outcomes if the issue is pursued by a disgruntled employee. This is essentially a risk management issue which falls within the scope of compliance policies.

From a strategic perspective, PM can be seen as a link between the organisation's objectives and employee performance, as Figure 20.1 shows.

Thus, PM systems focus employee activity on achieving objectives that contribute to the broader objectives of the business unit and the organisation.

An additional strategic element relates to issues such as employee engagement, attraction, retention and talent management. Research tells us that employees value performance feedback, especially when it enhances their job satisfaction and the development of their careers. Employees also value the opportunity to give feedback to managers. A PM policy that incorporates these kinds of elements can contribute to the creation of a positive work environment and to the reduction of undesirable outcomes such as excessive turnover or absenteeism.

Policy statement

The PM policy document should begin with a statement of the purposes of the PM system in the organisation. These purposes will vary according to the type of organisation, the maturity of the PM process in the organisation and other variables such as organisational culture and the business context, but should be similar to those outlined previously.

Roles and responsibilities

A functional PM system requires the participation of everyone in the organisation. The policy should outline these roles and responsibilities. Some of

Table 20.1 Performance management roles and responsibilities

Roles	Responsibilities
Executive management	• Sets strategic direction and organisational objectives • Communicates objectives to line management
Line management	• Defines performance criteria for employee roles • Communicates those criteria to employees • Observes and measures performance • Provides performance feedback to employees as per system requirements
Human resource management	• Designs and manages the system • Monitors and reports on system usage • Provides information and training to system users • Assists line managers to define performance criteria • Evaluates and updates the system
Employees	• Undertake roles with performance criteria in mind • Receive performance feedback from line management • Give feedback to line management on operational factors affecting performance

these roles might vary depending on the type of appraisal system being used but, in general terms, Table 20.1 gives a broad indication of the kinds of roles played by different participants.

The policy should also make clear which employees should take part in the process and whether or not there are any exceptions. Ideally, of course, everyone should participate, but there may be circumstances where some people are not appraised. These might include:

• temporary or short term employees – the policy should define the duration of employment for this classification (e.g. less than three months)
• contractors or workers from labour hire companies
• employees on extended leave (e.g. long service leave or parental leave)

Frequency and time frames

The policy should outline the various time parameters that apply to the process. Perhaps the most fundamental of these is how frequently the formal appraisal process occurs. In most organisations, appraisals occur annually, but this is by no means the only model. In some industries, particularly those that are highly dynamic (e.g. the technology sector) appraisals can be more frequent – perhaps six monthly or even three monthly. This is a policy decision that needs to be made based on the specific context. Most organisations

Figure 20.2 Stages in the performance management process.

opt for annual appraisals because the business planning and financial cycles are annual, and so outcomes from the business planning process can cascade down through the organisation in the shape of performance criteria. As a general rule, appraisals should not happen any less frequently than once a year. Longer time frames make the likelihood of non-compliance much higher and make the whole process more cumbersome. Too long a time frame will also lead inevitably to employees going for long periods without any performance feedback, and the potential retention and talent management benefits discussed earlier will be lost.

Having decided on the frequency, it is possible to schedule the various stages of the process. Most appraisal systems are structured around three stages (Figure 20.2). Again, though, the actual model that is adopted needs to reflect the particular organisation and the circumstances. So, for example, there might be two review points before the final appraisal if the context is more volatile. This allows for performance criteria to be adjusted to the changed circumstances and for employees to realign their efforts accordingly. Alternatively, the policy might simply allow for variations to the standard pattern on a needs basis.

The issue of the timing for new employees also needs to be addressed in the policy. It is common for new employees to hook into the cycle when the next one starts. However, this disadvantages people who join the organisation just after the beginning of a new appraisal cycle. They may be waiting nearly a year before the system picks them up. To avoid these kinds of anomalies, the policy should specify how new employees should be slotted into the process. For instance, it may be a policy requirement that managers conduct an objective setting session with new employees within a specified time after starting work. This might be soon after the employee's start date, or if there is a probationary or trial period, at the conclusion of that period when the new person's employment is confirmed.

Finally, the policy should specify exactly who is responsible for conducting the performance assessment and giving performance feedback. Usually this is the line manager who has direct supervisory responsibility, and there is a strong argument that it should be that person. However, in some cases, a higher level manager may have responsibility. If this is the case, it is likely to be a cultural feature of the organisation or perhaps simply reflect a tradition

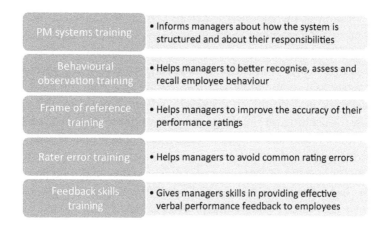

Figure 20.3 Performance appraisal training options.

that hasn't been changed for whatever reason. There is also scope for others to be involved in the process (though not necessarily responsible for it in a managerial sense) depending on the particular appraisal methodology the organisation is using – these circumstances are explored later in this chapter.

Process issues

A good PM policy needs to ensure that the process is effective and is conducted in a professional and proper manner. One policy option that would help in this regard is to specify that managers involved in the process undergo training to better equip them for their roles as performance assessors and givers of feedback. There are numerous training options for managers involved in the appraisal process (Figure 20.3).

Few organisations would routinely provide all of these types of training, but requiring that managers undergo some form of training is advisable, especially considering the degree of resistance that is often experienced. At the very least, PM systems training and feedback skills training give managers the fundamental knowledge and skills they need to fulfil their responsibilities. PM systems training ensures that managers are aware that a system exists and know how it works and what they are expected to do (so there can be no later claims of ignorance as an excuse for not participating). Feedback skills training enhances the quality of feedback that people get as well as increasing the confidence of managers to handle feedback scenarios competently. Whether or not it is feasible to make mandatory training a policy requirement will depend on the size of the organisation, its geographic characteristics and the cost of providing the training.

The location of the appraisal interview can be an important factor in its effectiveness. While it might seem obvious that interviews should be done in a private setting, there are (unfortunately) some managers who seem not to recognise this or who don't think it's important. Consequently, including this in the policy as a requirement will help ensure that even the most insensitive managers provide an appropriately private setting for the appraisal interview. Depending on the design of the workplace and the availability of other options, it may also be worth specifying that managers should conduct appraisal interviews in a neutral venue such as a meeting room. This would be preferable to meeting in their own offices where they might be perceived to have the 'home ground advantage' and where the employee might feel less at ease. There are also issues about the physical set up of the interview room and how this, too, can affect the dynamics of the interview. For instance, having a manager and an employee converse across a desk can be interpreted as being adversarial. And different chair heights can emphasise the power differential between manager and employee. However, whether or not it is feasible or necessary to address these kinds of issues in a policy document is debatable. In most cases, having a policy that specifies that interviews should take place in a private, neutral setting should suffice.

The involvement of third parties is another process issue that should be addressed in the policy. Normally, of course, appraisal interviews are one-on-one. However, on occasions, an employee may want another person to attend as a supporter and/or observer. This is often a union representative. Where this occurs, it implies a less than positive relationship between manager and employee, and it is not the ideal scenario. However, denying an employee the right to have a third party present is difficult to justify, and so the policy should allow for it as an exception but not as the general rule.

Indeed, procedural fairness at all stages is an important process issue that should be addressed in the policy document. This might result in policy requirements such as

- employee's right to comment on performance assessment outcomes
- employee's right to request a review of the outcomes
- provision of two-way feedback
- requirement for a formal written record to be kept
- requirement for both parties (manager and employee) to sign PM documentation

These kinds of policy provisions help to ensure a just and defensible process, minimising the likelihood that an employee will go away feeling dissatisfied. Of course, these provisions will not necessarily prevent employees objecting

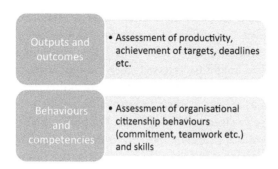

Figure 20.4 Types of performance criteria.

strenuously to the outcome of the appraisal process, especially where they have been rated poorly. The important thing from a procedural fairness perspective is that, if this occurs, the means exist by which they can voice their objection and pursue the matter if necessary.

Performance criteria

It could be argued that the criteria by which employee performance is judged are the most important components of the PM system. It is, therefore, necessary to ensure that those criteria are carefully considered and that they are consistent with job descriptions.

A fundamental question to consider in constructing performance criteria is 'what should we measure?' Broadly speaking, there are two approaches to defining performance requirements (Figure 20.4). PM systems can emphasise either or both of these aspects of performance. While there is a strong argument that a comprehensive PM system should include both, it is also true that behaviours and competencies are generally much more difficult to assess than outcomes and outputs. Necessarily, assessments of behaviours and competencies tend to be qualitative, which involves a degree of subjective judgement by whoever is making the assessment. There are potential issues with outcomes and outputs too. It is fair to say that in most organisational contexts, productivity and the successful achievement of targets and deadlines can be affected by factors not related to employee performance. These factors might include aspects such as the availability of resources, market conditions, management decisions or any number of other factors outside the employee's direct control. It is also true that in some contexts (e.g. the public sector) outcomes can be difficult to measure, especially where the work involves implementing and managing longer-term programmes and strategies.

PM policy needs to make clear what types of performance dimensions are to be included as performance criteria and whether they apply to all employees. It might, for instance, be conceivable that in a diverse organisation, some workers might be assessed solely on outcomes and outputs (sales staff, for example), while for others, behaviours and competencies are more important (such as service workers in hospitality, health or government). The inclusion of these kinds of provisions in the PM policy helps to ensure that the organisation applies appropriate thought to developing the performance criteria for all roles and that the choice is informed by the nature of the work, the objectives of the organisation and the economic context.

Methodologies

There are numerous ways to approach the appraisal process. Usually, an organisation's approach will incorporate two methodological aspects: review methods and rating methods (Figure 20.5).

There is almost no limit to the ways in which these review and rating methodologies can be combined to form a PM system. The choices will depend on various factors, including:

- the nature of the occupations
- the structure of the organisation
- the extent to which PM is established within the organisation
- the skills of those doing the assessments

Most PM policies do not specify which particular review and rating methods the organisation uses and to whom they apply. While it could be argued that this is more a procedural matter than a policy matter, it could equally be argued that including methodology as part of the policy ensures a consistent approach to PM and provides a more accurate guide for employees and managers. This is not to suggest that including a particular methodology in the policy is to enshrine it permanently. Following the systematic process outlined in Part II will ensure that any prescribed methodology is reviewed regularly and amended or changed according to need and its success or otherwise. If despite this, there is concern about lack of flexibility in the system, a policy provision could be included which allows for variations to the prescribed methodologies under special circumstances. For example, there may be a specialised area of the organisation where the nature of the work differs significantly from the rest of the organisation, or there may be a particular business unit or division with a unique structure or other atypical characteristics. A policy that allows variation to match circumstances is less likely to encounter resistance.

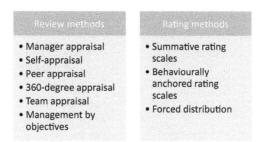

Review methods	Rating methods
• Manager appraisal • Self-appraisal • Peer appraisal • 360-degree appraisal • Team appraisal • Management by objectives	• Summative rating scales • Behaviourally anchored rating scales • Forced distribution

Figure 20.5 Performance management methodologies.

Another benefit of this kind of policy provision is that it allows different methodologies to be trialled for possible wider use. At the end of the day, specifying methodology as a matter of policy is optional rather than essential.

Managing poor performance

This is perhaps the most difficult and challenging aspect of PM, and for this reason it is essential that it be underpinned by a sound policy. Poor performance can come to light via the formal performance appraisal process, as part of the day-to-day supervisory process or as a result of a particular incident. From a policy perspective, it makes no difference how the poor performance is identified – what is important is the way in which it is managed.

Given the potential for conflict and litigation, procedural fairness is an important consideration. An effective policy for managing poor performance would include the following provisions:

- the obligation to advise employees of performance shortfalls
- the obligation to provide employees with appropriate means by which their performance could be improved
- the obligation to allow employees a reasonable time frame in which to demonstrate improved performance

As Table 20.2 shows, there are different approaches to different performance issues. The area of behaviours is potentially the most difficult issue given the possible consequences of continued poor performance (i.e. discipline, termination). Behavioural poor performance can include anything from tardiness to serious interpersonal issues. Often, the problems are not related to the work itself or to organisational factors but are personal in nature – related to the employee's personal circumstances or his/her personality. Behavioural issues are the ones most likely to cause employee grievance and, therefore, the ones

Table 20.2 Poor performance responses and consequences

Performance area	Responses	Consequences of non-improvement
Outcomes	Skills training Coaching	Transfer Demotion Termination
Outputs	Skills training Procedures training Job design changes	Transfer Demotion Termination
Behaviours	Counselling Personal development Mentoring	Discipline Termination
Competencies	Skills training Coaching	Transfer Demotion Termination

most likely to be challenged. A sound policy is an organisation's best defence against legal challenges (assuming that the policy is actually followed!).

Recognising and rewarding good performance

For many employees, the fact that their good performance is recognised and acknowledged by management is enough to maintain and enhance commitment and motivation. The PM system can also provide the means by which good performance can be recognised and rewarded in more tangible ways, and these should be part of the organisation's PM policy.

Linking the system to remuneration (e.g. pay increments, performance bonuses) is perhaps the most common way of doing this. Although the effectiveness of pay-for-performance systems is contested, the reality is that many organisations embrace them. The PM policy should make the linkages between good performance and pay rewards as explicit as possible. For example, it should specify the basis for allocating financial rewards, that is, what performance ratings are required to qualify for a salary increase or performance bonus. If a performance bonus system is in place, the criteria should be specific enough to eliminate any opportunity for, or perception of, bias or favouritism. From a policy perspective, it is problematic to have bonus systems where the criteria for receiving a bonus and/or the quantum of the bonus are determined at the discretion of individual managers – procedural fairness is as important an issue in rewarding good performance as it is for managing poor performance.

PM systems can also be linked to promotion or reclassification decisions. If this is the case, the same principles should apply. Criteria for promotion or reclassification should be clearly spelt out in the policy, and procedural fairness needs to be the guiding principle.

Linking remuneration and other financial or status rewards to the PM system may not suit every organisation. For example, public sector organisations may be restricted by the legislative or regulatory requirements of public sector employment, and organisations in the not-for-profit sector may not have the financial flexibility to reward high performing employees in monetary terms. In cases like these, other forms of non-financial reward are usually more appropriate and more achievable. These can include things as simple as employee awards (such as a certificate of recognition) or letters of commendation. Even though these forms of recognition are largely symbolic, they should still be based on clear policy guidelines that embrace procedural fairness principles ensuring they are not handed out capriciously. It could be argued that where the value of a reward is intangible, it is even more important that they be allocated in a consistent and accountable way. Not maintaining consistency and accountability will quickly diminish the credibility and meaning of any reward, transforming it from symbolic to shambolic.

Other policy linkages

As discussed in this chapter, PM policy links with both discipline and termination policy (in relation to managing poor performance) and with remuneration and rewards policy (in relation to recognising good performance). Where the PM system is linked to promotion or reclassification decisions, there is a link to the selection aspect of staffing policy as well. There are also two other policy linkages worth mentioning.

In many organisations, the PM policy is linked to the employee development policy, recognising that the PM process is an important tool for identifying training and development needs. The nature of that linkage needs to be made explicit in both policies. Most good PM systems include a section where both employee and manager commit to certain actions relating to performance improvement or future career development. This serves to validate the employee's need for certain kinds of training activities or programmes and can be seen as establishing eligibility for such programmes. This performance-based validation needs to be consistent with whatever eligibility provisions are contained in the organisation's employee development policy.

Similarly, where an organisation has a succession management policy, outcomes from the PM system can be the qualifying criteria for participation

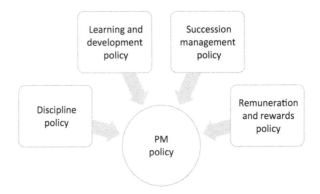

Figure 20.6 Performance management policy linkages summary.

in succession management initiatives such as leadership development programmes and mentoring programmes (Figure 20.6).

Legislative requirements

As mentioned at the beginning of this chapter, there is no legislative requirement for organisations to have a formal PM policy – it is just good management to do so. There are, however, certain pieces of legislation that impact on PM policies and practices. Equal employment opportunity legislation is relevant to PM. Hence, an organisation's PM policy needs to ensure equitable treatment for all employees regardless of gender, age, race, nationality, religious beliefs, political beliefs, sexuality, marital status or other characteristics covered by the legislation that applies in each jurisdiction.

Privacy legislation is also relevant in relation to the way in which PM documentation is used and managed. For instance, an individual's PM records should not be made available to people without a legitimate right to see them. Indeed, it is advisable that the PM policy contain specific provisions covering the proper use and management of employee performance records.

Industrial relations legislation may also impact obliquely on PM policy where it addresses issues such as unfair dismissal.

Summary

- Performance management policy is important because of the tendency for PM processes to be neglected if not actively driven.
- PM policy helps to ensure that the process reflects business strategies and is conducted in a fair and defensible way.

- The scope of PM policy is broad, and may include:
  - purposes
  - participation and time frames
  - process issues
  - training for appraisers
  - appraisal interviewing
  - involvement of third parties
  - performance criteria
  - methodology
  - managing poor performance
  - recognising and rewarding good performance
  - remuneration
  - promotion/reclassification
  - symbolic recognition
  - policy linkages
  - use and management of records.

Learning activity – case study 20.1

Reviving performance management

Jo has just been appointed as HR manager with the Department of Economic Development, a government agency with around four hundred employees. The department's workforce is largely professional, made up of economists and public policy specialists, along with assorted administrative support and corporate services staff.

On arrival, Jo undertook an audit of all HR systems and processes. One of the things she found was that while the department had a PM policy, it had not been reviewed or updated for more than ten years. It also appeared not to have been enforced for a long time because PM activity in the organisation was close to non-existent. In fact there were evidently only a couple of work teams who received any kind of formal performance appraisal, and that seemed to be largely due to the fact that the respective managers of those teams saw value in conducting the process, even if there were no negative consequences for not doing it. Needless to say, no one in the organisation knew what was in the PM policy, and most didn't even know there was one.

Jo's view is that the current situation is not acceptable, and that PM needs to be given a fresh injection of life within the department, beginning with a new policy.

Discussion questions

1. Review each of the policy options discussed in this chapter, and decide which ones would be appropriate to include in the new policy for the Department of Economic Development. What are the reasons for your decisions?
2. Consider the situation that Jo faces – no culture of PM and seemingly little interest in it. What barriers is she likely to encounter in trying to revive the practice of PM?
3. What approach would be best – a comprehensive policy with strong accountability measures to ensure compliance, or a smaller, simpler policy to ease the organisation back towards a culture of PM?

Learning activity – case study 20.2

Designing a performance management policy

Nick has recently been appointed as HR adviser at Digital Solutions, a software company. The company has been growing steadily since it began two years previously, and now has more than a hundred employees, mostly software engineers and various support staff. The culture of the business is quite informal, and there are no specific HR policies in place.

The owner of the company has told Nick that PM is a priority, as there have been some issues with some employees underperforming. Some of these cases have been caused, at least in part, by employees not having a clear idea of their roles or what is expected of them. The owner also wants a way to identify high performing employees so that he can take steps to reward and retain them. The industry is very competitive, and there is a good deal of movement between companies – skilled software engineers are in strong demand.

Nick understands that he needs to develop a policy that is consistent with the culture of the company and not too bureaucratic, but allows the company to address the issues identified by the owner.

Discussion questions

1. How frequently should performance reviews take place in this context?
2. What kinds of review and rating methods would be appropriate?
3. What training would people need?
4. What kinds of rewards might be appropriate for high performers?
5. Who should Nick consult in developing the policy?

Chapter 21

REMUNERATION AND REWARDS POLICY

Remuneration and rewards policy can be a good indicator of an organisation's culture and values; thus it can be seen as being primarily strategic. Traditionally, remuneration policies have been used to create order, reinforce hierarchical structures and direct employee behaviour. Modern remuneration policies, however, have more ambitious aims that include supporting organisational objectives, recognising and rewarding both team and individual outcomes, providing incentive and enhancing employee engagement and motivation.

The scope of remuneration and rewards has also broadened. Figure 21.1 shows the elements of modern remuneration and reward systems.

Policy principles

Remuneration and rewards can also be contentious. This alone is a good reason to have a comprehensive policy that clearly outlines the organisation's remuneration and rewards philosophy and practices. In broad terms, remuneration and rewards policy should be underpinned by the fundamental principles of fairness, alignment, competitiveness and compliance (see Figure 21.2).

The fairness principle has two elements. The first relates to the connection between contribution and reward. Employees whose contributions to the organisation are greater should expect to enjoy greater rewards. Contribution can mean different things in different organisations and can encompass elements such as outputs, outcomes, level of job complexity, level of responsibility and a range of other criteria. The second element of fairness is about procedural fairness – the way in which remuneration decisions are made. Remuneration decisions need to be made (and be seen to be made) impartially and with reference to objective criteria, rather than as a result of cronyism, organisational politics or patronage.

The alignment principle relates to comparative remuneration within an organisation between different employees and occupational groups. It is essentially about consistency. An aligned policy recognises that people doing comparable work and making comparable contributions should be remunerated

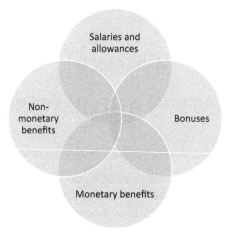

Figure 21.1 Elements of remuneration and rewards systems.

Figure 21.2 Remuneration and rewards policy principles.

Source: Adapted from Milkovich, G., Newman, J. and Gerhart, B. 2010. *Compensation* (10th edn). Boston: McGraw Hill/Irwin.

similarly. Internal consistency can be an issue in larger organisations where divisions or even individual business units may diverge from one another in terms of remuneration practices. Perceptions of inconsistency can fuel unrest within the workforce, and this is obviously something that most organisations would want to avoid.

The competitiveness principle recognises the effect of market forces on remuneration levels. Labour markets, like any other type of market, are influenced by supply and demand factors that can increase or decrease the value of certain skills. Some organisations adopt policies to set remuneration levels in relation to the market. This is usually expressed as a position within a certain percentile of the market. Not all organisations aim to pay at the top end of the market. Decisions about market positioning need to take account of a range of factors, including the capacity to pay and achieve a sustainable balance of remuneration, other forms of reward and organisational factors such as culture.

The compliance principle acknowledges that remuneration is framed by certain legislative and regulatory requirements. In general, regulatory instruments such as awards and industrial agreements set minimum levels of remuneration for specific occupations. Remuneration policies should commit the organisation to complying with whatever regulatory frameworks apply to it.

Remuneration systems

Remuneration systems can be divided into two broad categories: job-based systems and competency-based systems.

Job-based systems are more traditional and still prevalent in highly regulated employment environments like the public sector. They remunerate on the basis of the putative work value of a particular occupation. They are based, therefore, on work analysis or job analysis methodologies that attempt to measure job elements such as complexity and responsibility. The underlying assumption of job-based systems is that the value of a particular position depends on its intrinsic characteristics rather than on who is doing it.

Competency-based systems have gained greater prominence in recent times and are fundamentally different from job-based systems in that they pay the person not the job. These systems recognise that the value of a particular position can be influenced significantly by the person doing it. They also recognise that different employees bring different skills and characteristics to their roles, even where their jobs have the same title. Systems like these give organisations the capacity to recognise and reward highly skilled employees and to provide incentive for everyone to learn and undertake relevant professional development.

The reality is that most remuneration systems incorporate both job-based and competency-based elements. After all, some jobs are intrinsically more complex and more valuable than others, just as some employees are more skilled or more productive than others. The ultimate objective of an organisation's remuneration and rewards policy is to the get the balance right.

Increasingly, remuneration is being seen by organisations as a combination of fixed and 'at-risk' elements, especially for white-collar, professional and

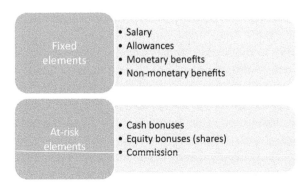

Figure 21.3 Total employment cost remuneration.

managerial employees. This is known as total employment cost (TEC) remuneration (Figure 21.3).

The proportion of fixed to at-risk elements will depend on the organisation and the nature of the work. Usually, at-risk elements comprise a relatively small percentage of total remuneration. There are some exceptions to this general rule, however. People employed in sales roles are often remunerated wholly or partly on the basis of commissions. Sales commissions can be seen as being at risk because they depend directly on outcomes. Executive remuneration can also include a comparatively high at-risk component which is usually based on the achievement of high level strategic objectives.

Pay scales and increments

In larger organisations with a range of different occupations and job classifications, it is common for remuneration to be structured around pay scales that specify the salary (or TEC) range for particular roles, often with specific pay points. Traditionally, people began at the bottom of the pay scale and progressed through it by means of annual increments. However, most organisations now adopt a more flexible approach, where starting salaries can be anywhere on the scale. This is an attempt to accommodate individual differences and market factors within a job-based system.

It is increasingly common for organisations to have a smaller number of wider pay scales. This is known as broadbanding, which increases the level of flexibility that organisations have to recognise the skills and experience of individual employees and to respond to market factors. Overlapping bands provide even greater flexibility, allowing organisations to recognise and reward very experienced or highly competent people who may not necessarily

Table 21.1 Example of a broadbanded pay scale

	Step 1	Step 2	Step 3	Step 4	Step 5	Step 6	Step 7	Step 8
Band 5	100,000	106,000	112,000	118,000	124,000	130,000	136,000	142,000
Band 4	80,000	84,000	88,000	92,000	96,000	100,000	104,000	108,000
Band 3	65,000	68,000	71,000	74,000	77,000	80,000	83,000	86,000
Band 2	50,000	52,500	55,000	57,500	60,000	62,500	65,000	67,500
Band 1	40,000	41,500	43,000	44,500	46,000	47,500	49,000	50,500

be seeking promotion (Table 21.1). Where an organisation uses pay scales, the remuneration policy should specify whether or not people are required to begin at the bottom of the scale or whether there is capacity to appoint people at higher levels within the scale. If a more flexible approach is adopted, the policy should outline the basis on which the starting salary is determined.

The basis for awarding increments should also be specified in the policy. Traditionally, increments were awarded annually, one incremental point at a time. It is more common today, however, for increments to be based on performance rather than time served, and for employees to be able to progress more rapidly, perhaps advancing two or three incremental points in one step. Obviously, this requires a strong link between the remuneration system and the performance management system. A variation on this theme in competency-based systems is to link increments to successful skills development or to the acquisition of relevant qualifications and/or certification.

In smaller organisations, the need for formal pay scales and increments is less pressing. Indeed, it could be argued that having too formal a system may actually have a negative impact by creating unnecessary bureaucracy and reducing flexibility. It is common in smaller organisations for remuneration to be negotiated directly with the proprietor or manager without there being any policy at all. This is not necessarily a bad thing, though the principles discussed earlier should still be evident in remuneration decisions.

Performance pay

Performance pay is one of the 'at-risk' elements discussed earlier and is usually awarded as a cash bonus. As the name suggests, it recognises and rewards outcomes and outputs and can act as an incentive for employees to direct their efforts towards achieving goals that are important for the organisation. While performance pay has its critics, it remains a common component of many organisations' remuneration policies. The main policy issue in relation to performance pay is whether it is applied to individuals, teams or the organisation as a whole. This will depend on the nature of the organisation and the work. Performance pay can also be linked to performance appraisal outcomes, with bonuses being awarded to employees who achieve high performance ratings. Ratings might reflect tangible measures such as outcomes and outputs, as well as intangible measures such as behaviours. Including less tangible measures can make the system more contentious because ratings are more subjective. Nonetheless, the inclusion of behavioural components can reinforce and reward desirable behaviours rather than just rewarding results, which can be affected by factors outside the employee's control.

Remuneration policies should clearly outline performance pay arrangements, covering issues such as who is eligible, how the bonuses are determined, the form of the bonuses (e.g. cash or shares) and how frequently they are paid.

Retirement benefits

The notion of employers providing for their employees' retirement is well established. Approaches vary across jurisdictions. Australian employers, for example, are required by law to contribute 9.5 per cent of an employee's gross salary to an approved superannuation (retirement) fund. This will rise gradually to 12 per cent by 2025. Retirement funds can be employer-managed, union-managed or independently managed (say, by a financial institution). In some cases, employees can choose which superannuation fund that employer contributions are paid into. This usually depends on the legal framework that applies in that jurisdiction.

Remuneration policies should confirm the organisation's commitment to meeting any legal requirements that apply in their jurisdiction. Some employers contribute more than the legal minimum, usually as part of a competitiveness strategy or to enhance attraction and retention. If this is the case, the policy should state the level of superannuation contributions and any conditions that might apply to contributions in excess of the minimum requirement (e.g. qualifying periods).

There is no doubt that retirement benefits can be a powerful attraction and retention factor. As this is an important aspect of remuneration and rewards, it is wise to include a description of available benefits and how they are administered in a remuneration and rewards policy.

Salary packaging

Many organisations in Australia now offer employees the option of packaging their total remuneration in a way that reduces their income tax liability and increases their take-home pay. Expenses like vehicle leases, additional super-annuation contributions, insurance premiums and even mortgage payments and children's school fees can be deducted from employees' gross pay as a 'salary sacrifice', thereby converting that component of their pay from salary to fringe benefit. Doing this essentially transfers the tax liability from employee to employer, with employers paying fringe benefits tax on the value of the deductions. While in theory it is possible to package 100 per cent of gross income, most organisations would not offer such an option because of the cost. Salary packaging policies, therefore, need to specify what deductions are allowable and how much of their gross income employees can package.

As with superannuation and retirement benefits, different arrangements apply in different jurisdictions. Where salary packaging or similar arrangements are in place, the provisions relating to them should be included in the policy.

Non-monetary benefits

Benefits are essentially tangible non-monetary rewards that are of value to employees. Broadly speaking, benefits can be categorised either as workplace rewards (benefits available to all employees) or performance rewards (benefits given in recognition of outstanding performance).

Workplace rewards can include:

- discounts on goods and services
- provision of vehicles and/or car parking facilities
- access to counselling or other support services
- gym and health club memberships
- provision of child care facilities

Performance rewards are usually one-off benefits such as dinners, movie tickets, travel or holidays. Of course, there are other less tangible forms of rec-ognition such as letters of commendation and certificates of merit, but these would generally be covered in the organisation's performance management policy rather than falling within the purview of a remuneration policy.

Remuneration policies should outline the kinds of workplace and perform-ance benefits available to employees and any conditions attached to those benefits, such as qualifying periods for new employees. Eligibility criteria should also be specified in the policy. For example, benefits may only be avail-able to permanent or ongoing employees rather than to casual or temporary employees. Some more valuable benefits like vehicles may only be available to managerial employees. These kinds of policy decisions need to take account of the costs and level of sustainability as well as fairness and equity principles.

In addition, the policy should specify how performance benefits are awarded. It is common for these kinds of rewards to be linked to performance appraisal outcomes or other measurable results. They may also be based on nominations by managers, colleagues or customers.

Decision-making policy

All remuneration decisions should be governed by a clear decision-making policy that allocates responsibility for salary determination, pay increases, payment of increments and allocation of bonuses.

Some larger organisations convene remuneration committees to make these kinds of decisions. Committee members can include senior management, line management, employees, unions and HR. The make-up of the committee will depend on the nature of the organisation and its culture.

Other organisations allocate responsibility to specific roles. For instance, the CEO or HR manager may be the ultimate decision-maker, but line managers may be responsible for making recommendations.

In many cases, general pay increases are determined through formal industrial agreements. Alternatively, pay levels may be linked to movements in the consumer price index or to the achievement of organisational objectives. Whatever the method, the remuneration policy should incorporate an explanation of the organisation's approach to general pay-setting.

Inevitably, disputes and disagreements will arise over remuneration issues. The policy should, therefore, include provisions relating to dispute resolution. Where the organisation has a grievance policy, this may be the most appropriate avenue for dealing with disputes, and so the remuneration policy should refer specifically to that policy. Where there is no formal grievance policy, or where the organisation prefers remuneration issues to be dealt with separately, the remuneration policy should set out the provisions for dealing with disputes and nominate the final arbiter. Internal dispute resolution policies would generally relate only to individual cases. They would not include provisions relating to industrial disputes, which are governed by legislation.

Executive remuneration

Executive remuneration is one of the most contentious issues in contemporary HR. In Australia as well as in other jurisdictions, there has been much public and political debate about the appropriateness of executive remuneration levels and the connection (or lack of it) between remuneration and company performance. The high level of public scrutiny makes executive remuneration policy particularly important. It is common for corporations to have fairly loose executive remuneration policies that refer to attraction, retention and market forces as the primary drivers of remuneration levels. Policies such as these have the advantage of providing maximum flexibility, but it could be argued that they actually provide very little guidance to decision-makers about what may or may not be acceptable to shareholders or to society in general.

A more comprehensive executive remuneration policy might include provisions relating to

- the mix of fixed and 'at-risk' elements
- the method of determining bonuses
- the size of base salaries in relation to average earnings within the company
- the size of termination payments and the method of calculating them

Much of the public concern about executive remuneration revolves around the seemingly unlimited discretion that boards have in determining salaries, bonuses and termination payments. Greater transparency would seem to be the fundamental issue. Organisations adopting more transparent, more specific policies are less likely to incur the wrath of shareholders, governments and the public.

Summary

- Remuneration and rewards policy generally covers issues relating to salaries and allowances, bonuses, superannuation and benefits.
- Policies should embody the principles of fairness, alignment, competitiveness and compliance.
- If there is a specific policy in relation to market competitiveness, this should be stated explicitly in the policy document.
- Approaches to remuneration can be job-based or competency-based. It is also possible to apply competency-based principles within an essentially job-based system by using pay scales and increments.
- Policies should cover the operation of pay scales and increments where these are used to classify jobs and roles.
- Performance pay arrangements should also be covered where these exist. The basis for awarding performance-related bonuses should be made clear in the policy.
- Superannuation options, salary packaging arrangements and the availability of non-cash benefits should also be outlined in the policy.
- Policies should allocate responsibility for remuneration decisions and for dealing with disputes and disagreements.

- Executive remuneration policies can be contentious if not sufficiently detailed. These policies should embody the same principles as those for other employees and be able to withstand public scrutiny in terms of transparency.

Learning activity – case study 21.1

Designing a pay policy

'Buildings by Design' is an architectural firm specialising in the design of residences and small- to medium-sized commercial buildings. The business's owner, Joe, started the firm ten years ago. It now employs around 80 people, including architects, draftsmen and women, financial and contract management specialists, and administrative support staff. Joe's approach to remuneration has always been person-based. That is, he would negotiate a remuneration package with each individual when they were employed and review the arrangement every 12 months. This has worked well in the past, but recently things have become more complex.

About three months ago, Joe agreed to a 15 per cent salary increase for Simon, one of his more experienced and capable architects. Not long after this, another architect, Laura, who had been given a 5 per cent increase a few months before, approached him to have her salary reviewed again. She said that Simon had told her about his 15 per cent pay increase and that she felt that her 5 per cent was inadequate by comparison. Although he didn't say it to Laura, Joe's view was that Simon was worth more to the company. He undertook to consider Laura's request.

This left Joe with something of a dilemma. As the owner of the business, he did not want to relinquish the right to set salary levels. By the same token, he could see that, without a consistent approach, his remuneration decisions could be seen to be subjective, even capricious, and that this could have a negative effect on employee morale, retention and productivity. He also knew that there was potential for salary costs to blow out if not properly managed, and that this could affect the viability and sustainability of the business.

Joe subsequently sought advice from an HR consultant, who recommended that he create pay scales for each different class of employee and grant annual increments within those scales based on satisfactory job performance. Starting salaries within the scale would be negotiated on appointment, as per Joe's current practice.

In the meantime, Laura has again approached Joe asking if he's made a decision about her request for a pay review.

Discussion questions

1. Are Joe's concerns valid? Does he really need a different approach to pay-setting, or can he continue to manage things the way they are as long as he can justify his decisions?
2. What would be the advantages of having a more defined system of remuneration such as the one suggested by the consultant?
3. Would pay scales give Joe sufficient flexibility to differentiate between high performers and those whose performance was merely satisfactory?
4. Is there a way of balancing Joe's desire to retain a measure of decision-making autonomy and flexibility with greater consistency and transparency?
5. How should Joe respond to Laura's request?

Source: Fazey, M. 2017. *Cases in HR Practice and Strategy* (3rd edn). Prahran: Mirabel Publishing, pp. 65–66. Used with permission.

Learning activity – case study 21.2

Pay increments: Individual vs collective performance

Anita has just been appointed as HR manager for Elite Energy, a large gas and electricity supplier. Only a few days after she began the job, she received a written submission from one of the company's senior managers, Eric, questioning the validity of the company's remuneration policy. Currently the company awards annual pay increments on a collective basis. The size of the increment depends on company performance against a matrix of key performance indicators (KPIs). Each division has a set of KPIs against which their performance is measured. Hitting or exceeding KPIs contributes to a positive pay outcome, but missing KPIs affects the outcome negatively. Once the numbers have been calculated, a final pay outcome for the company is generated. If the result is positive, everybody receives the same increment. If the overall result is negative, pay levels are held at their current level rather than reduced. Last year, the system resulted in a 3 per cent pay increase for everybody in the company.

Eric's issue is that results tend to vary significantly across divisions. In fact, one particular division had failed to meet its KPIs for the past three years, which had the effect of dragging down the overall result. Eric had calculated that his division's results in the previous year warranted a 6 per cent increase, but they had only gotten 3 per cent because of the underperforming division, and this had caused some resentment. Other higher-performing divisions were similarly affected. Eric requested that Anita review the company's remuneration policy with a view to assessing whether it was delivering equitable outcomes and was sustainable in the long term.

Discussion questions

1. What are the advantages and disadvantages of the current policy?
2. Is it fairer to award pay increases on a division-by-division basis, based on each division's performance against its KPIs (i.e. higher-performing divisions would receive higher pay increases)?
3. How might Anita test Eric's assertions about people in high-performing divisions being resentful?
4. Is a collective system the best approach? Would a system based on individual performance rather than collective performance be better? If so, why? If not, why not?

Chapter 22

EQUITY AND DIVERSITY POLICY

Although equity and diversity are different issues, they are closely connected; therefore it is common to deal with them in a single policy. Broadly speaking, equity and diversity policies are about creating and maintaining workplaces that are characterised by fairness (equity) and inclusiveness (diversity), where individual differences are accepted and respected and where employment decisions are made on the basis of relevant, objective criteria.

In most jurisdictions in developed economies, equity and diversity principles are underpinned by legislation that precludes discrimination on the grounds of gender, race, nationality, religion, disability, age and a range of other personal characteristics; thus there is a strong compliance aspect to equity and diversity policy. Equity and diversity policy can also be seen as a culture-shaping policy with ethical, social and business dimensions.

Traditionally, equity and diversity policies have been directed towards specific groups, including women, people with disabilities, people from culturally and linguistically diverse backgrounds and indigenous people (often referred to collectively as 'EEO groups'). In more recent times, however, the concept of diversity has broadened to include individual differences such as personality, values and socio-economic background.

The nature and extent of an organisation's equity and diversity policy can reflect either its existing culture or the culture to which it aspires. The cultures of many organisations have evolved significantly in the 30 or so years since the first anti-discrimination legislation was proclaimed in Australia. Others have not. Most organisations fall within one of the three cultural development stages represented in Figure 22.1.

One of the problematic issues with equity and diversity policy is that, even in organisations which have reached the 'commitment' stage of cultural development, the policies themselves are sometimes little more than statements of good intention. In order to function effectively, policies need to detail specific actions and responsibilities, as well as expressing the intent of the policy. This is even more important where an organisation is attempting to facilitate cultural change (e.g. progressing from a 'compliance' culture to a 'commitment'

Figure 22.1 Stages of cultural development.

culture). Policies that espouse particular values but do not actively encourage or enforce them usually come to be regarded with some cynicism. An effective equity and diversity policy does more than just state a philosophical position – it outlines exactly *how* the organisation will promote and maintain the values it espouses.

Roles and responsibilities

Equity and diversity policies should assign clear responsibilities across the organisation. This helps to reinforce the message that equity and diversity are integral to the day-to-day management of the organisation. Some organisations have equity and diversity officers, usually located within HR. While this is not in itself a bad thing, if equity and diversity issues are the only assigned responsibility of the officer, the issue might be marginalised by others who see it as someone else's responsibility. Policies should, therefore, outline a matrix of responsibilities similar to those in Figure 22.2.

Given the cultural nature of equity and diversity, it is important that it be driven from the top. Including equity and diversity responsibilities in management job descriptions and performance appraisal criteria is an effective way of affirming responsibility. Of course, organisational culture reflects everyone's behaviours, not just management's, and so equity and diversity policies should also make clear that all employees are required to uphold the principles of

Figure 22.2 Equity and diversity responsibilities.

fairness and inclusiveness in their interactions with each other as well as with customers and clients.

Training

Providing equity- and diversity-related training is one tangible way that organisations can demonstrate commitment. Many organisations provide equal employment opportunity (EEO) awareness training to managers and employees; indeed, some organisations require it. This type of training typically outlines the requirements of legislation and provides examples of how equity and diversity principles can be applied to decision-making. Programs like this also reinforce the fact that discriminatory behaviour is not always overt or intentional.

Cultural awareness training may also be appropriate in organisations that employ people from different cultural backgrounds or where customers and clients are culturally diverse. This type of training promotes understanding of cultural differences and helps to prevent negative stereotyping.

Managing diverse work teams can be challenging. Consequently, diversity management training may also be useful to help managers accommodate individual differences and needs, as well as managing conflicts that might arise within teams.

All these kinds of training fall within the category of 'affective' – that is, training that deals with values and attitudes. While it could be argued that it is difficult to change values and attitudes through training, it is incumbent on organisations that embrace equity and diversity to provide the means by which employees can align their behaviours with those expected by the organisation. There is also a risk management aspect to the provision of equity and diversity training. Legally, employers can be vicariously liable for discriminatory behaviour by employees if they cannot demonstrate that positive measures have been taken to prevent such behaviour. Having an appropriate policy in place and providing equity and diversity training are effective ways in which organisations can demonstrate that they have taken such positive measures.

Equity and diversity policies should, therefore, include details of the types of training that are available and whether or not completion of the training is a requirement.

Employment conditions

While basic employment conditions are usually enshrined in industrial relations legislation, awards and employment agreements, these rarely include provisions that specifically address equity and diversity issues. Additional conditions and entitlements designed to accommodate diverse needs can be included in equity and diversity policies. These might include provisions such as those outlined in Figure 22.3.

Parental leave can be paid, unpaid or a combination of both. Traditionally, parental leave has been available only to mothers, but more progressive policies may also include leave entitlements for new fathers who wish to take on an active parenting role. The duration of the leave and whether or not it is paid, unpaid or a combination of the two will depend on the capacity of the organisation to fund and sustain it, as well as its level of commitment to family-friendly policies and management practices.

Cultural leave provisions respect significant social and religious obligations that might apply to people from different cultural and ethnic backgrounds. Given the diversity of these kinds of obligations, it is difficult to address specifics in a policy (i.e. to specify the exact circumstances to which cultural leave applies). It is sufficient for these types of policies to be couched in general terms, allowing employees to use the leave according to their own requirements. As with parental leave, the amount of leave that is available for these purposes will depend on capacity and sustainability, but in most cases, an entitlement of a few days per year is adequate.

It is becoming increasingly common for awards and employment agreements to include 'personal leave' provisions that combine traditional sick leave entitlements with leave covering other forms of personal commitments, including caring for family members who may be ill or disabled. However, where provisions like these do not exist as part of mainstream leave entitlements, they can be incorporated into equity and diversity policies.

Special needs provisions may accommodate people with disabilities or those with specific cultural, religious or family needs. These provisions might include wheelchair access and the provision of modified work stations or equipment and hygiene facilities for people with disabilities, or the provision of facilities

Figure 22.3 Employment conditions and entitlements that support equity and diversity.

for religious observance, such as prayer rooms for Muslim employees who need to pray at certain times of the day. Special needs provisions can also include child care facilities for employees with young children. While having full-time on-site child care facilities is really only viable in larger organisations, there are other ways that organisations can support employees with family respon- sibilities, such as providing school holiday care programs or after-school care facilities. Some office complexes provide child care facilities for the employees of organisations, which are tenants in the same building. Subsidising the cost of accessing these facilities or subsidising the cost of off-site child care either directly or indirectly (e.g. through salary packaging arrangements) are also effective ways of accommodating the needs of people with families.

Policies should outline the kinds of employment conditions that the organ- isation offers to support equity and diversity.

Policy linkages

Equity and diversity issues may also be addressed directly or indirectly in other HR policies. It could, in fact, be argued that the incorporation of these types of issues into mainstream policies is indicative of a truly integrated approach to equity and diversity. These linkages should be outlined in the organisation's equity and diversity policy. Table 22.1 summarises the possible policy linkages.

Reporting and accountability

The axiom 'what gets measured gets done' applies very much to equity and diversity. As discussed earlier in this chapter, a vital role for HR is the meas- urement and reporting of equity and diversity outcomes. A range of quanti- tative and qualitative data should be available in most organisations to help

Table 22.1 Equity and diversity policy linkages

Staffing policy	Advocating non-discriminatory recruitment and selection practices
Code of conduct	Prohibiting racist, sexist or other discriminatory behaviours
Dress codes	Respecting and accommodating cultural differences
Grievance policy	Providing an avenue of redress for employees affected by unfair or discriminatory actions or decisions
Discipline policy	Taking strong action against discriminatory or intolerant behaviour or actions
Workplace flexibility	Accommodating family and other significant social responsibilities

Table 22.2 Equity and diversity measures

Quantitative measures	Qualitative measures
Representation of EEO groups in overall employment	Employee perceptions of culture and management practices
Number and outcome of grievances concerning fairness and equity	Feedback from exit interviews
Number of disciplinary cases concerning fairness and equity	Feedback from performance appraisal processes
Number of employees accessing flexible work arrangements	Feedback from development activities (e.g. 360-degree feedback outcomes)
Participation of EEO groups in training and career development activities	
Representation of EEO groups in different occupations (e.g. management, professional, technical)	
Participation in EEO awareness, cultural awareness and diversity management training	
Percentage of management positions with equity- and diversity-related responsibilities included in job descriptions and performance criteria	

management assess the organisation's performance in relation to equity and diversity issues. The sources of such data will vary according to organisational resources but might include HR information systems, HR audit outcomes, employee surveys, focus groups and exit interview outcomes. Table 22.2 summarises the kinds of measures that might be undertaken.

Many organisations use a balanced scorecard approach to organisational measurement, where a range of different measures are used to gauge organisational performance. The inclusion of key equity and diversity measures in the overall matrix of performance indicators is an effective way of ensuring accountability and demonstrating the level of commitment to creating a fair and inclusive culture.

Target-setting should also be an integral part of the measurement and reporting process. Targets can be expressed in terms of the measures outlined in Table 22.2, especially the quantitative measures. As a general management principle, target-setting is useful because it specifies desired outcomes in key areas and focuses attention on those outcomes. Policies should include equity and diversity targets for this reason.

Individual employees also need to be accountable for upholding equity and diversity principles. This can be facilitated through the performance management process as well as through the application of grievance, dispute resolution and discipline policies.

An effective equity and diversity policy should outline the various measurement criteria and accountability mechanisms that the organisation uses to monitor and promote fairness and inclusiveness.

Affirmative action

Affirmative action is the term used to describe policies and programs designed to address inequities. These might include:

- identifying certain positions to be filled by members of specific EEO groups
- training and development programs which are open only to members of specific EEO groups
- recruitment campaigns targeting people from specific groups or socio-economic backgrounds

In general, affirmative action policies and programs are designed to boost the representation of particular groups which are underrepresented in the workforce when compared with their representation in the general community. They are also used to overcome barriers to career development, such as the underrepresentation of women or members of certain ethnic groups in management or other senior positions.

While affirmative action policies and programs are allowable under anti-discrimination legislation, they can be contentious because they are interpreted by some as being inherently unfair. Equity and diversity policies should include a statement of the organisation's position on affirmative action and outline any affirmative action initiatives that exist, the rationale for them and their duration.

Summary

- Equity and diversity policies are used to promote fairness and inclusiveness.
- Policies should be more than statements of intent – they should outline how the organisation intends to achieve its equity and diversity goals.
- Policies should outline roles and responsibilities as well as specifying the training and/or special employment conditions provided by the organisation to promote and facilitate a fair and inclusive culture.
- Linkages to other HR policies with equity and diversity dimensions should be outlined in the policy.
- Measurement, reporting and accountability provisions at both organisational and individual levels should also be included in the policy.
- The policy should address the organisation's approach to affirmative action, and where such initiatives are used, outline their rationale and duration.
- Employment conditions and entitlements that support equity and diversity should also be outlined in the policy.

Learning activity – case study 22.1

Affirmative action – the best policy?

Kate is an HR policy officer working in the Office of Public Sector Employment, a government agency responsible for HR policy and strategy across the whole government workforce. She has been invited to be part of a committee formed in response to a recent research report on women in leadership in the public sector. The report found that the percentage of women in leadership roles had been in decline for several years and was now only 18 per cent.

The report identified the discontinuation of special women's leadership programs as a major cause of the decline and recommended that these kinds of programs need to be re-introduced as a matter of urgency. It also recommended a return to quota-setting for women in leadership roles (i.e. numerical targets that public sector agencies would be accountable for achieving). At the initial meeting of the committee this approach was strongly endorsed, and Kate was given the task of developing some specific policy proposals for the committee's consideration.

As part of the policy development process, Kate convened a focus group of young women who would be the intended beneficiaries of the new policies – high performers with potential to develop into the next generation of leaders. The strong feeling of the focus group members was that 'women only' programs and quotas were a throwback to the past and would not be valued by their intended recipients. The women certainly wanted opportunities for leadership development, but they wanted those opportunities to be integrated, not gender-specific.

Discussion questions

1. What factors might have led to the percentage of women in leadership declining?
2. What would be the advantages and disadvantages of the kinds of affirmative action policies being advocated by the committee?
3. Are the focus group participants right? Are affirmative action policies outdated?
4. Who else could Kate consult with, and what kinds of questions could she ask?
5. How should Kate proceed with her assignment?

Learning activity – case study 22.2

Embracing equity and diversity for the first time

Sue is an HR adviser with CM Engineering which provides construction and maintenance services to the mining, energy and infrastructure industries. The company employs more than six hundred people and has contracts with several major mining and energy companies.

Sue reports to Hugh, the HR manager. Recently Hugh called her into his office to discuss the need for an equity and diversity policy. The catalyst for this was that one of the large mining companies with which CM Engineering had contracts had recently made equity and diversity a strategic priority. Part of that commitment was the implementation of a policy requiring their contractors to be able to demonstrate a similar commitment to equity and diversity. In short, if CM Engineering was not able to meet this requirement, it would not win any further contracts with the company. One of its most lucrative contracts was coming up for renewal in about six months' time, and Hugh has asked Sue to develop and implement an equity and diversity policy for their company as quickly as possible.

Sue knows that the company has not previously embraced equity and diversity at all, and the company's leadership has never previously raised or discussed the issue. The workforce is very much male-dominated, and there is little cultural diversity among employees. She knows that achieving a genuine cultural shift within the company is going to take some time. She also wonders whether the company's commitment to the policy will be genuine given that the impetus for it is pragmatic (i.e. the desire to retain their contracts with the mining company).

Discussion questions

1. Does it matter that the desire to retain contracts is the driving force behind the policy? Is Sue right in being sceptical about the level of commitment?
2. How much consultation should she do in the development of the policy? Given the current lack of interest and understanding among the company's leaders, would it be better to develop a draft policy without consultation?
3. What kinds of policy provisions would be appropriate to include?
4. What kinds of accountability mechanisms should be built into the policy?
5. What other HR policies might need to be modified to incorporate equity and diversity principles? How might they change?

Chapter 23

WORKPLACE FLEXIBILITY POLICY

Workplace flexibility is one of the most significant HR issues to have emerged in recent years. Many organisations already have flexibility policies though not always as separate policy documents. Some organisations incorporate flexibility provisions as part of their equity and diversity policies, while others see flexibility as being primarily an employee benefit and incorporate it into their remuneration and rewards policies. Still others treat it as a staffing policy issue. There are obviously strong connections between flexibility and these other policy areas, but whether or not flexibility is bound up with other policies matters little. For our purposes, workplace flexibility is sufficiently important and complex to be treated as a stand-alone policy.

Both employers and employees value employment flexibility, though it is sometimes difficult to get the balance just right. Perhaps the biggest problem with flexibility is that there is often a gap between policy and practice, which means that while flexible work arrangements are available in theory, employees are frequently denied access to them. In addition, those who do access them often feel marginalised because they are excluded (usually inadvertently) from organisational communications, meetings and training opportunities. Career progression can also be affected. An effective policy can help to remedy these problems by addressing access and equity issues. Indeed, many flexibility policies suffer from the same shortcoming as equity and diversity policies – they are statements of good intention that are not sufficiently detailed and not managed strongly enough to achieve sustainable cultural change.

For employees, being able to access flexible work arrangements enhances the capacity to balance work with family responsibilities and/or other aspects of life. For organisations, flexibility has the potential to reduce overtime costs, reduce absence rates and enhance attraction and retention, as well as providing operational flexibility. However, where flexibility policies are too restrictive or badly managed, these potential benefits can be lost.

Dimensions of flexibility

Workplace flexibility can take several different forms. Figure 23.1 shows the main types of flexible arrangements that can be included in a flexibility policy.

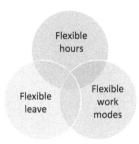

Figure 23.1 Dimensions of flexibility.

Flexible hours can include part-time work, job sharing, flexitime (where employees can 'bank' excess hours and take time off later) and compressed work weeks (where employees work longer days in return for a four-day week or nine-day fortnight). Flexibility of work hours is the most prevalent form of flexibility available.

The most sought after form of flexible work modes is home-based work. It is unusual for employees to work from home all the time, but there is high demand for opportunities to work from home some of the time (e.g. two or three days per week). Home-based work can also be ad hoc – where employees can work from home on a particular task or project, perhaps for a day or a few days depending on the project. Though not yet widely available in Australia, working from satellite offices is an emerging trend in work mode flexibility. This kind of work mode involves employees who might be based in a head office or other city-based location accessing work facilities in the suburbs or regional areas close to where they live.

Some of the flexible leave options have already been discussed in Chapter 19 in the context of leave management policy. These include using annual and long service leave flexibly (e.g. extended half-pay leave), purchased leave (where employees sacrifice salary in return for more leave) and unpaid leaves of absence.

Not every organisation will be able to offer every flexibility option, and so workplace flexibility policies need to define the specific types of flexible arrangements that are available to employees (Figure 23.2).

Access and eligibility

One of the reasons that employees are often frustrated by being unable to access flexible work arrangements is that the existence of ill-defined flexibility policies raises their expectations. For this reason, policies should be very clear about access and eligibility conditions. Some flexibility options may simply

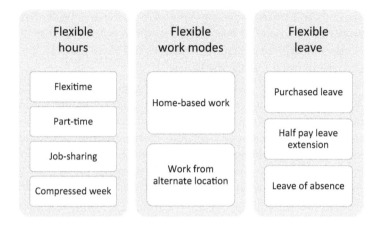

Figure 23.2 Summary of flexible work options.

not be feasible for some employees. For example, home-based work would not be an option for employees whose work revolves around direct customer service, such as in a retail or hospitality environment. Similarly, flexible hours arrangements may need to take account of work flow and hours of business.

Decisions about access and eligibility policy need to be specific to the organisation and take account of actual business requirements. They should not be arbitrary or overly restrictive. Where there are restrictions, the rationale for them needs to be outlined in the policy. Doing so will reduce the number of inappropriate applications, and therefore, the number of instances where access is denied. At the same time, organisations should avoid scenarios where certain groups of employees are deemed ineligible for any form of flexible work arrangement. Given the range of flexibility options that exist, it is difficult to envisage circumstances that would entirely preclude access to at least some of those options.

Approval and decision-making

Some flexible work arrangements such as flexitime and flexible leave options are available to all employees as general conditions of employment. Others are employee initiated and tailored specifically to individual needs. In these cases, it is common for line managers to have decision-making authority for flexible work applications. This is quite appropriate, though problems can arise where the approval criteria are vague or non-existent. While it is true that managing a flexible workforce can be challenging, this should not in itself be sufficient reason to deny an application. Managers need to be accountable for their decisions, and there needs to be consistency across the organisation; therefore the approval criteria need to be spelled out in the policy. In most cases, the primary criterion will be operational viability, but there may also be criteria relating to cost or other managerial issues.

Application processes should not require the employee to justify their application for a flexible arrangement. Doing this implies that approval is based on someone else's judgement of whether the reason is valid rather than on whether or not it is operationally viable. In other words, the onus should be on the decision-maker, not the applicant. The policy should state this.

Approvals are normally granted for a specified period. Where there is doubt about the sustainability of a particular flexibility arrangement, a trial period may be appropriate. Indeed, it may be a good policy option to require that where a flexible arrangement is being taken up for the first time, the initial approval period is relatively short (say, three months). This allows both employee and manager to assess the workability of the arrangement before committing to a longer period. It would also be sensible for the policy to define a maximum agreement period (say, a year) rather than allow open-ended arrangements. This doesn't prevent flexible arrangements from being ongoing, but it allows for regular review.

The policy should also require a flexible work agreement to be entered into for the specified period. This agreement should outline both employer and employee responsibilities. It should also include provisions requiring managers to ensure that the employee is not excluded from normal communication processes or from access to training or information that would otherwise be available to them.

Performance management

It is important that employees working flexibly are effectively managed and have access to the same performance management processes as everyone else. Equity is an important consideration here – employees with flexible work arrangements should not be subject to more stringent performance management requirements simply because they are working flexibly. At the same time, they should be aware that their continued access to flexible work arrangements is dependent on satisfactory work performance, and so performance criteria and expectations need to be clearly communicated. The policy should affirm this.

Change or termination of flexible arrangements

Policy provisions for changing or terminating flexible work arrangements need to be carefully considered. Obviously, circumstances can change both for employees and organisations, and so it is reasonable for policies to include a 'get out' clause. However, change or termination provisions should not be able to be invoked without justification.

Employer-initiated changes or terminations may be the result of changed business requirements or because of unsatisfactory performance by the employee. Regardless of the reason, decisions to change or terminate flexible work arrangements need to take account of the fact that employees may not be able to rearrange their lives at short notice, and so a reasonable period of notice should be specified in the policy.

Employee-initiated requests to change or terminate flexible arrangements will usually result from changes to personal or family circumstances. Changing or terminating agreed work arrangements may have management implications (e.g. salary budgets, staffing plans, project management plans); therefore, as with employer-initiated changes, a reasonable notice period should be specified in the policy.

Review and evaluation

It is good management practice to review and evaluate flexibility arrangements regularly, and so the policy should make provision for this.

For organisation-wide flexibility options such as flexitime and flexible leave, an annual audit should be undertaken to determine the level of usage and to identify any management issues.

Individually negotiated flexibility arrangements should be reviewed at the end of the agreed period. It is important that both manager and employee inputs be included in the review. Employee input helps to determine whether or not the required levels of equity and inclusiveness are being observed.

Evaluation criteria will vary according to the nature of the flexibility option and the organisation. The overall objectives of the review and evaluation process are to determine how successful the arrangement has been, both from a management perspective and from an employee perspective, and to assess its sustainability. Criteria need to reflect these objectives.

Summary

- Workplace flexibility policies need to be more than a statement of possibilities. They need to detail the conditions and management arrangements for flexible work options.
- In general, flexible work options fall into one of three categories: flexible hours, flexible work modes and flexible leave.
- Access and eligibility criteria need to be specified in the policy, including the rationale for any restrictions.

- Approval and decision-making criteria also need to be detailed in the policy. Approvals should not be open-ended and should be subject to review.
- Policies should affirm that normal performance management processes and practices will apply to employees working flexibly. There should not be extra or more demanding performance criteria placed on employees simply because they are working flexibly.
- Policies should include provisions for changing or terminating flexible work arrangements but should not allow changes to be imposed without justification. They should also include a reasonable notice period for changes, whether those changes are initiated by the employer or by an employee.
- Review and evaluation processes should also be outlined in the policy, both for flexibility options that are open to everyone and for individual arrangements.

Learning activity – case study 23.1

A flexitime audit

Julie is an HR adviser with Indian Ocean Oil, an oil company with five hundred employees in its head office. A year ago, the company introduced flexitime for all head office staff. This allowed people to clock on and off using swipe card technology and to manage their own hours within the requirements of their particular jobs. Employees were able to build up excess hours and, with the approval of their managers, take time off periodically. The system was very well received by employees.

Julie has recently conducted an audit of the system's first year of operation. The audit showed that the system was generally working as it was intended and that the vast majority of employees and managers were satisfied with it. However, there were some worrying issues as well:

- Some employees had built up enormous credits over the past year and appeared not to have taken any time off. One employee had more than 200 hours in credit, several more had accrued 100 or more credit hours and credits of 40 hours were not uncommon. In all, about 10 per cent of employees had credits in excess of 40 hours.
- At the other end of the scale, about 6 per cent of employees were in debt. One employee was 80 hours in the red, and a significant number appeared to be permanently in deficit. The company's flexibility policy includes reference to the availability of flexitime and the basic features of the system, but there are no provisions covering its management.

Discussion questions

1. Why are excessive credits and deficits a concern for management?
2. What short-term measures might be appropriate for reducing credits and deficits?
3. What kinds of additional policy provisions could Julie propose to help control the level of credits and deficits in the longer term?

Learning activity – case study 23.2

A home-based work application

Janice is the HR manager for Steinberg Wells, a stockbroking and invest-ment firm with its office in the heart of the CBD. Janice has been with the company for about six months and has formed the view that, while fun-damentally sound, the company's employment practices are very trad-itional and the management culture somewhat conservative.

This view was confirmed when she received a formal submission from Brian, a 55-year-old market analyst with more than ten years' service with the company. Brian's role involves analysing market data using the company's sophisticated IT systems and preparing reports on market trends and significant market developments for the company's brokers and investment fund managers. Brian had recently applied to his manager to work from home two days a week but had been refused permission to do so. He was now seeking a review of that decision. His application to work from home included the following information:

- Brian wished to phase into retirement over the next few years, and working from home part of the time was a good way of doing this.
- He had recently moved to a property on the outskirts of the city (his intended retirement home) which added considerably to his commuting time and travelling expenses.
- Much of his work could be done away from the office provided he had access to the company's systems. He had consulted IT on this point, and they had advised that there would be no problem in setting up remote access for him.

At first glance, Janice thought that Brian's application was quite reasonable. She then arranged a meeting with Alan, Brian's manager. Alan is a long-serving employee, strongly committed to the company and steeped in the company's culture of hard work. Alan expressed the view that the arrangement would not be operationally viable for several reasons:

- Allowing the work-from-home arrangement would set a precedent and might well result in a flood of applications from others wanting to work from home too.
- It was not possible to properly supervise someone working from home and not possible to know whether or not they were actually working.
- While much of Brian's work involved working independently, he was also part of a team. His absence for 40 per cent of the week would have a negative effect on team cohesion.
- Giving Brian remote systems access could pose data security risks.

Alan also observed that Brian had no dependents or other domestic commitments, and so there was no compelling reason for him to be at home more often.

This would indeed be a first for Steinberg Wells – nobody had ever sought a virtual work arrangement before, and there is a culture of long working hours. There is no flexible work policy in place either. Under the company's existing decision-making policies, Janice has the authority to overturn Alan's decision if she believes that doing so is in the broader interests of the company.

Discussion questions

1. Are Alan's objections valid? If so, which ones and why? If not, why not?
2. Does it matter what Brian's reasons for seeking a flexible work arrangement are? Should this be a factor in the decision-making process?
3. What might be the consequences if Janice support's Alan's decision?
4. What might be the consequences if she supports Brian?
5. Is there anyone else Janice should talk to before making her decision?
6. What should her decision be?
7. How should she communicate that decision to the relevant parties?
8. Is there a case for a flexible work policy to be developed and implemented regardless of the outcome of Brian's application? If so, what provisions should it contain? If not, why not?

Chapter 24

STAFFING POLICY

Staffing is perhaps the most visible HR function. Ask most people what the main role of HR is, and they will most likely say 'hiring and firing'. For this reason, staffing policy is a particularly important policy area. It is also quite broad in scope, with several different elements (Figure 24.1).

Staffing policy essentially encompasses the whole employment life cycle from recruitment to termination. Many aspects of the employment relationship are regulated by legislation, awards and industrial agreements, and so there are limitations on the kinds of policies that organisations can legitimately enact. Even so, there remains sufficient scope for organisations to make policy choices that reflect different business needs, different contexts and different cultures.

One of the consequences of the globalisation of business is the emergence of international HRM as a specialised field. International staffing policy incorporates the same kinds of elements as outlined in Figure 24.1, though there are additional dimensions that do not apply to domestic staffing scenarios. International staffing policy is also dealt with in this chapter.

Recruitment

The most fundamental recruitment policy issue is whether or not the primary recruitment source is internal or external.

An internal selection policy requires that positions are advertised only within the organisation in the first instance (i.e. preference is given to existing employees). Positions are advertised outside the organisation only if there are no suitable internal applicants. Essentially, an internal recruitment policy is a 'promote from within' policy. Conversely, an external recruitment policy requires that positions are routinely advertised on the open market, with internal and external applicants given equal consideration. There are both advantages and disadvantages to each policy option (Table 24.1).

Labour market conditions and strategic factors may both affect policy choices. In a tight labour market, organisations are more inclined to 'grow their

Table 24.1 Internal versus external recruitment policy – advantages and disadvantages

	Internal	External
Advantages	Provides career opportunities for existing employees Helps to retain corporate knowledge Helps to ensure a return on investment in training and development Affects morale positively	Bigger talent pool Regular injections of new ideas and different ways of thinking Status quo is more likely to be questioned
Disadvantages	Talent pool is smaller Fewer new ideas are brought into the organisation Negative cultural features may be perpetuated	Fewer career opportunities for existing employees May contribute to higher turnover May be less effective in a buoyant labour market

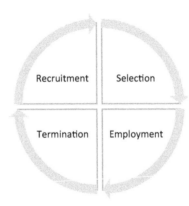

Figure 24.1 Elements of staffing policy.

own', and so an internal recruitment policy may be favoured. Where the labour market is less buoyant, organisations may feel that accessing the broadest possible talent pool is a better option. Business strategies that emphasise diversification or organisational renewal might lead to an external recruitment policy because of its greater potential to inject new ideas and skills.

It may be preferable for an organisation to have a flexible policy, allowing decisions to be made on a case-by-case basis. Some positions or occupational groups may be quarantined for internal applicants, while others may not. For instance, recruitment for unique or specialist roles that have no definite career path within the organisation will clearly be quicker and more effective when the open market is accessed. Similarly, where a position is new or it is already known that the internal talent pool is limited, there would seem little point in following an internal recruitment policy. For positions where corporate knowledge is considered to be important, it is likely that promotion from within will be the better option.

Recruitment policies should state the organisation's position on internal and external recruitment, depending on the culture it wants to project and the business context. Where a flexible approach is adopted, the policy should specify who has decision-making authority regarding whether the position is advertised internally or externally.

Organisations that adopt an internal recruitment policy generally have career paths built into their structures and will inevitably do most of their recruitment at entry level. Entry-level jobs are usually training positions. These can be formal training arrangements (e.g. apprenticeships, traineeships and graduate development programmes) or less formal arrangements where the training is largely on-the-job and doesn't necessarily lead to a qualification. Regular intakes of entry-level employees may be strategically wise, especially in large organisations, and so recruitment policies may include provisions requiring this for certain occupations. The size of the intake will obviously vary according to organisational needs and economic circumstances, and so it would not generally be appropriate to specify numbers. However, a policy that commits the organisation in principle to planned entry-level recruitment will help to support career structures and workforce planning activities and minimise the problems caused by skills shortages.

Where an organisation has an external recruitment policy, consideration needs to be given to the recruitment method. There are numerous ways to access potential job candidates, including newspaper and internet advertising, recruitment agencies and referrals by existing employees. In circumstances where the organisation wants to control recruitment costs, it may specify certain preferred recruitment methods in its policy. For instance, it may want to limit the amount of recruitment done through agencies because this can be quite costly. In some cases, organisations have contractual arrangements or special deals with particular publications, recruitment websites or recruitment agencies; these preferred suppliers would need to be specified in the policy. The inclusion of recruitment methods in the policy is optional and should be done only where there is a specific reason for doing so.

Selection

The purpose of selection policies is to ensure that the process is fair and equitable and that it results in the best outcome. Policies also outline the roles and

Table 24.2 Selection policy – methodology and process issues

Methodology	Process issues
Selection criteria	Should selections be based on assessment against formal criteria drawn from job descriptions?
Interviews	Are interviews required? If so, should they be structured or unstructured? Under what circumstances would phone interviews be appropriate?
Testing	Is formal testing required? If so, what kinds of tests are appropriate?
Reference checking	Is reference checking required before a recommended candidate can be appointed?
Applicant ratings/ rankings	Are formal ratings or rankings required? If so, what systems should be used?
Documentation	Is a formal report required outlining the rationale for selection decisions?

responsibilities in the selection process. Selection policies should apply equally regardless of whether candidates are sourced internally or externally. The extent to which selection processes are standardised will vary according to an organisation's size and culture. In most cases, however, it is advisable to specify at least some methodological requirements to ensure that the process is not simply a subjective exercise and can be defended if challenged. Table 24.2 summarises some of the methodological issues that might be included in selection policies.

Selection processes can be complex and time-consuming, especially where there are a lot of process-related policy requirements. This can be resource-costly and can also result in preferred candidates being lost to other job offers. At the same time, 'quick and dirty' selection processes can result in poor decisions and are difficult to defend if challenged. Policymakers need to strive for an appropriate balance between rigour and pragmatism.

The same balance needs to be applied when considering roles and responsibilities. Some organisations prefer a centralised approach with multiple participants, while others prefer a more devolved approach with fewer people involved in the process. Table 24.3 outlines some of the policy issues relating to roles and responsibilities.

Whatever policy choices are made, they need to be context-specific. This means that they need to reflect the size, nature and culture of the organisation and be consistent with any applicable regulations (such as in the public sector). They also need to de defensible in terms of fairness and equity and discourage practices that might negatively affect morale or the organisation's reputation as an employer. Such undesirable practices include:

Table 24.3 Selection policy – roles and responsibilities

Roles	Responsibilities
Number of participants	Can the process be carried out by a single selector, or is a selection panel required? If so, how many people should be on the panel?
Management involvement	Is there a requirement for the line manager of the vacant position to be involved?
HR involvement	Is there a requirement for a representative from HR to be involved?
Training	Is there a requirement for selectors to have undergone selection training?
Approvals	Do selection decisions need to be ratified by a higher level decision-maker?

Nepotism: giving jobs to family members without consideration of others

Patronage: giving jobs to friends or supporters on a political basis to reward or to ensure loyalty

Discrimination: excluding candidates because of their gender, race, nationality, disability, marital status, sexuality, political views, religious beliefs, pregnancy, union membership or any other grounds covered by anti-discrimination legislation

Good selection policies should result in open, competitive, transparent processes that are efficient and that maximise the likelihood of the best candidate being chosen.

Employment

As already observed, many aspects of the employment relationship are regulated by law and industrial relations instruments such as awards and agreements. However, there remain several aspects that are best addressed at the organisational level through policy. Figure 24.2 outlines these kinds of employment issues.

Probation/trial periods

It is common for organisations to impose probation or trial periods for new employees as a way of confirming the person's suitability for the job. It also gives employees the opportunity to assess the job and the organisation before making a longer-term commitment. Employment policies should

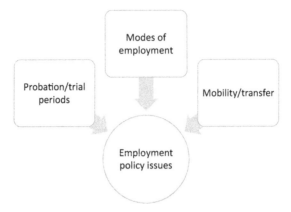

Figure 24.2 Employment policy issues.

specify whether or not a period of probation is required and if so, its duration. Probation periods are usually between three and twelve months, depending on the job and the organisation. Longer periods are generally not recommended.

The policy should also specify how the decision to confirm or not confirm the person's continuing employment should be made and by whom. It should specify the grounds on which a decision not to confirm continuing employment can be made; valid reasons should be based on job performance and behaviour. Probation periods should not be an easy 'get out' clause for employers, but they should allow for appointments to be annulled if there are legitimate reasons for doing so.

Modes of employment

Modes of employment encompass the range of different employment arrangements that are possible (e.g. full-time, part-time, casual, permanent, fixed-term). Employment modes can also include alternatives to traditional employment arrangements, such as the use of independent contractors or labour hire companies. Many organisations utilise a range of employment modes because doing so maximises the flexibility of the workforce and the organisation's capacity to respond to changing market conditions. However, the use of contingent or non-permanent workforces can also be contentious. Social commentators and trade unions often criticise the overuse of contingent workforces because non-permanent forms of employment do not provide the same entitlements or security as more traditional forms. Having a 'modes of employment' policy is one way of minimising the potential for controversy.

The primary purpose of policies like these is to prevent the unfettered growth of the contingent workforce. Limiting the contingent workforce can help to prevent conflict, as well as controlling costs, given that the cost of contingent workers is usually more than for permanent workers. Such a policy might state a preference for certain employment modes over others, or limit the use of non-permanent modes. It may also define the circumstances under which contractors or staff from labour hire companies can be used and outline any restrictions on their use (e.g. limiting their period of engagement).

Modes of employment policies should also address the issue of changing work modes. Most organisations would want to be able to modify employment modes if needed, for instance, changing casual employees to permanent part-time employees or vice versa. Similarly, employees might want to change their modes of employment for a range of reasons. Policies should, therefore, outline provisions for doing this, including details of who has decision-making authority. Work mode changes can be contentious too, especially where employees feel that their employment conditions are being diminished. This needs to be taken into account when developing the policy. Ideally, the policy should require management-initiated work mode changes to be supported by a strong business case and approved by a senior manager. Employee-initiated requests for change need to be assessed against operational requirements, and while it is obviously desirable to accommodate reasonable requests, the policy should make it clear that employees should not expect requests to be automatically supported.

Mobility/transfer

Workforce flexibility can also require employees to be moved to different parts of the organisation or to different locations because of operational needs, restructuring or other staff moves. Mobility may also be part of an organisation's approach to career development. Employees may also have reasons to want to transfer. It is therefore advisable for larger organisations with multiple divisions or locations to have a policy covering staff mobility/transfer. While employers do have the right to transfer employees as business needs dictate, there are obvious disadvantages to compulsorily moving employees against their will; therefore mobility policies should attempt to balance organisational needs and employee needs. Table 24.4 outlines the policy issues that should be addressed.

Mobility/transfer policy should also prohibit the use of compulsory transfer as a disciplinary measure or for political reasons. Such practices are both ethically questionable and legally dangerous.

Table 24.4 Mobility/transfer policy issues

Policy issue	Policy considerations
Basis for transfer	What business circumstances warrant management-initiated staff transfers? Can employees request transfers? If so, on what basis are they assessed?
Employee rights	Can an employee decline a transfer? If so, under what circumstances?
Notice periods	How much notice does an employee need to be given when being transferred?
Duration	Are transfers for an agreed period? If so, what return rights do employees have?
Relocation support	Where an employee is being relocated, what support does the organisation provide? (e.g. relocation costs, company housing, family support etc.)

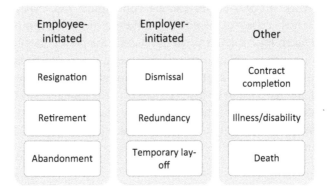

Figure 24.3 Termination categories.

Termination

The end of the employment relationship can be prompted by different sets of circumstances (see Figure 24.3). In many cases, the separation occurs organically and without trauma. However, this is not always the case. Termination policies help to ensure that separations are managed appropriately and that the organisation is not exposed to unnecessary legal risk.

The categories outlined in Figure 24.3 form a useful framework for termination policies. This is one aspect of staffing policy which is regulated in a broad sense by industrial relations legislation and industrial instruments like awards, collective agreements and individual employment contracts. Policies obviously need to be consistent with what is prescribed in these instruments.

Table 24.5 General termination policy issues

Policy issue	Policy consideration
Exit interviews/ surveys	Are departing employees required to participate in an exit survey or interview? If so, when is it conducted or administered and by whom?
Financial	Employer's right to recover money owed by employee. Employee's right to receive payment for accrued salary, allowances and unused leave
Security	Employee obligation to return security items such as keys, swipe cards and ID cards
Property	Employee obligation to return property belonging to the organisation (e.g. vehicles, equipment, laptops)
References	What is the organisation's policy on giving references and/or statements of service?

They also need to deal with issues not covered specifically in the regulatory framework.

General policy issues

Regardless of the method of termination, there are several policy issues that apply to all separations and that should be included as general policy provisions. These are outlined in Table 24.5.

Employee-initiated termination

Resignation is the most common form of termination. The main policy issue for resignations is the period of notice that is required. This is often part of the employment contract or agreement. Where this is the case, the policy needs to address whether or not the standard notice requirement can be varied or waived and if so, under what circumstances. Where notice periods are not specifically included in contracts or agreements, the policy needs to specify the requirement.

Retirements are expected to increase significantly over the next 20 years, as the ageing workforce phenomenon gathers pace. Traditionally, retirement policies have specified compulsory retirement ages. However, recent case law has determined that this is now considered to be unlawfully discriminatory. In any case, expected labour shortages caused by the bursting of the baby boomer bubble have made retention of older workers a strategic priority for many organisations, and they are actively encouraging people not to retire. Allowing older workers to phase into retirement by accessing flexible work arrangements is an effective strategy for this purpose. One policy provision that would help in this regard is a requirement for line managers or HR to meet with workers when they turn 55 or 60 to discuss their retirement intentions. This would help organisations to understand and accommodate the needs of older workers and to encourage continued participation in the workforce. Staffing policies should include special arrangements like these.

The least common but perhaps most problematic of employee-initiated terminations is abandonment. Abandonment occurs when an employee simply stops coming to work and does not resign or advise the employer of the reason for their absence. From a legal perspective, declarations of abandonment can only be made legitimately where an unauthorised absence continues for an extended period with no contact or communication by the employee. Termination policies should define the point at which abandonment is deemed to have occurred, as well as the organisation's obligations to make reasonable efforts to contact the absent employee. There is no hard and fast rule about how long an absence constitutes abandonment, but case law decisions indicate that it would need to be weeks rather than days.

Employer-initiated terminations

Dismissals generally result either from disciplinary issues or from job performance issues. Hence, policy concerning dismissals is very much bound up with discipline policy and performance management policy. Given that issues around managing misconduct or unsatisfactory performance are covered in these policies, the dismissal policy need only concern itself with the mechanics of actually terminating the person's employment. The main issue concerns notice periods. In circumstances where an employee is being dismissed, having that person work out the required notice period may be problematic; therefore the policy will usually give the employer the option of paying the dismissed employee in lieu of notice to enable them to leave immediately.

If not covered in the discipline and/or performance management policies, the dismissal policy should include a requirement for each case to be fully documented. This helps the organisation defend its actions if the dismissal is challenged.

The issue of constructive dismissal should also be addressed in the policy. Constructive dismissal occurs when the employer effectively provokes an employee's resignation through mistreatment or by putting them in an untenable position. Constructive dismissal is unlawful and should be prohibited in the policy.

Policies concerning the management of redundancies are very important, especially considering that redundancy programmes can generate considerable

Table 24.6 Voluntary vs involuntary redundancy

	Voluntary	Involuntary
Advantages	Less stress Less likelihood of industrial action or legal action	Allows specific targeting of surplus positions Better chance of retaining best people
Disadvantages	May lose best people May result in too many volunteers	Very stressful for everyone More potential for controversy

amounts of conflict, ill-feeling and bad publicity if not managed appropriately. Fairness, equity and consistency are important principles that should underpin redundancy policy. Perhaps the most fundamental policy issue is whether or not redundancies should be voluntary or involuntary. Both options have advantages and disadvantages, as outlined in Table 24.6.

Of course, it may be prudent for organisations to keep their options open rather than commit themselves to one or other option in the policy. If this is the case, the policy should allow for either option, depending on circumstances. Voluntary redundancy programmes tend to work best when the organisation is simply trying to reduce overall employee numbers without targeting specific areas or occupations.

Decision-making should also be addressed in the policy. This is especially important in situations where reductions are being made within particular occupational groups where there may be many employees doing the same work. It is important that the policy specify the criteria on which decisions are made. Some organisations embrace a 'last on, first off' policy while others base decisions on performance. Regardless of whether decisions are based on seniority, performance or other factors, care needs to be taken that they do not discriminate unlawfully. For instance, targeting older workers for redundancy because they are close to retirement age is likely to be considered to be unlawfully discriminatory if challenged. The policy should make clear that decisions should not be based on criteria that would breach anti-discrimination legislation. In most cases, decision-making relates to involuntary redundancy scenarios, but it is also possible that voluntary redundancy programmes will require a decision-making process if there are more volunteers than required. If this is the case, the same principles should apply – legality, fairness, equity and consistency.

Access to outplacement services should also be addressed in the policy. Outplacement services are provided to redundant workers to help them make the transition to a new job or career. These services can include career and personal counselling, aptitude testing, training and assistance with job applications. It is generally only larger organisations that have the capacity to offer these kinds of services, which are usually delivered under contract by specialists. However, where they are offered, the policy should address issues like eligibility and whether or not there are any limitations on the kinds of services offered or on the duration of the transition period.

Depending on the jurisdiction, legislation may prescribe minimum entitlements for redundancy pay (as in Australia). Some organisations, however, offer more generous redundancy packages or, at least, want that option available as a way of encouraging volunteers or in the interests of goodwill. If this is the case, it should be mentioned in the policy.

Temporary lay-offs are sometimes used as an alternative to redundancy to help organisations ride out periods of economic downturn. This practice needs to be underpinned by a policy that specifies the maximum duration of lay-offs and how periods of lay-off affect employees' entitlements. It is common (and reasonable) for lay-off periods to count as service for the purposes of leave accrual and salary increments.

Other termination scenarios

The most straightforward of the 'other' termination scenarios is contract completion (i.e. when a temporary or fixed-term appointment expires). The main staffing policy issue that needs to be addressed with contract completions is re-engagement. It is common for temporary contracts to be 'rolled over' (i.e. renewed for another fixed period) where there is more work that needs to be done on a particular project or where new work is available. Given our earlier observations about contingent workforces, however, it may be advisable to place some restrictions on the number and/or duration of rollovers as a way of limiting the organisation's dependence on contingent workers. Another approach might be to have a policy that bestows permanent status on temporary or fixed-term employees whose employment continues unbroken for an extended period. This would also help keep the numbers of contingent workers to a minimum, but care would need to be taken that it not be used by managers as a way of avoiding the normal recruitment and selection policies for permanent appointments (which are often more rigorous than for temporary appointments). If not controlled adequately, ongoing roll-over of contract staff may also lead to staff numbers and costs blowing out.

From time to time, it becomes necessary to terminate the employment of an employee because of chronic ill-health or disability. Although unpleasant, this is quite legitimate in circumstances where the employee is no longer able to carry out their duties. From a policy perspective, the main consideration is to ensure that any decisions to terminate on medical grounds are justified. The policy should specify the kind of medical evidence that is required to justify termination. It should also allocate decision-making authority, preferably to a senior manager. Additionally, there should be a requirement to fully document the termination decision and the rationale for it. The existence of a chronic medical condition or disability is not in itself sufficient grounds for termination. Termination is only justifiable where the condition or disability renders the employee incapable of fulfilling the requirements of their position. Termination on medical grounds should not be treated as an easier alternative to terminating people for disciplinary or performance-related reasons.

In circumstances where an employee dies, financial entitlements are obviously paid to the deceased worker's estate. There are few issues requiring a policy response, except perhaps to confirm that the termination date should be the date of death. The same provisions for returning security items and company property continue to apply, although one would hope in these circumstances that they are enforced with less urgency and more sensitivity.

International staffing

As mentioned at the beginning of this chapter, international staffing has become a significant HR function in organisations that operate globally. It is worth treating this aspect of staffing policy separately because of the many unique factors that apply. Figure 24.4 shows these unique policy dimensions.

International recruitment policy

Organisations generally take one of four policy positions in relation to international recruitment exercises:

Ethnocentric: staffing from parent country nationals (PCNs)
Geocentric: staffing from host country nationals (HCNs)
Polycentric: staffing from anywhere; third-country nationals (TCNs)
Regiocentric: staffing from a particular region (e.g. Asia Pacific)

The policy choice is influenced by a range of factors relating to the business itself, its strategic outlook and the location of the appointment. Cultural and political factors in the host country may also influence the policy choice. Among Western countries, the ethnocentric approach, for example, an Australian company sending Australians to overseas postings, remains the predominant policy.

Figure 24.4 Dimensions of international staffing policy.

Expatriate employment policy

Employment conditions for employees who are posted overseas are usually different from those of domestic employees. Policies need to specify the particular conditions that apply. Table 24.7 summarises the main policy issues.

Expatriate support policy

Employees undertaking overseas postings require much higher levels of support than domestic employees. This support is important to help ensure that the posting is successful. Support strategies should begin before the person takes up their overseas position and should continue for the duration of the posting. Support is particularly important where the posting is to a less developed country, a country with a significantly different culture or a country which is politically volatile. Table 24.8 outlines some of the main policy considerations for employee support.

Repatriation policy

Repatriation policies are essentially retention policies. They help to ensure that employees returning from overseas postings are successfully re-integrated and that their careers continue to progress in a positive way. It is common for returning employees to feel disconnected from the organisation, especially if they have been overseas for an extended period. It is also common for them

Table 24.7 Expatriate employment policy issues

Policy issue	Policy considerations
Remuneration	Are expatriates entitled to special salary rates and/or allowances while working overseas?
	What taxation arrangements apply?
Leave	Are expatriates entitled to additional annual leave or other forms of leave while working overseas?
Tenure	What is the period of the overseas posting?
	Are there provisions for early return? If so, under what circumstances?
Travel and relocation entitlements	Is there provision for an exploratory visit before accepting an overseas posting?
	Are there provisions for home visits during the period of the overseas posting?

Table 24.8 Expatriate support policy issues

Policy issue	Policy considerations
Preparation	What preparatory training is required before taking up an overseas posting (e.g. language skills, cultural awareness, political/contextual issues, business practices, legal framework)?
Accommodation	Is company housing provided?
	If not, what assistance is available to find suitable accommodation?
Family support	What family support services are provided (e.g. schooling, work for partner)?
Health care	What health care services are provided for employees and their families?
Safety and security	What measures are in place to ensure the safety and security of employees and their families?
Socialisation	What expatriate social networks exist?
	What orientation programmes exist for employees and their families once they have arrived?

to find themselves put into makeshift jobs because there has been insufficient planning for their return. Experiences like this increase the likelihood of resignation. Repatriation policies, therefore, need to ensure that the transition is as smooth and orderly as possible and that both employee and organisation benefit from the international experience. Table 24.9 lists some possible repatriation policy provisions.

Table 24.9 Repatriation policy issues

Policy issue	Policy considerations
Communication	How is the employee's connection with their home base maintained while they are away?
	What provisions exist for keeping the employee advised about developments and changes at home?
Deployment	How are employees assigned to new positions on their return?
	Is there an agreement that guarantees a mutually acceptable home posting?
Re-orientation	What re-orientation programmes exist for returning employees?
	How does the organisation utilise the skills and knowledge that the employee has gained from their overseas experience?
Career development	Is career counselling/advice available to returning employees?
	What assistance is given to help returning employees plan their future careers with the organisation?

Summary

- Staffing policies encompass recruitment, selection, employment and termination, as well as international staffing.
- The provisions of staffing policies need to be consistent with the conditions of applicable awards, industrial agreements and employment contracts, and they must comply with relevant legislation.
- Recruitment policies generally outline the organisation's preference to recruit internally (i.e. promote from within) or externally and may specify certain preferred recruitment methods.
- Selection policies are about ensuring a fair and equitable process that is efficient and results in the most suitable candidate being chosen. They should also allocate roles and responsibilities in the selection process.
- Employment policies generally cover areas that are not included in awards or employment agreements. Typically these include probation or trial periods, modes of employment and mobility/transfer issues.
- Termination policies generally cover a range of termination scenarios and are designed to ensure that terminations are managed consistently while protecting the organisation from the legal risks of unlawful or unfair dismissal.
- International staffing policies usually cover recruitment, employment, support and repatriation issues. They are designed to maximise the organisation's return on investment, as well as enhance the job performance of employees and their ongoing connection with the organisation.

Learning activity – case study 24.1

The right person for the job?

Alison is the HR manager for RMI, a risk management and insurance company with around three hundred employees. She has been in the role for only a few weeks, having come from the public sector. She is excited to be working in a new industry. So far, she has been impressed with the company's culture, which emphasises getting things done with a minimum of fuss.

Recently, though, an issue has arisen that troubles her. Part of her role is to sign off on staff promotions and appointments. A selection file has landed on her desk recommending an appointment to an entry-level graduate position in the company's marketing department. The recommended appointee is the daughter of one of the company's senior managers. On examining the file, Alison could find no evidence that the position had been advertised, or that any other candidates had been considered. When she asked the marketing manager, Steve, about it, he told her that the senior manager had approached him when he heard that there was a position becoming available and suggested that his daughter, who had just graduated from university, would be an excellent candidate. Steve had agreed to consider her. Subsequently, she submitted her CV, and Steve arranged an informal interview with her, after which he decided that she was suitable for the role.

The lack of process and accountability worried Alison, as did the fact that Steve reported directly to the senior manager in question. Did he feel pressure to employ his boss's daughter? Was she, in fact, the best person for the job, given the number of marketing graduates out there? Alison decided to seek advice from her boss, David, the corporate services manager. David seemed less concerned about it than Alison was.

'You're not in the public sector any more, Alison,' he said. 'We're not restricted by bureaucratic regulations here. Our culture is all about getting things done rather than being slaves to the process.'

When Alison questioned whether the company was getting the best person for the job, David replied that it wasn't so much about getting the best person; it was about getting a suitable person. Sure, they could spend a lot of time and money advertising the position and going through a rigorous selection process, but at the end of the day, they really just needed someone who could do the job satisfactorily, and Steve had made the judgement that his boss's daughter could do that.

Although she can see the rationale behind David's response, she remains uncertain about the ethics of appointing the relatives of senior managers without any real selection process. Isn't this nepotism? Doesn't it set a dangerous precedent for the future? While it was true that selection processes in the public sector could be somewhat time-consuming, they were designed so that every selection decision was transparent and those making the decisions were accountable. Alison believes that these principles should apply regardless of the organisation or industry. She also feels some pressure to sign off on the appointment, given that David seems to have no problem with it. To resist might damage her standing in the company, something she doesn't really want to do so soon after starting work there.

The company has no selection policy at all. This concerns Alison, and she would prefer that there was more rigour and transparency in the way selections were done.

Discussion questions

1. Do Alison's concerns about rigour and transparency override the argument that making a direct appointment is quicker and cheaper?
2. Does the company need a selection policy? What would be the advantages and disadvantages of a formal policy?
3. What policy provisions could Alison suggest that would prevent situations like this arising in the future without being overly bureaucratic and costly?
4. Should she sign off on the appointment? If so, why? If not, why not?

Learning activity – case study 24.2

Developing an international staffing policy

Ashleigh works in HR in the Sydney head office of a global financial services company. The company has been operating successfully in the Asia Pacific region for more than 20 years, and in more recent times it has expanded into India and the Middle East.

Recently, the company decided to implement an international placement programme as part of a professional development strategy. It was decided at senior management level that someone from Sydney should undertake a placement at the company's newest office in Doha, Qatar. After a formal selection process, David (a 32-year-old accountant) has been selected for a two-year posting. David has been with the company for four years and is considered to have great potential for a future leadership role. His partner, Lucy, is a primary school teacher. Neither of them has been to the Middle East before. They have no children as yet, but are planning to start a family before too long.

This initial posting will be considered as a pilot programme, with an assessment being made at the end of the two-year period about whether to make a long-term commitment to the strategy.

The company has always had a policy to employ local people, and so this is its first international staffing exercise – there are no international staffing policies in place and no previous experiences to learn from. A remuneration package has already been negotiated with David, but as yet no other details have been determined. In fact, no one in the company has really thought about it.

Ashleigh has been assigned responsibility for managing the programme, and has decided that the best place to start is to develop an international staffing policy. David's appointment doesn't take effect for another three months, and so there is some time for her to develop the policy and implement it before he is due to leave.

As a first step, Ashleigh meets with David. He is excited about the opportunity and looking forward to the experience very much. He confirms that Lucy is arranging to take a leave of absence from her teaching job and plans to accompany him on the posting. He also remarks that while he knows that Qatar is one of the more stable countries in the Middle East, he is a little worried about safety and security because the rise of pro-democracy movements in several nearby countries has made the region more politically volatile in recent times. Ashleigh agrees to look into this for him.

She also contacts HR at the Doha office. They are aware that David is coming, though they don't seem particularly enthusiastic about it. In fact, they seem quite uncooperative, which puzzles Ashleigh somewhat. When she asks whether there is company housing available, they tell her that there is no company housing and that David will need to find his own accommodation. Ashleigh adds this to her growing list of things to do.

Discussion questions

1. Who are the stakeholders in this case, and what are their interests?
2. Should the company also be assisting Lucy to find work in Doha?

3. How might Ashleigh address the safety and security issue?
4. Is there any training or other preparation that David should undertake before beginning his posting?
5. Why is the Doha office so unenthusiastic about the placement? What implications does this have for Ashleigh and for David?
6. Are there other risks that might cause the appointment to fail? If so, what policy provisions could Ashleigh develop to manage those risks?

Source: Fazey, M. 2017. *Cases in HR Practice and Strategy* (3rd edn). Prahran: Mirabel Publishing, pp. 99–101. Used with permission.

Chapter 25

LEARNING AND DEVELOPMENT POLICY

Almost every organisation provides some form of learning and/or development to its employees. Indeed, learning and development can represent a significant investment in terms of money and time, and so it makes sense for organisations to have policies underpinning its management. Increasingly, learning and development are being seen by both employees and organisations as attraction and retention factors; this is another good reason to ensure that the system is underpinned by a comprehensive policy that defines the organisation's approach to skills and career development. A good employee development and training policy covers several different dimensions, as outlined in Figure 25.1.

Programmes

Operational training

Operational training is the most fundamental aspect of organisational learning because it focuses on the knowledge and skills that employees need to do their jobs right now. Approaches to operational training will vary according to the nature of the organisation, the job and the industry. Typically, operational training will cover some or all of the following:

- induction
- safety
- computer applications
- processes and procedures
- customer service
- product knowledge
- equipment and machinery operation
- formal entry-level training (e.g. apprenticeships, traineeships)
- training for special roles (e.g. first aid officers, fire wardens)

Operational training policy should clearly define what training is mandatory and when it should be received. It may also be appropriate to specify what operational training is provided in-house and what is provided externally.

Figure 25.1 Dimensions of learning and development policy.

The policy should also specify the kinds of operational training that need to be periodically refreshed or updated. For instance, in an industrial environment, refresher safety training may be required every six months or so. Computer applications and product knowledge training obviously need to be updated when new versions or new products appear, and people with special roles like first aid officers need to undertake regular refresher training in order to maintain their certification. The policy should commit the organisation to providing the required refresher or update training in a timely way.

Formal entry-level programmes such as apprenticeships and traineeships usually require employers to enter into a formal training agreement. Where an organisation is a party to these kinds of agreements, the policy should commit to providing the required training in accordance with the provisions of the agreements.

A lot of operational training is informal in nature and carried out on-the-job as part of the normal range of operational activity. It is not necessary to try to capture this type of training in a policy document. In fact, it would be virtually impossible to do so.

Studies assistance

Many organisations provide assistance and support to employees undertaking relevant part-time studies. The policy needs to outline the types of assistance provided and to clearly and unequivocally identify the kinds of studies that attract assistance (this can be a contentious issue if not adequately defined). Generally speaking, studies assistance can take two forms: study leave and financial support.

Study leave is provided to enable employees to attend classes and/or exams during business hours. It can also provide leave to prepare for exams or to undertake private study (e.g. research, writing assignments). Traditionally, study leave policies required employees to undertake at least the same number of study hours in their own time as they were taking in leave, but contemporary approaches tend to be more flexible. One example of a flexible study leave policy is for approved employees to receive a notional allocation of study leave hours at the beginning of each semester or academic year, which they can then use as they need them. It is important that study leave policies balance organisational needs with employee needs, allowing line managers to manage their employees' study leave around the operational requirements of the job.

Financial support is becoming increasingly sought after as the costs of professional education continue to rise. Obviously, the level of support an organisation can provide depends on its financial resources. Some larger organisations fully fund their employees' professional studies while others subsidise the cost to varying degrees. The policy should outline the level of support that is available and the arrangements for its payment. The most common option is for organisations to reimburse the cost on successful completion of a unit or subject, with no reimbursement being payable if the employee withdraws or fails. Some other organisations may pay tuition fees up front, although this can create administrative problems in case of withdrawal or failure. Financial assistance can also include reimbursement for the cost of textbooks or other required resources, again, usually dependent on successful completion.

The issue of return on investment can also be addressed through policy. Most organisations that provide financial assistance to employees undertaking professional studies would want to guarantee at least some return on their investment. For this reason, 'golden handcuff' policies are becoming more common. These types of arrangements ask employees to commit to a minimum agreed period of continuing service in return for the organisation's financial support of their studies. If the employee leaves the organisation before that period has elapsed, they are obliged to repay some or all the money they have accepted in studies assistance. These kinds of arrangements are quite legitimate and are often underpinned by formal, legally enforceable agreements. Policies should include details of arrangements like these.

Continuing professional development

Most professions require practitioners to undertake a certain minimum amount of continuing professional development (CPD) each year in order to maintain their professional status and accreditation. Common forms of CPD include conferences, seminars and short courses as well as formal study. Many organisations support CPD by funding or subsidising activities that count towards CPD requirements. Policies should identify the occupational groups to which CPD requirements apply and detail the kinds of assistance provided.

In addition, some organisations fund or subsidise membership fees for professional associations, recognising that membership gives people access to relevant publications, research data and networks of their professional peers. This should also be included in the policy if it is offered. It is not always easy to determine whether an association is a bona fide professional body or something else; therefore it is worthwhile defining in the policy the specific associations that the organisation recognises for this purpose.

Management development

Any organisation large enough to have a formal organisational structure should be concerned about the professional development of its managers. Many organisations are very focused on developing future managers (which is discussed in the next chapter) but tend to neglect the needs of existing managers. After all, management is not like riding a bike – something you need to learn only once. Management is an evolving field with new ideas and new management practices being developed constantly. Experienced managers need to keep abreast of these developments in the same way as professionals in other fields do through CPD. Indeed, the same principles that apply to CPD should apply to ongoing management development.

Management development policy is a good vehicle for ensuring that existing managers understand that they have an obligation to continuously develop their skills and knowledge and not to stagnate, and that the organisation will support them in this endeavour. One possible approach to management development policy is to require managers to undertake a certain minimum amount of management development activity each year and to be accountable for this through the performance management system. Eligible activity should also be defined in the policy (e.g. workshops, seminars, conferences, formal studies). The policy should also define which positions in the organisation count as management positions for purposes of the policy. Targeting will depend on a range of factors, including the size of the learning and development budget.

Personal development

Personal development programmes can include a range of learning activities that are not directly related to a person's job, but which help to develop personal traits or characteristics that can lead to enhanced job performance. Programmes like these might cover such topics as stress management, interpersonal skills, assertiveness, self-awareness or potentially anything that is inwardly focused. Attitudes to personal development programmes can vary, and therefore, policies about supporting them also vary. Indeed, the level of support (or non-support) for people undertaking personal development programmes is a good reflection of that organisation's culture. Organisations that value employees as human capital and consider expenditure on employee development as an investment are more likely to support personal development programmes than organisations that consider employees to be commodities and training expenditure to be a cost.

The training and development policy should include a statement about the relevance of personal development programmes and whether or not the organisation supports them in principle.

Processes

Eligibility and access

Because many organisations utilise different modes of employment, learning and development policy needs to define who is eligible to participate in the various programmes on offer. Obviously, all permanent employees should be eligible, but the status of temporary or casual employees needs to be clear. A more inclusive policy will incorporate temporary and casual employees, at least for operational training, though longer-term development programmes may be restricted to permanent employees only.

The status of independent contractors and people engaged through labour hire companies also needs to be outlined in the policy. Technically, independent contractors are self-employed, and workers from labour hire companies are employed by the labour hire company itself. Thus there is an argument for excluding these categories of workers from access to training and development opportunities on the grounds that they are not employees. Some organisations might prefer to include contractors and other contingent workers in essential operational training such as safety training, but it would be unusual to include them in longer-term development programmes. One option for including workers like these might be to allow them access to programmes on a 'user pays' basis. Such a policy provision might also stipulate that contractors and contingent workers cannot displace bona fide employees from programmes (i.e. preference goes to regular employees, with spare places being made available to others on a 'user pays' basis).

It is also important to ensure that employees accessing flexible work arrangements are not deliberately or inadvertently excluded from training and development opportunities. The policy should state this explicitly and commit the organisation to facilitating access to training and development opportunities for all employees regardless of their employment mode.

Needs assessment

Ideally, training and development needs should be identified through a systematic process. Such a process would involve the collection and analysis of data from different sources (e.g. business plans, workforce data and performance appraisal data). In reality, however, it is common for needs assessment to be ad hoc or non-existent. Having policy provisions that cover the needs assessment process can be an effective way of ensuring that a more structured approach is adopted and maintained.

HR should bear the ultimate responsibility for determining and prioritising needs across the organisation, but line management should also be involved in the process either through the provision of specific data or through a consultation process. The policy should outline roles and responsibilities and the timing of the needs assessment process. Some organisations publish a quarterly or six-monthly training and development plan. The requirement for a formal plan should also be included in the policy.

Nomination and approval

A fundamental process issue for all organisations is how employees gain access to particular courses or development programmes, and so the policy should outline the nomination and approval process. It is common for organisations to have formal nomination and approval processes, whereby employees can either self-nominate or are nominated by their managers. Self-nominations still need to be approved by the person's manager. The basic principle behind processes like these is that line managers are in the best position to decide whether the proposed training is relevant and whether or not the person's absence from the workplace is operationally manageable.

There may be occasions where there are too many nominations for a particular programme. In cases like these, the policy needs to specify who has authority to determine who is accepted. This is usually HR.

Evaluation and follow-up

Internal programmes

Programmes that are developed and run in-house, either by internal training specialists or by consultants or service providers, need to be evaluated to

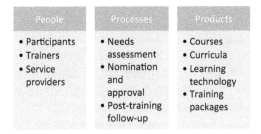

People	Processes	Products
• Participants • Trainers • Service providers	• Needs assessment • Nomination and approval • Post-training follow-up	• Courses • Curricula • Learning technology • Training packages

Figure 25.2 Dimensions of training evaluation.

determine the extent to which they are meeting needs and giving value for money. There are different evaluation models, some of them very complex. However, most organisations adopt a pragmatic approach to evaluation rather than adhering to a particular theoretical model. In broad terms, evaluation can cover any or all of the dimensions outlined in Figure 25.2.

The policy should commit the organisation to some level of evaluation of its internal programmes. This should go beyond simple participant reactions and incorporate analysis of other elements of the kind outlined in Figure 25.2. The particular approach to evaluation will vary from organisation to organisation. While it is true that not all organisations include evaluation in their training and development policies, it is also true that, like needs assessment, evaluation tends not to be done well or not done at all if not enshrined in policy.

External programmes

Most organisations allow employees access to public training programmes that might be run by professional associations, universities, consulting firms or other training providers. External programmes can be a useful adjunct to internal programmes and have the advantage of exposing employees to people from other organisations and industries. It is often difficult to judge the quality of an external programme in advance, so sending people can be something of a gamble. Given that external programmes are generally more costly per head than internal programmes, it is worth gathering feedback from participants to help determine whether future investment in the programme is warranted.

A useful policy provision in this regard would be to require people who have attended an external programme to provide a feedback report when they return to the workplace. This could be a relatively simple pro forma that people complete and send to HR. The data could then be made available to employees and managers considering the same programme, and poorly rated programmes or providers could be identified and avoided.

Post-training follow-up

Lack of post-training follow-up and support is an unfortunate reality in many organisations. This can result in the benefits of training being reduced or lost altogether. However, it is an issue that can be addressed through policy by requiring managers to personally follow-up with employees who have just completed a training or development programme. The primary objective of the meeting would be to facilitate the transfer of the new learning to the workplace. It could also help to identify which aspects of the training could be shared with other team members.

Such a policy might operate as an honour system (i.e. there is no direct accountability mechanism) or require that the meeting be documented in some way as evidence that the policy requirement has been met. A policy provision like this should specify the timing of the meeting (which should preferably be the day the employee returns to the workplace) and whether or not it needs to be documented. It should apply both to internal and external programmes.

Administration

Funding

Learning and development funding policies can take several different forms, as outlined in Figure 25.3. Where funds are fully or partially devolved, the policy should state the basis on which funds are allocated to divisions or business units (e.g. an amount per employee). Where there is partial devolution, the policy should differentiate between the types of training and development that should be funded from the central pool and what should be funded from devolved funds. Some organisations have been known to devolve funds (notionally at least) to individual employees who have discretion to spend the notional amount allocated to them as they choose. However, such policies tend not to optimise the use of funds, and so they are not recommended.

Record-keeping and measurement

Good record-keeping is essential in training and development. Indeed, in some environments, it is crucial to maintaining safety and for ensuring that employees have the proper certifications to carry out their jobs competently.

Apart from keeping accurate employee training records, there is a myriad of other training and development information that could be collected and recorded. Learning and development policy should define what records need to be kept and what measurements should be made and recorded. Recording

Figure 25.3 Training and development funding policy options.

requirements will vary according to the type of organisation and its occupational profile, but the fundamental purpose is to ensure that the organisation knows how and where its investment in training and development is being spent and can track the training provided to individual employees. Most modern HR information systems are able to gather these kinds of data quite readily (Table 25.1).

The learning and development policy should specify the minimum data that the organisation needs to collect and define the various roles and responsibilities. Measurement allows organisations to form a holistic picture of their training and development activities and to pinpoint anomalies and trends.

Summary

- Learning and development policies should cover programmes, processes, evaluation and administration.
- Programme-related policies should focus on operational training (especially mandatory training) as well as developmental initiatives such as studies assistance, CPD, management development and personal development.
- Process-related policies should cover eligibility and access issues, needs assessment and nomination and approval processes. Inclusiveness and equity should be the principles underpinning these policies.
- Evaluation policies should specify the types of evaluation that should be carried out to determine quality and value for money. A pragmatic approach rather than a theory-based approach is recommended.
- A policy requiring managers to follow-up with employees on their return from training is a good way of enhancing the transfer of learning to the workplace and maximising value.

Table 25.1 Learning and development measurement options

Participation	Expenditure
Number of hours of training and development (by division, business unit, individual)	Total expenditure
Participation rates (% of employees undertaking training and development)	Distribution of expenditure across the organisation
Types of training carried out	Expenditure per employee
Ratio of internal vs external training	Cost per hour of training.

- Administration policies should outline the method of allocating funding for training and development, as well as defining the minimum requirements for record-keeping and measurement.

Learning activity – case study 25.1

Enhancing professional development

Rachel is the HR manager for Callan, Brownrigg and Marsh (CB&M), a large and prosperous accounting and consulting firm doing a variety of accounting, auditing and business strategy work for corporate clients at the big end of town. Their team of about two hundred accounting professionals are all qualified either as certified practising accountants (CPAs) or as chartered accountants.

The company recruits a new intake of accounting graduates every year, usually 10–12 people. Graduates are expected to commence professional studies with CPA Australia or the Institute of Chartered Accountants within a year of joining the company and to successfully complete their professional studies within three years. Completion of the professional study programme makes them fully fledged CPAs or chartered accountants. Once fully qualified, employees are expected to maintain their professional status by undertaking the required amount of continuing professional development (CPD) each year, currently 30 hours.

In addition, more experienced accountants are encouraged to undertake further postgraduate studies such as an MBA to enhance their knowledge of business strategy.

Traditionally, people have funded their own studies and CPD activities and have done them in their own time. This has been an accepted part of the culture at CB&M, a way of demonstrating commitment to the profession and to the company. People who do these things successfully are considered to be in line for a partnership at some point in the future.

In the past two years, however, turnover has increased markedly, especially among younger employees, and the labour market for both graduates and experienced accounting professionals has become very tight. This has seen some rival accounting firms and other large corporate employers beginning to offer incentives, including financial subsidies and time off work for people to undertake their professional studies and CPD and to complete MBAs and other relevant postgraduate programmes.

In order to compete in the marketplace, Rachel has put forward a policy proposal designed to make CB&M a leading firm in terms of professional development. The proposal includes provisions for:

- full funding of professional accounting studies (up to $10,000 per person)
- full funding of MBA or other relevant studies (up to $30,000 per person)
- 60 hours per year paid study leave, which can be taken at any time (e.g. on a regular basis to attend lectures and/or in blocks)
- full funding of up to 30 hours a year of CPD activity (up to $5,000 per person per year)

The estimated direct costs are $700,000 per year, plus about another $100,000 in indirect costs (i.e. paid study leave). The firm's partners are divided over the proposal. Some feel that it will have a positive effect on their ability to compete in the labour market and on employee commitment and turnover. Others believe that it is not justified, too costly and too risky. Rachel has been invited to a special meeting with all partners to discuss the proposal in more detail.

Discussion questions

1. What are the risks of enacting a policy such as the one Rachel is proposing?
2. Can those risks be managed? If so, how?
3. Is the policy too one-sided? Should there be more of a shared responsibility for professional development?
4. If the policy is implemented, how might its success (or otherwise) be measured?

Source: Fazey, M. 2017. *Cases in HR Practice and Strategy* (3rd edn). Prahran: Mirabel Publishing, pp. 87–89. Used with permission.

Learning activity – case study 25.2

Access to development opportunities

Erin is the learning and development manager for Social Justice Commission, a government agency involved in developing social policy and managing the delivery of social services through a network of providers. She has recently implemented a development programme that involves talented people undertaking six-month secondments to different parts of the organisation in order to gain wider experience. This is part of the agency's strategic workforce plan. The rationale for the programme is that it contributes to the development of the next generation of leaders and policy specialists, as well as enhancing retention.

The programme has been very popular, with many people applying. Erin has developed a nomination policy that requires applicants to address a number of criteria and to outline their existing experience and skills and the skills and knowledge that they would like to develop. As with other development programmes, each applicant requires the support of their line manager to undertake a secondment.

Soon after advertising the second round of placements under the programme, Erin received a meeting request from Ben, a young policy officer. Before meeting, Erin did some research into Ben and discovered that he was a highly regarded policy officer, who was a consistently high performer with considerable potential. On meeting, Ben explained that he had applied for the secondment programme, but his application had been blocked by his line manager, Graham, who had indicated that he hadn't supported Ben's application for 'operational reasons'. Ben was understandably frustrated at not being given the opportunity to participate and asked if there was any way that Erin could intervene. Erin agreed to speak informally to Graham.

She subsequently met with Graham and explained that Ben had asked her to look into the reasons why his application for the secondment programme hadn't been supported. Graham responded by saying that he was simply asserting his right as per the policy. He went on to say that Ben was his best policy officer and he could ill afford to lose him, adding that there was no guarantee that Ben would ever return to his position on completion of the secondment. Indeed, the experience of the first round of placements was that people tended to be promoted or transferred at the end of the period of secondment.

While Erin understood Graham's perspective, she had some sympathy for Ben. She also wondered whether Graham's view was a little narrow, and not consistent with the broader objectives of the agency's strategic workforce plan.

Discussion questions

1. Should Erin try to change Graham's mind about releasing Ben to undertake a secondment?
2. Is it appropriate for the policy to assign decision-making authority to line managers? Does this lead to decisions that don't take account of the bigger picture?
3. Should Erin advise Ben to lodge a formal grievance against Graham? This would allow a more senior manager to review Graham's decision and overturn it if it was deemed to be inappropriate.
4. Alternatively, should she amend the policy to allow her or a more senior manager to override line managers' decisions?

Chapter 26

SUCCESSION MANAGEMENT POLICY

Succession management is a system for identifying and preparing candidates to take up key roles in the future. Leadership and management are the most common key roles covered by succession management initiatives, but it can also apply to professional, technical or other specialist roles, depending on the nature of the organisation and its business. Succession management has assumed greater strategic importance in recent times because of the ageing workforce phenomenon. In many organisations, the key roles are occupied by members of the baby boomer generation who are approaching retirement age. Many of the feeder positions for those key roles (i.e. positions from which people are usually promoted into key roles) are also occupied by baby boomers. Consequently, organisations that have not previously had formal succession management policies are developing them, and organisations that do have them are reviewing them.

Traditional approaches to succession management

The concept of succession management (or succession planning) is not new. Traditional approaches involved the hand-picking of candidates for future appointment to specific key roles. Occupants of those key roles would effectively anoint a successor, who would then be given exclusive access to development opportunities to prepare them for their eventual promotion.

However, there are inherent problems with a system like this. First, it is not equitable, relying entirely on the subjective judgement of the decision-maker. Indeed, it has the potential to cause resentment among those overlooked. Second, where the occupants of key roles choose their successors, there is a high likelihood that the person chosen will be someone very much the same as the incumbent in terms of their ideas, values and management styles. This leads to a perpetuation of existing cultural features and management practices, which is not conducive to innovation or diversity. This is sometimes known as 'cloning'. The third and perhaps most obvious problem is that the whole plan is thrown into disarray if the chosen successor leaves the organisation. This was less an issue in the past, when people tended to stay with their employers long term. However, the new generation of employees is far less inclined to do this and more likely to seek new opportunities and experiences every few years.

The upshot of all these issues is that traditional approaches to succession management are no longer consistent with the values and characteristics of today's workplaces.

Contemporary approaches to succession management

Given the potential problems with the traditional approach to succession management, more equitable, less risky approaches have been developed and are becoming increasingly common. These approaches emphasise the creation of 'talent pools' rather than identifying a single successor. Talent pools, as the term suggests, are groups of employees with potential for promotion into key roles. Talent pool members are generally identified with reference to specific criteria, and often, a formal selection process is undertaken to allow potential talent pool members to put forward their credentials.

Once formed, the talent pool then undertakes appropriate development opportunities. These can be undertaken collectively (e.g. participation in in-house leadership development programmes) or individually (e.g. accessing external programmes). Typically, people would undertake a combination of collective and individual development activities according to their particular needs. When key positions become available, interested talent pool members apply and a merit-based selection process is undertaken (Figure 26.1).

In smaller organisations, the same sort of process might be undertaken without the creation of a formal talent pool. In other words, interested people would undertake development activities and compete on merit when key positions fall vacant. In larger organisations, there may be multiple talent pools reflecting the diversity of key roles in questions (e.g. leadership and management roles, senior professional or technical roles, specialist roles).

A succession management policy needs to clearly outline the organisation's approach to succession management and the process. A process like the one just discussed implies several policy connections, and so succession management policy needs to be consistent with the other policies outlined in Figure 26.2.

Identification of key roles

The policy should describe the roles that are subject to succession management. Usually these would be a few very senior roles, but depending on the organisation and the circumstances, there could be quite a large number of such key roles. Logic would suggest that the targeting of succession management

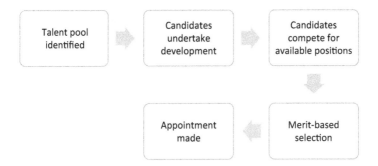

Figure 26.1 Contemporary succession management process.

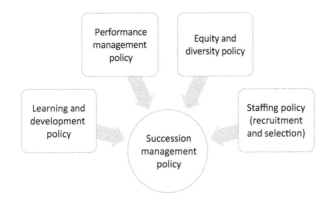

Figure 26.2 Succession management policy connections.

should not be based solely on the seniority of positions. It should identify roles which would be difficult to fill when the incumbent retires, resigns or leaves the organisation for whatever reason. In some organisations, this might include middle management and certain other mid-level professional, technical or specialist positions. Ideally, the organisation's HR planning process would identify these roles.

Entry to talent pool

Where formal talent pools are being created, the policy should define both the criteria and the method of selection. The criteria might be based on demonstrated competencies, qualifications, experience or other assessable factors and should not be too restrictive. The selection process should involve more than one person. Ideally, a panel of senior people who are the occupants of key roles should be involved in selecting the talent pool.

In most cases, interested employees would nominate themselves by submitting an application. However, it may also be desirable to include a policy provision which allows for people to be nominated by their manager or by a colleague. If this option is included, it should not replace the selection process. People nominated in this way would need to be assessed in exactly the same way as self-nominees, and obviously, if they do not want to be included, they would not participate in the selection process.

As discussed earlier, it is possible in larger organisations that several talent pools might be formed for different key roles. This leaves open the possibility that some people might seek inclusion in more than one talent pool. For example, a young professional may aspire both to leadership roles and senior professional roles. Where multiple talent pools are being created, the policy should cover scenarios like this. Ideally, organisations would not want to restrict talent pool membership, but there may be practical considerations such as whether or not a person has the time and capacity to undertake two or more sets of development activities. This needs to be taken into account when formulating the organisation's policy position.

The overall size of the talent pool needs to be considered too. A balance needs to be struck between being appropriately inclusive and maintaining the quality of the pool. Operational issues need to be considered too – a large talent pool will inevitably mean that a lot of people will be undertaking development activities off-the-job. This may not be sustainable. As a general rule, the policy should specify the maximum number that can be included in the talent pool.

Review and renewal of talent pool

Talent pools are inherently dynamic. Inevitably there will be some natural attrition as people leave the organisation or are promoted, meaning that the pool will need to be renewed regularly. The timing and frequency of entry opportunities should, therefore, also be included in the policy. For most organisations, an annual intake is appropriate. The timing of the process will depend on the particular organisation.

Membership of the talent pool should not be indefinite, and so the continuing eligibility of existing talent pool members will also need to be assessed on a regular basis. The frequency should be the same as the frequency with which membership of the pool is renewed (i.e. annually in most cases). The policy should define the means by which assessments of continuing eligibility are made and by whom. The obvious mechanism for assessing continuing membership is the performance appraisal process, though some organisations may want to include other measures such as successful completion of prescribed courses. Whatever the methods, they need to be as objective as possible. Poor job performance or failure to complete required training may, therefore, result in a person's membership of the talent pool being terminated.

Termination of talent pool membership may also occur for disciplinary reasons, and if this is the case, the policy should say so. However, given the investment that the organisation is making in its talent pool members, terminating membership is not something that should be done lightly. The policy provision governing termination for disciplinary reasons, therefore, might allow some flexibility where the disciplinary breach is relatively minor.

Appeals

Membership of the talent pool is likely to be prized by career-minded employees, and competition for entry may well be keen. Similarly, people whose membership of the talent pool is terminated may seek some redress. It is, therefore, advisable to include appeal provisions in the policy. Typically, appeal provisions would allow people whose applications have not been successful or who have been ejected from the talent pool to put their case and have the decision reviewed.

Alternatively, where the organisation has a grievance policy in place, this could be the appropriate vehicle for dealing with appeals. Although appeals can be time-consuming and frustrating, they at least underscore the transparency and openness of the processes, and demonstrate in a very tangible way the organisation's commitment to equity and organisational justice.

Summary

- Succession management policies should embrace contemporary approaches that involve the creation of talent pools and are underpinned by equity and merit principles.
- Policies should clearly explain the process and criteria for entering the talent pool, including the timing and frequency of intakes.
- Policies should also define the maximum number of people who can be part of the pool at any one time and, where necessary, outline the provisions for participating in different talent pools.
- Continuing membership of the talent pool should be contingent on job performance, skill development and behaviour. The policy should, therefore, include guidelines for determining ongoing membership and the conditions under which a person's membership may be terminated.
- An appeals process should be available in the interests of organisational justice and transparency.

Learning activity – case study 26.1

Managing the talent pool

Alison works in HR for Ardent Financial Services, a national company that provides financial advice, investment services, mortgage broking services and other financial services to individual and corporate clients. In response to the demographic profile of its leadership group, two years ago the company created a talent pool to prepare the next generation of leaders. Part of Alison's role involves managing the talent pool and the company's approach to succession management more generally.

One of the provisions of the succession management policy requires that continuing membership of the pool be reviewed every 12 months. This is done by seeking input from each member's immediate supervisor. Alison has developed a pro forma for this purpose, which asks a number of questions about the person's ongoing work performance.

Alison recently received an assessment from the supervisor of Grant, an existing talent pool member, recommending that his membership of the pool be terminated due to unsatisfactory performance. Grant was subsequently notified of the recommendation and, as per the policy, given the opportunity to respond. His response made the following points:

- The relationship between him and his supervisor had deteriorated over the previous 12 months, and that this was the likely reason for the negative recommendation.
- He did not believe that his performance was unsatisfactory. His most recent performance appraisal did not indicate any deficiencies.
- He was undertaking part-time postgraduate study towards a master's degree in leadership and was doing well.
- He also questioned whether job performance in an operational role alone was a valid criterion for determining a person's leadership potential.

Discussion questions

1. Is relying on supervisors' judgement too subjective? Is there a more objective way of assessing performance?
2. Should Grant's good academic performance override his job performance?
3. Is Grant right about the tenuous relationship between operational competence and leadership potential? If so, how might people's leadership potential be assessed more accurately?
4. How should Alison deal with the case from here?

Learning activity – case 26.2

Succession management: What is the best approach?

Andrew has recently become HR manager for the Department of Business Regulation (the DBR), a state government agency with around five hundred employees. Like most public sector organisations, the DBR has an ageing workforce. In fact all of its senior managers and leaders are aged over 45; more than half have already reached 55 and are eligible to retire at any time. The department has traditionally had a stable work-force. The specialised nature of the work has meant that there have been few people recruited from outside except at entry level.

Andrew has prepared a proposal for a succession management strategy to help ensure that the DBR can replace its existing leaders when they retire. The proposed strategy is consistent with contem-porary approaches to succession management and with public sector regulations and standards. It involves the creation of a 'talent pool' within the department, made up of employees with leadership potential, who would then participate in a range of development initiatives to pre-pare them for future roles as leaders. When a leadership position became available, talent pool members would have the opportunity to apply for it and be considered on their merits.

However, when Andrew presented it to the DBR's executive committee for endorsement, there was some concern that creating a talent pool would effectively create an elite group within the organisation. It was considered that this would not be good for the culture which had always been very egalitarian.

At the same time, the committee acknowledged that there was a pressing need to prepare a new generation of leaders. However, they remained uncomfortable about the cultural impact of a talent pool and asked Andrew to rethink the policy to see if the same outcome could be achieved in a different way.

Discussion questions

1. Are the executive committee's concerns justified, or are they being needlessly pessimistic?
2. Are there other approaches to succession management that might be effective and appropriate for the organisation?
3. Should the DBR be looking outside the organisation more? As well as developing people internally, should it be trying to change the

introspective culture by actively recruiting managers from other government agencies or from the private sector?

4. How should Andrew respond to the executive committee's request?

Source: Fazey, M. 2017. *Cases in HR Practice and Strategy* (3rd edn). Prahran: Mirabel Publishing, pp. 146–47. Used with permission.

Chapter 27

EMPLOYEE SAFETY, HEALTH AND WELL-BEING POLICY

One of the fundamental legal and moral responsibilities of employers is to provide a safe, healthy working environment. This requires them to take reasonable steps to protect employees from injury, illness or harm. Work safety and health is governed by very detailed legislation and regulations which often run to hundreds of pages. Government agencies responsible for administering this legislation and regulatory regimes are typically empowered to impose significant financial penalties on organisations that breach them. Safety and health are also important priorities for many trade unions, and a significant potential cause of industrial disputation. So there are strong compliance and risk management aspects to safety, health and well-being policy.

In addition to reducing the likelihood of incurring hefty fines or loss of productivity through industrial action, a safer, healthier workplace also contributes to reductions in workers' compensation claims and, therefore, to workers' compensation premiums.

However, there is also a strategic dimension. Increasingly, organisations are making a connection between employee safety, health and well-being and increased productivity, increased employee commitment, reduced absence rates and lower turnover. Clearly, employees value policies and practices that enhance their quality of work life. Such policies and practices, therefore, contribute strongly to an organisation's reputation and competitiveness in the labour market.

The ageing workforce phenomenon is another significant strategic driver for safety, health and well-being policy. With an increasing number of older workers in the workforce and people being encouraged to retire later rather than sooner, the need to keep people healthy and productive for as long as possible has assumed greater importance than ever before. Indeed, it could be argued that there is a growing trend towards a more holistic approach to employee safety, health and well-being. A comprehensive, coherent policy is the foundation for an effective holistic approach.

Figure 27.1 Employee safety, health and well-being policy framework.

A policy framework

When developing safety, health and well-being policies, the framework outlined in Figure 27.1 provides a useful structure. Because of its complexity, work safety and health has long been regarded as a specialist area of HRM. Many organisations employ safety and health specialists to manage these functions, particularly in industries like manufacturing, mining and construction. While this is appropriate, there is also a danger that occupational safety and health will be perceived as being somehow separate from the rest of HRM. A framework like this one will help to reinforce the message that everyone in the organisation has a vested interest and a responsibility to help create and maintain a safe, healthy work environment and that safety, health and well-being connect strongly with other HR policy areas, such as those outlined in Figure 27.2.

Workplace safety

Prevention

Preventive policies can cover a range of workforce management issues, including:

- safety processes and procedures
- requirements for protective clothing
- processes to maintain a clean, hygienic environment
- requirements for machinery and equipment maintenance

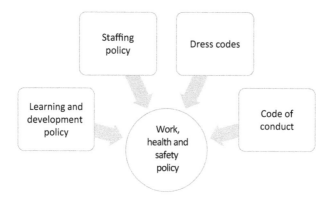

Figure 27.2 Employee safety, health and well-being policy connections.

- specialist safety and injury management roles
- drug and alcohol testing
- ergonomic workstation design and assessment
- protection from violence and abuse

Many of these measures are self-evident, particularly in industrial environments. Legislation and regulations often prescribe certain preventive processes for particular industries; therefore policies need to be consistent with whatever requirements apply. Policies should also include requirements for employees at all levels to report workplace hazards and for the organisation to act on them in a timely way.

While safety is very much culturally engrained in industrial environments, it tends to be less so in commercial or white-collar settings where the potential for injury is not so obvious. In these environments, poor workstation design can lead to a range of chronic injuries and medical conditions such as tendonitis and back complaints, which can be very costly for employers. The eyes can also be affected by continual exposure to computer monitors. Indeed, during the 1980s, when many organisations introduced information technology for the first time, these types of injuries reached epidemic proportions. An appropriate policy response to scenarios like this is to require workstations to be assessed regularly to ensure that they are ergonomically sound. Routine eye testing for employees doing screen-based work would also be an appropriate preventive policy measure.

The issue of protection from violence and abuse from clients and customers is becoming increasingly important, especially in organisations where employees have direct public contact. In some cases, employees have even been stalked or harassed outside the workplace by disgruntled or disturbed clients or customers. Policies such as those that protect the identity of employees have been enacted in organisations to help prevent these types of incidents occurring. Other measures include requiring employees to use only their first names when dealing with clients, and requiring that employees report incidents where they are verbally threatened or abused. It may also be appropriate to have a policy that enables the organisation to withdraw service from clients or customers who have acted in an abusive or threatening manner.

Training

As discussed in the chapter on learning and development policy, safety training often falls into the category of mandatory training. This can include (depending on the industry):

- safety awareness training
- first aid training
- manual handling training
- driver training
- ergonomic awareness training
- certification for machinery operation and other potentially dangerous occupations

Policies should specify the training that should be undertaken by employees in particular occupations and should also mandate refresher training to ensure that employee knowledge and awareness is maintained. The inclusion of safety management training in management development programmes would also be an appropriate policy requirement in many industries.

Management and support

Safety management and support policies generally encompass emergency management, crisis management and injury management.

Emergency procedures covering fire, accidents, bomb threats or other adverse workplace events should be enshrined in policy. The policy should include requirements for regular fire drills or other exercises designed to heighten awareness and ensure that emergencies are managed effectively. The policy should also define emergency management roles and responsibilities.

Crisis management generally covers extraordinary situations where employees are in potential danger. These might include extreme incidents like robberies, terrorist attacks or natural disasters. Crisis management policies should be designed to ensure that the danger to employees is minimised, that all employees are accounted for when a crisis occurs and that, where a crisis is ongoing, there is effective communication. Post-crisis support services such as access to counselling should also be covered in the policy. Crisis management policies might also include arrangements for business continuity and media liaison. Because of the complexity and interconnectedness of crisis management issues, policy responsibility may not lie with HR. If this is the case, HR should ensure that the policy adequately covers employee safety issues and that HR has a central role in the crisis management process.

Less dramatic, but equally important is the issue of injury management. This is the process of managing the rehabilitation and return to work of injured workers. Injury management policies should ensure that injured workers receive appropriate medical treatment and that they return to work as soon as is practicable. This might include provisions for graduated return to work (i.e. where a recovering employee may return on a part-time basis and ease back into full-time work over time). It might also allow for recovering workers' jobs to be modified temporarily so as not to risk re-injury (e.g. excluding heavy lifting). Injury management may also encompass redeployment provisions where workers are unable to return to their original position because of the ongoing effects of their injury. Injury management policy provisions should cover those suffering from psychological ailments such as stress as well as those with physical injuries.

Employee health and well-being

Prevention

As previously mentioned, employee health and well-being has emerged as a significant strategic issue in recent years, primarily as an attraction and retention issue. Policies are mainly concerned with facilitating the long-term health and well-being of employees. Prevention issues covered in policies of this nature might include:

- quit smoking programmes
- weight loss programmes
- exercise and fitness programmes
- subsidisation or salary packaging of gym memberships
- health checks
- flu vaccinations
- work–life balance initiatives

One of the major policy issues in this area is privacy. Most people would oppose the idea of compulsory health checks or requirements to undertake a weight loss programme or a quit smoking programme. Societal values support the idea that, ultimately, health is a personal issue and a personal responsibility. However, there is an argument that where a health issue such as obesity is affecting an employee's work performance adversely, there is an employer right to take appropriate action. As a general rule, however, policies in this area should emphasise voluntary rather than mandatory participation in illness prevention initiatives such as those listed above.

The capacity of the organisation to provide services like these is also an issue that should be considered when developing the policy. It may not be financially viable to provide a comprehensive range of initiatives. Policy decisions need to reflect the costs and potential benefits. An organisation may choose to provide some but not all of the services listed or to subsidise the cost to employees rather than pay for the entire cost. When embracing preventive health and well-being initiatives for the first time, it might well be prudent for organisations to begin modestly and expand the range of services over time as resources allow. Sustainability is important because employees will generally react negatively to the withdrawal of services; therefore the potential for enhanced attraction and retention could be damaged or lost altogether.

Training

Health awareness training can form an important part of preventive strategies. Training such as this is generally about raising awareness of the risk factors for chronic diseases and promoting healthy lifestyles. Training initiatives are often accompanied by health checks or by employer-sponsored events like healthy lunches. As discussed in the previous section, these types of initiatives should be voluntary rather than mandatory, and they should reflect the organisation's capacity to provide them.

Management training is also important. Managers need to be skilled in and knowledgeable about issues like managing chronically ill or injured workers, maintaining safety standards and managing emergencies or crises. There is a case for making this type of training mandatory for all managers. A policy that requires managers to undergo this type of training will not only enhance management practices but will also help to demonstrate the organisation's commitment to employee safety, health and well-being – a useful thing to be able to do in case of litigation.

Management and support

Many larger organisations have employee assistance programmes which give employees access to confidential counselling and support. Programmes like these can help employees cope with work and personal problems and are generally valued highly.

Given the increasing prevalence of stress and stress-related absences in modern workplaces, the provision of stress management programmes can be useful. These usually take the form of workshops or seminars that raise awareness of stressors and provide participants with skills to help them deal effectively with stressful situations.

Peer support programmes can perform a similar function in organisations where employees are exposed to stressful incidents such as customer abuse or threats. Peer supporters are employees who are trained to debrief colleagues in the immediate aftermath of an unpleasant incident. The aim is to help employees deal with the emotions that such incidents arouse so that they can return to their duties as soon as possible. Peer supporters are also trained to recognise where professional counselling or other assistance is needed.

All of these management and support initiatives incur costs to the organisation. Although most organisations would see these costs as being necessary to help prevent the even greater costs of increased workers' compensation premiums, lost productivity, absenteeism or litigation, there remains a danger that in periods of economic downturn they could be seen as being dispensable. Providing these kinds of services as a matter of policy can give them greater legitimacy and make it more difficult for organisations to discontinue them. This is not to suggest that they should be continued indefinitely, however. If they are enshrined in policy, they become subject to the same policy review processes as any other HR policy, which means that their usefulness and value are assessed systematically rather than as a knee-jerk reaction to changed economic circumstances.

Global issues

The globalisation of business has increased the level of international mobility among the employees of organisations operating across national borders. Indeed, many companies have operations in countries and regions that potentially pose additional safety, health and well-being issues.

Exposure to HIV/AIDS and other contagious diseases can be a significant risk in some parts of the world. In addition, many less developed countries have only rudimentary health systems and facilities, and so the risk of employees becoming ill but not receiving medical treatment in a timely way are significantly increased. Organisations that deploy staff to countries or regions where this is a risk need to develop policies that help protect employees. These might include the provision of vaccinations or other protective measures, or provision of emergency evacuation to a location where appropriate medical aid can be accessed.

Organisations deploying staff in areas that are politically volatile should recognise the risks of violence, terrorism or other issues caused by civil unrest or warfare and develop policies that guarantee employees some level of safety. Policies covering these kinds of situations should commit the organisation to providing ongoing security arrangements and, where the situation becomes untenable, emergency evacuation.

Employees who travel overseas regularly may also be at risk of developing travel-related health problems such as deep vein thrombosis. International travel policies should require appropriate preventive measures to be taken by employees travelling by air and should also commit the organisation to providing medical treatment if this becomes necessary.

Summary

- Employee safety, health and well-being policy has strong compliance elements; it also has increasing strategic importance as issues related to the ageing workforce become more prominent.
- Policies can be framed around the concepts of prevention, training, management and support.
- Safety policies should reflect whatever legislative or regulatory requirements apply to the organisation or industry and the particular risks posed by the type of work undertaken by employees, including abuse by clients or customers.
- Employee health and well-being policies are primarily strategic in nature because their objectives include maintaining the health and productivity of existing employees and creating a work environment that is conducive to enhanced attraction and retention.
- Organisations operating globally need to include policies that address the specific risks involved in international travel and residence in parts of the world with elevated risks of disease or physical conflict.

Learning activity – case study 27.1

An employee health programme: Weighing up costs, risks and benefits

City Insurance is a general insurance company with about three hundred employees. Some months ago the HR manager put a proposal to the company's executive to sponsor an employee health and fitness programme. The rationale for the proposal was that it would:

- improve employee commitment at a time when retention is a big issue
- improve morale, which a recent employee survey had shown was beginning to decline

- provide a vehicle for employees from different business units to interact, which would help to break down the 'silos' that existed in the company
- act as an attraction factor for potential new employees
- reduce sickness and absence rates
- produce long-term productivity benefits

The executive subsequently approved a pilot programme. At its conclusion, the programme was to be evaluated and a decision made about the long-term viability of adopting it as policy. A health and fitness consultant was engaged to run the pilot programme, which included an exercise programme (isometric exercise, running and gym work) plus measurement and monitoring of health and fitness levels. Twenty employees signed up for the pilot programme, which ran for three months. At the end of the pilot programme, HR undertook an evaluation that included surveying participants, analysing costs and HR data for the 20 participants and researching outcomes from similar programmes elsewhere. The evaluation resulted in the following findings:

- Employee reaction to the programme was outstanding. Everyone who participated loved the programme, and attendance at the various exercise and assessment sessions was excellent.
- Employees reported that the programme enhanced their perception of the company and was likely to be a positive factor in terms of retention.
- Employees also reported positive effects from their interaction with colleagues from other business units whom they would not otherwise have had contact with.
- There was a strong view among participants that the programme should be ongoing (i.e. not just limited to three months). While some of them had continued to keep fit independently, the majority had not.
- The health and fitness levels of all participants increased significantly. Almost everyone recorded an improved body mass index, improved blood pressure and lung capacity, and better flexibility.
- During the three months of the programme, sick leave for the 20 participants actually increased. This was mainly due to several people sustaining minor injuries and muscle strains that required treatment.

Research by HR in relation to workers' compensation coverage revealed that injuries or adverse medical events that resulted from an employer-sponsored exercise programme were compensable. While the existence of such a programme would not in itself affect the company's workers' compensation premiums, if there were claims in future, this would result in increased premiums.

While there was general support in the literature and some anecdotal evidence of positive effects, HR was unable to find any hard data supporting a link between corporate health and fitness programmes and increased productivity or long-term reductions in sickness or absence rates.

The direct cost of the pilot programme was $25,000. There were also indirect costs resulting from the increased sick leave among participants.

Discussion questions

1. What are the costs, benefits and risks associated with the programme?
2. Should the company continue with the programme? If so, why? If not, why not?
3. Are there other policies that might achieve similar results for the company?

Source: Fazey, M. 2017. *Cases in HR Practice and Strategy* (3rd edn). Prahran: Mirabel Publishing, pp. 78–80. Used with permission.

Learning activity – case study 27.2

Addressing employee safety and well-being

The Social Support Agency is a government organisation providing income support and related services to people in need. Georgia has recently been appointed as HR manager for the Southern Region, which includes four service delivery centres with a total staff of 240 people.

Not long after commencing, Georgia is contacted by a union representative, Gary, who tells her that the union has some concerns about employee safety and well-being in the service delivery centres. She arranges to meet him a few days later. At the meeting, Gary says that the union has become aware of a disturbing number of incidents where client service officers have been verbally abused, threatened and even physically assaulted. These incidents seem to have escalated over the past few months and are most likely connected with the implementation of new government policies in relation to income support, tightening the eligibility criteria for new claimants and applying more stringent criteria for existing claimants. According to Gary, this has resulted in an increased number of angry clients, some of whom have taken out their frustration on client service officers.

Georgia is concerned by these claims and undertakes to investigate further. She subsequently meets with the managers of the four offices in her region. They confirm that such incidents have increased in recent times but are certainly not new. Indeed, all four tell Georgia that client abuse is part and parcel of the role and has been a regular occurrence for many years. This also worries Georgia. When she asks the managers what policies and programmes they have in place to deal with this, they respond that the agency has a one-day 'dealing with difficult clients' workshop that most client service officers attend, usually within a few months of starting.

Georgia then convenes a focus group of client service officers who confirm that client abuse and threats are commonplace. Some of the incidents they recount include:

- verbal abuse by phone and face to face
- verbal threats, including threats against officers' families and threats by clients to commit suicide if their claim is not approved or their payments are not reinstated
- in several cases, officers had been harangued on social media by disgruntled clients
- some officers had been physically assaulted by clients, though not seriously. These incidents had taken place both at the front counter and in interviewing booths
- one officer had been stalked by a client who approached her in public places and verbally abused her on several occasions

The officers also expressed the view that the agency did little to prevent incidents like these or to support people who were on the receiving end and that management seemed unconcerned about them. This accorded with Georgia's feelings after meeting with the managers, whose views seemed to be that this was part of the job and that people just needed to learn to cope with it.

Georgia comes to the conclusion that the current situation is unacceptable and that significant changes are needed.

Discussion questions

1. What might be the consequences if the current situation continues?
2. What kinds of prevention, training and support policies and programmes might be appropriate to ameliorate these risks?
3. Given management's current attitude, how should Georgia sell these new policy and programme ideas to the organisation?
4. What objections might she encounter? How should she respond to them?

Chapter 28

EMPLOYEE PRIVACY POLICY

Most people value their privacy, and societal values support people's rights to privacy. This applies as much in the workplace as in any other context. For this reason, organisations should have employee privacy policies that effectively balance employer and employee rights. Workplace privacy has three main aspects, shown in Figure 28.1.

In most jurisdictions there is legislation addressing privacy issues, although this is not always specific to workplace privacy. There is, however, a good deal of case law concerning employee privacy issues, and this is usually the best guide for policy development.

Personal information

Policies concerning the management of personal information should be based on the principle that personal information should only be used for the purpose for which it was originally provided. This includes information provided in job applications and for employee records, such as:

- private residential addresses
- private phone numbers
- private email addresses
- photographs
- bank account details
- tax file numbers
- any other information held by the employer which could identify the employee

Policies should prevent employers from releasing employee details to third parties such as financial institutions, debt collectors, marketers or sales representatives without the employee's permission. Many organisations also have policies that prohibit the release of employee details to people purporting to be relatives or friends of employees. In fact, some organisations will not

Figure 28.1 Aspects of workplace privacy.

even confirm whether or not a person is an employee unless the enquirer can verify their identity and relationship to the employee in question. This can be annoying for people with a legitimate reason for contacting the employee, but it also helps protect employees from unsolicited and unwanted attention. It can also be seen as a security measure that helps to safeguard employees from potential harm at the hands of estranged partners, disgruntled customers or anyone with an ulterior motive.

Recruitment and selection processes generate significant amounts of personal information, and so it is important that privacy policies include specific provisions covering the management of this information. A fundamental principle should be that application forms and other recruitment or selection processes only require the provision of *relevant* information. That is, information relevant to determining the person's job skills, qualifications and capacity to do the job for which they have applied. While some employers would profess to want to find out about the 'whole person', including details of their family circumstances or activities outside work, it is not appropriate to seek personal details that are not work related. The issue of medical information can also be contentious, but the same principle applies. There is an obligation on job applicants to disclose any medical information that affects their capacity to perform the job safely, and it is legitimate for employers to require new employees to undergo a medical examination to determine their fitness for the specific job to which they have been appointed. However, it is not appropriate for employers to seek general medical information that is not job-related. Privacy policies should, therefore, include a statement about the provision and use of medical information.

It is common for third parties such as consultants to be involved in recruitment and selection processes, and so policies should include a requirement for applicants to be informed if third parties are involved in the process.

Additionally, where information is to be gathered from former employers as part of that process, the policy should require that permission be granted by the applicant by having applicants sign a statement to that effect on the application form.

Privacy policies should also deal with the management of employee records and personnel files. Personnel files should be kept securely, with access limited to people with a legitimate right to see them. The same principles should apply whether the records are electronic or paper-based. Policies should affirm employees' rights to inspect their records at any time and to correct any mistakes. Generally speaking, job applications and related documents should be kept no longer than is necessary unless there is consent from applicants. This means that where an organisation wants to keep a person's application for consideration for future positions, it needs to specifically seek the person's permission to do so. Performance appraisal records should also be subject to privacy provisions that restrict access only to those who have a right to see them (e.g. immediate supervisors).

Monitoring

The use of communication technology (internet, email and phone) is usually the main focus of employee monitoring in organisations. While there is no specific legislation in this area in most jurisdictions, case law supports employers' rights to monitor the usage of communication technology for quality control, security purposes or simply to help ensure that the technology is not abused. This type of monitoring can include:

- logging calls made from office or mobile phones
- recording calls, especially those involving customers
- monitoring websites visited and downloads
- monitoring email content
- blocking prohibited email content

Policies should affirm this employer right and outline in broad terms the method by which the monitoring is carried out. Policies should also make employee obligations clear. In some cases, policies covering the usage of information and communication technology (ICT) are not considered to be HR policies and are developed and managed by ICT departments. Obviously there are strong connections with privacy policy and also with discipline policy and codes of conduct. Thus it is important that monitoring policies are consistent with related HR policies, even if the ICT usage policies themselves do not fall within the purview of HR.

The following guidelines are useful for framing privacy policies relating to the monitoring and usage of ICT and the internet:

- The policy should be promulgated to staff, and management should ensure that it is known and understood by staff. Ideally the policy should be linked from a screen that the user sees when they log on to the network.
- The policy should be explicit as to what activities are permitted and forbidden.
- The policy should clearly set out what information is logged and who in the organisation has rights to access the logs and content of staff email and browsing activities.
- The policy should refer to the organisation's computer security policy. Improper use of email may pose a threat to system security, the privacy of staff and others, and the legal liability of the organisation.
- The policy should outline in plain English how the organisation intends to monitor or audit staff compliance with its rules relating to acceptable use of email and web browsing.
- The policy should be reviewed on a regular basis in order to keep up with the accelerated development of the internet and information technology. It should be re-issued whenever significant change is made. This would help to reinforce the message to staff.

Most organisations are reasonably tolerant of employees using business communication facilities for private purposes provided that it does not breach organisational policies (e.g. code of conduct, ethics, internet and email usage). However, privacy policies should make clear that, where employees choose to do this, they do so knowing that their activity is likely to be monitored in some way.

Surveillance

Legislation generally prohibits covert surveillance by anyone, including employers, except where it has been sanctioned in the interests of law enforcement, criminal investigations or national security. This covers:

- covert video surveillance
- covert computer surveillance
- listening devices
- tracking devices

There are differences between the legislation in different jurisdictions. However, in general, legislation does not prevent employers from undertaking some forms of employee surveillance provided that it is not done covertly. Indeed, video surveillance is common in some workplaces. While employee surveillance is not something that most employers would consider necessary, in some contexts where security is important, it may be justified as a means of preventing theft, for example. 'Big brother' style surveillance, where employees are routinely watched or tracked without specific reason, is more problematic.

The use of listening devices is generally prohibited by legislation unless there is consent. In an employment context, it is difficult to envisage a scenario in which the use of listening devices would ever be justified, with or without consent.

Similarly, legislation prohibits the use of tracking devices unless there is consent or the existence of the device is clearly indicated. There is an argument that using tracking devices on company vehicles can be justified on safety grounds, especially where the vehicles cover long distances and traverse remote areas (such as in long-haul trucking). In general, however, the use of tracking devices simply to keep tabs on employee movements is difficult to justify.

Policies should affirm the organisation's commitment to observing its legal responsibilities in relation to surveillance. Where lawful overt surveillance is undertaken, the policy should outline the rationale for doing it and the methods by which it is done. Given that legislation differs in each jurisdiction, policymakers need to ensure that the policy complies with whatever legislation applies.

Summary

- Privacy policy should balance commercial interests and security issues with employee rights and be consistent with societal values.
- Employee privacy encompasses three main areas: personal information, monitoring and surveillance.
- Privacy of personal information relates mainly to recruitment and selection processes, performance appraisal data and employee records such as personnel files.
- The fundamental principles underpinning the gathering and storage of information are that only information relevant to the person's employment should be collected, and access to that information should be restricted to those who have a legitimate right to see it.
- Monitoring of employee use of internet, email and phone facilities is generally accepted as being legitimate, though employees are entitled to know that routine monitoring is occurring.
- Workplace surveillance is generally prohibited by legislation if it is covert. By contrast, overt surveillance is generally acceptable.

- The use of tracking devices can be justified in some circumstances as a safety measure, but in most cases, there would appear to be very little reason to use this type of surveillance.
- Privacy policy is primarily a compliance policy, and so it should directly reflect whatever legislation applies in the organisation's particular jurisdiction.

Learning activity – case study 28.1

Privacy and health issues

David is an HR adviser for Rapid Transport, a trucking company involved in both short and long haulage. Recently, he met with company's operations manager, Roy, regarding one of their truck drivers, Bob. Bob is in his late forties and has been with the company for ten years. He has been a reliable employee. He is also grossly overweight, a heavy smoker and not very physically fit. Roy tells David that Bob had recently had three weeks off on sick leave. Although he had provided a medical certificate, it did not indicate the nature of the illness. Bob seemed reluctant to talk about it other than to say that he was fine now. David told Roy that it was standard practice for medical certificates to not specify the nature of the illness and that it was a privacy issue.

Roy then explained to David that he suspected Bob had suffered a heart attack and that this was the cause of his absence. When David asked how he had formed this conclusion, Roy said that it was just rumour. Nonetheless, he was concerned about Bob's ongoing health given his obesity, lifestyle and the heart attack rumours. He also observed that Bob had not appeared to change his habits at all, and if he had in fact had a heart attack, he might well be in line for another one, and that this posed a safety issue given that he was a professional driver.

He then suggested that the company institute a policy requiring all drivers to undergo a full medical examination every year to determine their overall state of health and their fitness for work. This could be justified on safety grounds. He also suggested that the company be able to send employees on programmes for weight loss, for example, if their health was found to be problematic. David undertook to look into it.

Discussion questions

1. Should the company be able to compel Bob to reveal details of his illness?

2. Is a policy requiring annual medicals for drivers reasonable, or is it an intrusion on employees' privacy?
3. Is it appropriate for employers to require employees to participate in weight loss programmes or other health programmes?
4. How should David proceed from here?

Learning activity – case study 28.2

Monitoring as a strategic tool

Antrobus and Associates is a large accounting firm operating in the CBD. Like most employers of accounting professionals, it is struggling to attract and retain people because of an acute skills shortage. Turnover is increasing, and in the past three months or so, the company has lost some of its best accountants to better offers from other companies.

At a recent strategic planning meeting of the company's leadership group, one of the firm's partners put forward a suggestion for reducing turnover and increasing retention. The suggestion was that, since the company already routinely monitored employees' internet and email usage, it should use this technology to identify any employees who were accessing recruitment websites or receiving emails from recruiters. Those employees could then be invited to renegotiate their employment contracts with a view to making them more attractive, thereby (hopefully) persuading the employee to remain with the company rather than seeking a position elsewhere.

The IT manager has confirmed that the technology would be capable of this kind of monitoring and that doing so would be in line with company's IT usage policy, which clearly states that internet and email usage is monitored. The suggestion has now been referred to Gary, the firm's HR manager, for a response.

Discussion questions

1. What privacy issues are raised by the proposal?
2. Are there risks to the company of using monitoring technology in this way?
3. Would it work?
4. What should Gary's response be?

Chapter 29

SOCIAL MEDIA POLICY

The rapid rise of social networking has created some significant issues for organisations and their employees. Perhaps more than anything else, the widespread use of social media such as Facebook and Twitter has highlighted the fact that it is becoming increasingly difficult to separate employees' work lives from their private lives. Broadly speaking, social media issues for organisations fall into four categories – productivity, discipline, privacy and security – as shown in Figure 29.1.

Social media also pose some significant risks, both for employers and for employees. These risks can be addressed through policy, yet many organisations have been slow to react to the new landscape. Some international studies have shown that less than half of all organisations have a social media policy.

Productivity

The immediacy of social media is one of its attractions for users. Consequently, many users, particularly younger ones, feel compelled to spend significant amounts of time each day connected to social media. Indeed, as many parents and teachers have noticed, many young people seem incapable of staying away from social media for more than about five minutes! In the workplace, this can create a productivity issue if people are spending inordinate amounts of time tweeting or accessing Facebook. Organisational responses to this can vary (see Figure 29.2).

The compliance approach usually sees organisations blocking access to social media sites through their own systems, although the effectiveness of this is questionable given that it does not stop people from accessing the sites using mobile devices. Indeed, this is probably the preferred mode of access for the majority of users. The best that can be achieved by blocking access through the organisation's systems is to send a message that people should not be using social media during work time. This is rather a heavy-handed approach, however, and is unlikely to have the desired effect.

Figure 29.1 Social media issues related to HRM.

Figure 29.2 Organisational responses to productivity issues.

A risk management approach accepts the inevitability of people accessing social media while at work, but attempts to put some limits on it. For example, the policy might specify that people should access social media only during designated breaks. It might also specifically preclude accessing social media during meetings, training sessions or other work activities. Most people would see restrictions like these as reasonable. The success of a policy like this would, of course, depend on it being consistently applied by supervisors.

The strategic approach uses people's liking for social media to enhance organisational communication. Some progressive organisations have set up their own internal social networks. Typically, these are modelled on external social media sites and allow people to share both personal and professional information. People are encouraged to participate in the network and use it to source information and expertise within the organisation. Realistically, this is really only an option for larger organisations which have the resources to set it up and maintain it and sufficient employee numbers to make it dynamic.

Many organisations now use external social media (especially Facebook) for marketing and business development. Where this is the case, it is important that there be policies in place to regulate this. These are dealt with in the next section.

Discipline

Employee misuse of social media has led to a significant body of case law and an increasing understanding of the risks for employers and employees. Case law has established that organisations are entitled to take disciplinary action against employees who misuse social media to the detriment of their employers. However, disciplinary cases can be complex, and some employees have been successful when challenging disciplinary action taken against them. The best way to ensure a consistent approach to disciplinary issues is to have clear policies.

Employee misuse of social media can encompass many things. These include:

- making statements that denigrate the organisation's reputation or undermine its interests
- disclosing confidential or proprietary information
- using the organisation's intellectual property or infringing on others' intellectual property rights
- criticising customers, suppliers or other business partners
- making statements supporting competitors
- posting illegal content
- using social media to defame, vilify, bully or harass others

Misconduct such as this essentially breaches employees' common law obligations of fidelity to their employers. In addition, there are obvious risks to organisations when these kinds of things happen, including the risk of being held vicariously liable for workplace discrimination, bullying or harassment. Many of these risks arise from the fact that many people's social media profiles include their employer's name, and thus they are easily identified with that organisation.

Social media policies should be specific about the kinds of behaviours that are unacceptable. Organisations should also ensure that employees are aware of the policy by using active information strategies (as discussed in Chapter 11).

Some organisations have attempted to mandate employees' reporting negative comments made on social media either by other employees or by people outside the organisation. Such attempts have typically met with opposition from employees, unions and the general public. In any case, such a policy would be almost impossible to police. Policy provisions like this should be avoided.

The issues we have discussed so far relate to people using their personal social media accounts. Where employees are required to use social media for business purposes (i.e. they are operating a social media account on behalf of their employer), the same conditions should apply. In addition, policies relating to employer social media accounts should remind users that the account is owned by the organisation and not by the individual or individuals operating it. User names and passwords should, therefore, be held by the employer and access should end when the employee leaves the organisation or moves to a different position within the organisation.

Privacy

Research has shown that approximately 45 per cent of employers routinely use social media profiles for background checking of job applicants. While the ethics of this practice are debatable, the fact is that it is widespread whether people like it or not. It could be argued that doing this is little more than unwarranted voyeurism. Typically, however, employers or prospective employers who advocate the practice argue that they are looking for things that help paint a more complete picture of the person and their 'fit' with the organisation. Hence, the kinds of comments and photographs that they post are central to the judgements that are made. Proponents of this kind of background checking would also point out that social media profiles are in the public domain, and thus there is nothing improper about looking at them, and that people who do not want to have their profiles seen by people they don't know simply need to apply the appropriate security settings. The biggest risk of using social media profiles for background checking is that subjective or possibly even discriminatory selection decisions might be made based on assumptions which may or may not be accurate.

Inevitably, opinions within organisations about the validity of this practice will vary. Some organisations will embrace it; others will not. The purpose of policy in this area is to make the organisation's position absolutely clear and to ensure that there is consistency in the way that job selection decisions are made.

Where the organisation wants to use this method as part of its selection processes (or at least to have this option), the policy should require that all applicants are advised of this fact, preferably as part of the job advertisement itself. It should also require that the applicant give specific permission for their profiles to be used for this purpose. This can be done relatively easily via an application form. The policy should also make clear that under no circumstances should applicants be required to provide passwords or to change their security settings to allow access. To do so would be a clear invasion of privacy. Ultimately, policies like these recognise that social media profiles are owned by individuals who have the right to control who sees them and how much they see.

Where the organisation wants to prohibit the use of social media profiles for background checking, the policy should specifically state that under no circumstances should social media profiles be used as part of the selection process. Of course, it could be argued that this will not necessarily stop people looking at applicants' profiles 'unofficially'. It does, however, send a clear message that selection decisions need to be justified on the basis of something more substantial than an applicant's social media profile. Using selection panels rather than having individuals make selection decisions is a good way to minimise the likelihood of the policy being 'unofficially' breached.

Security

The advent of social media means that it is easier than ever to find people online, and to discover things about them. In some occupations, this can make employees vulnerable to people with ulterior or inappropriate motives. For example, police officers may be targeted by criminals or anyone with a grudge against the police for any reason. Schoolteachers, social workers or other service providers may be targeted by students or clients. In these cases, the students/clients may be seeking social connections with their teachers/service providers. Most organisations consider it inappropriate (and indeed unethical) for professionals to develop social relationships with people under their care, and so approaches like these are undesirable.

Some individuals in these kinds of occupations choose to use a pseudonym on social media. This certainly makes it more difficult to be tracked down. Organisations that employ people in occupations such as those mentioned above or in other roles that could leave them vulnerable to unwanted social media attention may consider adopting a policy that requires employees to use pseudonyms on social media. This might be a contentious policy, however, as some people may consider it an unwarranted intrusion into their personal lives. Alternatively, a softer policy recommending (rather than mandating) that employees take steps to protect their online identities may be more appropriate.

Policy connections

Social media policy connects with several other HR policy areas (see Figure 29.3), and needs to be consistent with them. It may also connect with

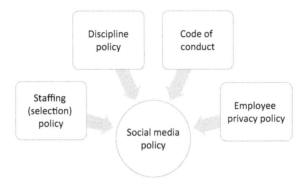

Figure 29.3 Social media policy connections.

non-HR policies such as those dealing with ICT usage. It could be argued that policy provisions dealing with social media usage could simply be incorporated into these other policies. This is certainly an option. It could also be argued, however, that, given the prominence of social media–related issues in contemporary workforce management, having a specific social media policy is likely to have greater impact than having social media policies embedded in other policies where they may attract less attention.

Summary

- Social media policy encompasses four main aspects: productivity, discipline, privacy and security.
- Productivity policies that are not too heavy-handed or prescriptive are likely to be more successful than policies that attempt to stop people from using social media in the workplace altogether.
- Policies should explicitly define the kinds of misconduct that might result in disciplinary action. These should reflect employees' common law obligations, as well as the statutory legal obligations of employers for which they can be held vicariously liable (e.g. discrimination).
- While the use of social media profiles for background checking is not unlawful in itself, there are risks to employers of making decisions based on them.
- Organisations that wish to use social media profiles as part of the selection process should do so in an open and transparent way rather than secretively, and their policies should reflect this.
- Policies requiring employees to protect their identities on social media can help prevent unwanted or inappropriate contact by students, clients, customers or others with whom employees have professional contact.

- While it is possible to incorporate social media policies into other policies, having a specific social media policy is a good way of ensuring that the policies are prominent and widely known. Consistency with selection, discipline and privacy policies, as well as with the organisation's code of conduct, is necessary where organisations enact specific social media policies.

Learning activity – case study 29.1

Social networking and professional responsibility

Rose is the HR coordinator at Moorcroft College, an independent secondary school employing 120 teachers and support staff. The school has a policy that prevents teachers from social networking with students. However, recently there have been some concerns raised by teachers about other aspects of social media. Rose has had conversations with teachers who have experienced persistent friend requests from students, as well as friend requests from parents. Even where friend requests had been declined, students were often able to see their teachers' profiles and sometimes commented inappropriately on postings. There had also been an incident at another school where the disgruntled parent of a student who had been suspended had tracked down a teacher through social media and threatened him.

The school's principal had contacted Rose recently to suggest an amendment to the social media policy that required all teachers to use pseudonyms on social media so that they would be more difficult to track down. He asked Rose to investigate the feasibility of such a policy.

Discussion questions

1. How should Rose approach her assessment of the principal's policy suggestion? Who should she consult with?
2. Would teachers be supportive of a policy like this? What might be some of their objections?
3. Would it make a difference? Are there other ways of protecting teachers' identities on social media?

Learning activity – case study 29.2

Selection and social media

Amy works in HR for a small mining company. The company has a head office in the city and mine sites in several remote locations. Mine site workers live on-site for three weeks and then have a week off. Accommodation and meals are provided by the company. The on-site workforce consists predominantly of young male workers. Although the company has strict rules governing behaviour while living on-site, there are sometimes incidents that need to be dealt with (e.g. disagreements, personality clashes). Creating an environment on-site that minimises the likelihood of problems is an important priority for the company.

Amy has recently participated in a selection process for a position as an on-site cleaner and kitchenhand. She and Daniel, a manager from the company's operations division, undertook the selection process and interviewed a number of candidates. Both agreed that there was one outstanding applicant, a young woman named Cherie who had similar experience on a mine site and who performed particularly well in the interview.

As per the company's selection policy, Amy and Daniel forwarded Cherie's application details to Graham, the head of the operations division, for approval of her appointment. The following day, Daniel called Amy and told her that Graham had not approved the recommendation to employ Cherie and had instructed them to recommend another candidate. Amy was quite taken aback, given how clearly superior Cherie's application was. She asked Daniel why Graham had disagreed with the recommendation. Daniel replied that Graham had told him that he had looked at Cherie's Facebook page and had not liked what he saw. Apparently he had formed the view that Cherie seemed like 'a bit too much of a party animal' and that this was not conducive to maintaining a peaceful mine site environment.

Amy feels angry that a sound decision is being questioned on purely subjective grounds, but isn't sure what, if anything, she can do about it given that Graham is a senior manager in the company.

Discussion questions

1. Is it ethical for Graham to check Cherie's social networking profile before making a decision to employ her?

2. Are his inferences about Cherie's lifestyle and suitability to work on-site reasonable?

3. What if Cherie's Facebook profile contained racist comments by her? Given the culturally diverse nature of the company's workforce, would that justify excluding her?

4. Is it reasonable for jobseekers to expect that prospective employers will check their profiles? If they're in the public domain, are they 'fair game' for anyone who wants to look?

5. Should jobseekers tone down their profiles to avoid giving a bad impression to possible employers?

Source: Fazey, M. 2017. *Cases in HR Practice and Strategy* (3rd edn). Prahran: Mirabel Publishing, pp. 43–44. Used with permission.

INDEX

Lightning Source UK Ltd.
Milton Keynes UK
UKHW011843210220
359140UK00001B/29